The Picture Postcard

Reimagining Ireland

Volume 103

Edited by Dr Eamon Maher,
Technological University Dublin – Tallaght Campus

PETER LANG

Oxford • Bern • Berlin • Bruxelles • New York • Wien

The Picture Postcard

A New Window into Edwardian Ireland

Ann Wilson

PETER LANG

Oxford • Bern • Berlin • Bruxelles • New York • Wien

Bibliographic information published by Die Deutsche Nationalbibliothek. Die Deutsche Nationalbibliothek lists this publication in the Deutsche Nationalbibliografie; detailed bibliographic data is available on the Internet at http://dnb.d-nb.de.

A catalogue record for this book is available from the British Library.

Library of Congress Cataloging-in-Publication Data

Names: Wilson, Ann, 1959- author.
Title: The picture postcard : a new window into Edwardian Ireland / Ann Wilson.
Description: Oxford ; New York : Peter Lang, 2021. | Series: Reimagining Ireland, 1662-9094 ; vol. 103 | Includes bibliographical references and index.
Identifiers: LCCN 2021006404 (print) | LCCN 2021006405 (ebook) | ISBN 9781788740791 (paperback) | ISBN 9781788740807 (ebook) | ISBN 9781788740814 (epub) | ISBN 9781788740821 (mobi)
Subjects: LCSH: Postcards--Social aspects--Ireland--History. | Ireland--Social life and customs--20th century.
Classification: LCC NC1878.7.I73 W55 2021 (print) | LCC NC1878.7.I73 (ebook) | DDC 741.6/83075--dc23
LC record available at https://lccn.loc.gov/2021006404
LC ebook record available at https://lccn.loc.gov/2021006405

ISSN 1662-9094
ISBN 978-1-78874-079-1 (print) • ISBN 978-1-78874-080-7 (ePDF)
ISBN 978-1-78874-081-4 (ePub) • ISBN 978-1-78874-082-1 (mobi)

© Peter Lang Group AG 2021

Published by Peter Lang Ltd, International Academic Publishers, 52 St Giles, Oxford, OX1 3LU, United Kingdom oxford@peterlang.com, www.peterlang.com

Ann Wilson has asserted her right under the Copyright, Designs and Patents Act, 1988, to be identified as Author of this Work.

This publication has been peer reviewed.

Contents

Figures

Acknowledgements

I want to thank the Thomas Dammann Junior Memorial Trust and the Irish Association of Professional Historians for financial awards that made possible the publication of this book with coloured illustrations. To both of these I am very grateful.

Thank you to Margaret O'Leary for giving me access to her grandmother's wonderful collection of postcards, and to Niamh O'Leary Moran for her generous sharing of her research on her family's history.

Thank you also to Hilda Haugh and Mary and Arthur O'Donnell, who allowed me to examine and photograph their amazing family postcard collections.

Thanks as well to Dan Breen in the Cork Public Museum, Deborah Baume in the Cobh Museum, and Sinéad Holland and Siobhan O'Neill in Portlaoise County library.

Thanks too for their help in various ways to Brian McCabe, Mark Carmody, Julia Gillen, Viv Gardner, Robert Demaine, and Peter Gilderdale, and all those who helped me in any way.

To Christabel Scaife and Anthony Mason at Peter Lang for their help and patience especially.

Also thanks to all the Wilson, Madigan, O'Leary and Nolan family members who were so helpful in response to my questions.

And above all thanks to Jim, for everything.

Introduction

> The Briton on holiday, the love-lorn swain, and the lazy correspondent made their own of the penny picture by post. They bought the coloured trifles by the dozen, and lavished their epistolary attentions on friends afar at a minimum of effort … The picture postcard was often a thing of beauty, but sometimes a tinted horror. To meet the demand for novelty, offences against good taste were doubtless perpetrated by manufacturers, but, speaking generally, the picture postcard craze had not specifically harmful results. (*Irish Independent*, 1907) [1]

This book examines the picture postcard craze as it manifested itself on the island of Ireland in the first decade of the twentieth century. Picture postcards were a huge international phenomenon during this period, and their production, distribution and use followed broadly similar patterns in most places, including Ireland. However, as elsewhere, the distinctive social, cultural and political local context inflected in very specific ways how the cards were used and the messages they communicated, and this will be the primary concern of this book. All of Ireland in the early twentieth century was still a part of the British empire, but the relationship between Britain and Ireland was fraught and unstable and both nationalist and unionist views across the island were becoming increasingly assertive. Ireland was also modernizing, but unevenly, and both the speed and slowness of this process generated specific anxieties about identity, prosperity and the roles of women. Picture postcards, because they were so cheap, accessible and attractive, were used by very many people to engage with these discourses, either publicly or privately, and at different levels. The cards themselves also often became the focus of discussions and opinion pieces, either being championed as a means of profit, education, enlightenment, useful promotion or much-needed entertainment, or castigated for spreading ignorance, illiteracy, lies, degrading stereotypes or (foreign) moral corruption. People in early twentieth-century Ireland could not avoid the picture postcard, as it was ubiquitous, and whether they liked it or not, or even knew it, they had to take it seriously as a communication medium.

Scholars vary slightly but not much in their assessment of when exactly the international picture postcard craze occurred. The Irish collector Niall Murphy sees it as taking place during the Edwardian era (1902–1910) 'although some will argue it ended in 1914 with the outbreak of the First World War'.[2] Others such as the Norwegian scholar Bjarne Rogan broaden the span so that it starts between 1895 and 1900 and fades out between 1915 and 1920.[3] During these years, hundreds of billions of picture postcards were produced and sold worldwide. Their enormous popularity was due to a range of factors: their visual appeal, their portability and the fact that they could be collected, gifted or sent through the post with added messages. Their imagery could be brightly coloured or black-and-white, photographic, illustrated or mixed media, and they depicted a huge range of subjects. They allowed individuals for the first time to quickly manipulate, repurpose and communicate with ready-made, varied and constantly updated imagery and text, in ways that could be compared to contemporary uses of social media. Postcard communication, especially everyday, casual interaction, was facilitated by the speed and frequency of postal deliveries during this era. Except for very remote areas, letters and cards could be guaranteed next-day delivery at the latest throughout Ireland and often travelled much faster in urban areas such as Dublin, where there were up to six mail deliveries a day.[4]

Postcards have up until recently primarily received attention from postcard collectors (deltiologists), and therefore books about them, while they often provided a well-researched history of postcard development, mainly focused on classifying and dating specimens, on identifying publishers, printers, artists and photographers, and on their value to collectors. In the last twenty-five years, however, some really interesting research has been published which examines postcards as multimodal historical artefacts, looking at their role in personal and public communication, in advertising and promotion, in perpetuating and constructing ideologies, and as mementos. Two significant collections of such research are *Delivering views: Distant Cultures in Early Postcards* (1998), edited by Christaud M. Geary and Virginia Lee Webb, and *Postcards, Ephemeral Histories of*

Modernity (2010), edited by David Prochaska and Jordana Mendelson. Other important work in this area has been done by Julia Gillen and the Edwardian Postcard Project in Lancaster University, Annebella Pollen in the University of Brighton, Bjarne Rogan in the University of Oslo and Peter Gilderdale in the Auckland University of Technology in New Zealand. In relation to Irish visual culture, Luke Gibbons' chapter 'John Hinde and the New Nostalgia' in his book *Transformations in Irish Culture* (1996) is ground-breaking in its analysis of John Hinde postcard imagery of Ireland from the 1950s to the 1970s.[5]

This book will use the material culture of the picture postcard as a lens through which to examine the Edwardian period in Ireland, thus approaching Irish history from a different angle than is usual, one that reveals new perspectives on networks of influence and communication. It will draw on newspaper debates on the postcard phenomenon, examples of collections of cards from the first decade of the twentieth century and Edwardian cards in collections put together later. The Edwardian collections examined were mainly put together by women, as casual collecting of postcards was seen by many as a suitable 'feminine' hobby, mainly practised by girls and young women. The cards in these collections feature a wide range of subject matter from many different countries and were published and printed by many companies, Irish and non-Irish. They thus provide a fascinating insight into the huge variety of imagery and ideas which became widely available in a short period of time to everyone in early twentieth-century Ireland. The postcards will be looked at not just for their mass-produced imagery and captions, but also for the text and other marks added to them by users and postal workers, marks which could augment, neutralize or contradict their original intended message, and which also highlight their status as material objects with social lives. The use of postcards as historical artefacts also allows the modern historian to eavesdrop on conversations and jokes from over a hundred years ago in a way that is very unlikely to happen with other media from that period. Postcards therefore offer a unique insight into the everyday life of Edwardian Ireland which adds considerably to our understanding of the period.

This study has two central approaches that need to be made clear. Firstly, Irish Edwardian postcard *culture* is looked at, as opposed to postcards *per se*. The picture postcard is taken as a starting point and its uses, valuing and role in Irish society are examined, as well as the kinds of images it constructed and the values it communicated to its consumers. There is more emphasis on the consumption of postcards and less on the details of their production. This is partly due to necessity, as detailed information on postcard production is patchy and in many cases unavailable, so that a comprehensive study is impossible, and partly because this approach provides greater understanding of the complexity of Irish society and culture at the time, contributing further to a picture so far constructed using other historical sources. Secondly, the postcard phenomenon is firmly situated as an international one, with a relatively seamless continuum between what was happening elsewhere and in Ireland, especially, but not only, in Britain. Postcards circulated easily around the world, as indeed did the discourse surrounding them, and newspaper articles often did the same. People in Ireland bought and received cards whose stages of production could have been located in a range of different countries, and read articles and opinion pieces about them that often were syndicated from non-Irish publishers. There were specific local and national versions of both, of course, and nationalist groups in particular put a lot of work into trying to provide specifically Irish cultural products and encouraging Irish people to consume them, but a considerable section of the population was uninterested in this, or unaware of it. The picture postcard therefore allows an examination of Edwardian Ireland not as an isolated case but as part of a broader nexus of commodity culture.

The chapters will be organized as follows:

Chapter 1, 'Edwardian Ireland and the picture postcard craze: Responses, debates and anxieties', provides an overview of the emergence of the picture postcard phenomenon in general, and specifically in relation to Ireland. Picture postcard imagery was largely dictated by market forces, and they penetrated all sectors of society, communicating values and concepts even to those who were unwilling or unable to engage with other media such as books and periodicals. Picture postcards were seen as a means of promoting Irish tourism and business, and as having generally the potential to cultivate a positive image of Ireland both at home and abroad, although some people worried about their negative influence on Irish society, especially on younger people with whom they were most popular. This chapter examines some of the discourse surrounding the postcard phenomenon in Ireland, relying a great deal on reports from Irish newspapers from 1900–1910.

Chapter 2, 'Collections, collectors and collecting', provides a brief overview of postcard collecting in Ireland, and describes the range of collections looked at in this book. These include postcards from the Edwardian period collected by the Cork Public Museum and by the Cobh Museum. Both of these institutions were (and are) driven by the aim to collect picture postcards featuring images of local scenes and people, in other words images judged relevant to the geographical areas represented and served by the museums. Both have in common the fact that the cards tend to be regarded mainly as photographic or illustrative representations, rather than three-dimensional material objects, and any added writing or postmarks are usually regarded as irrelevant. These collections are most useful for studying the way postcards constructed ideas and images of an area, especially in relation to the rapidly expanding tourism industry. The other collections examined in the course of writing this book were amassed, so far as can be determined, during the early twentieth century. The owners of these were Irish women based in Dublin, Belfast and Ennis, County Clare, and one Mayo-based man. All the collections are informal, and two were kept loosely in boxes rather than in albums. The principal one is an album containing 278 cards all posted between 1903 and 1907 to a young middle-class Dublin woman, Christina Jessop. Christina was a relative of the author's and as her collection could be more easily interpreted and contextualized because of family knowledge and sources, it was the most useful for this research.

Chapter 3, 'Postcards: A medium of private and public communication', looks at how the Edwardian postcard in Ireland became an important means of communication, looking at both the imagery on the front of the cards and written messages and other additions made by senders and postal authorities. Postcards, both pictorial and plain, were in common use by 1900 for business- and government-related enquiries, surveys and promotions. They were also used by individuals to make public and semi-public statements, sometimes defamatory and anonymous, as evidenced by the numerous libel cases reported in newspapers of the period. Mostly, however, they were used to communicate short personal messages such as making appointments, brief enquiries about health and well-being, and conveying congratulations and greetings on birthdays and occasions such as Christmas. To a considerable extent they facilitated the kinds of communication now carried out through texting, emails and social networking, as Esther Milne has shown in *Letters, Postcards, Email. Technologies of Presence* (2010) her investigation of the relationship between letter writing, postcards and modern electronic communication.[6] These messages are often short and appear banal and ritualistic to a modern reader, characteristics which Bjarne Rogan has attributed to the fact that they were 'activity-orientated communication' – communication whose purpose is to build and maintain social bonds, rather than to deliver information.[7] This provides the researcher with unparalleled insights into the everyday habits and language of the period, the 'murmur of small voices' as Naomi Schor has called it.[8]

Chapter 4, 'Irish identity: Empire, modernity and revival', examines how picture postcards were used during this period to construct a sense of Irish identity, as well as to challenge accepted ideas about it, both in their mass-produced imagery and the text and other markings added to them by users. Irish identity was the subject of much debate in the first decade of the twentieth century, and various concepts of it were promoted particularly by writers such as W. B. Yeats, Douglas Hyde and D. P. Moran, by organizations such as the Gaelic Athletic Association (founded 1884) and the Gaelic League (founded 1893), and by individuals and groups associated with the Irish Roman Catholic Church. Many people expected some form of political independence soon, probably in the form of Home Rule, and the necessity for developing a distinctively Irish culture came to be seen by many as both unavoidable and urgent. Just as in other more highly respected mass media, the discourses of nationalism, internationalism, tradition, modernity and empire were aired via the cheap picture postcard, and probably reached a much wider audience than through those media that required greater commitment, economic means or literacy.

Chapter 5, 'Ireland and the wider world: Travel, emigration and tourism', looks at postcards in relation to travel and emigration in the late nineteenth and early twentieth centuries, and at the construction of place and society in postcard imagery. Tourism was becoming a very significant industry by the early twentieth century, and many picture postcards therefore tended to reproduce an image of Ireland which was desired and sought by tourists, often a beautiful, wild and mostly unpopulated countryside punctuated by picturesque ruins. Cards representing Irish people frequently construct a delightful timeless Irishness, reassuringly free from jarring modern intrusions or unpleasantly obvious poverty, and representations of Irish people at work are also often pre-industrial and romanticized. Postcard imagery, however, was also 'world-making' in the sense that it constructed a world view for Irish people of the wider world beyond their shores, and in this way could be very influential in shaping how Irish people were both viewed and viewed others.

Chapter 6, 'A suitable hobby for young ladies: Postcards and women's lives in Edwardian Ireland', discusses the lives of women in early twentieth-century Ireland, using the postcard collections as a starting point. These allow insights into day-to-day lives, social circles, entertainment, work and specific interests. The women whose collections will be looked at were from a range of geographical areas and social classes, and the cards they collected show evidence of different interests. However, none of these women were from that small social elite whose actions and life-events merited public recording and celebration, nor from the group of women whose lives were so poor and desperate that their names appear only on workhouse and court records. They came, instead, from those classes in the middle whose lives generally were of no particular interest except to their circle of relatives and friends, and their postcard collections offer one of the few windows into their world.

All the card collections contain numerous representations of glamorous, mostly female, music-hall performers. These types of postcards were extremely popular with young females around the world, as Veronica Kelly has pointed out in her discussion of the phenomenon in Australia, and Ireland seems to have been no exception.[9] They became a powerful tool for the promotion of musical comedy and celebrity culture, both frowned upon in Ireland by many nationalist and religious groups as imported, trashy and morally corrosive. As images in their own right, however, they produced a glowing version of femininity characterized by luxury, leisure, charm and glamour, a version that most young Irish women in the early twentieth century could only yearn to emulate.

In my research, picture postcards turned out to be extraordinarily useful (and fascinating) as a means of accessing relatively hidden aspects of Irish life in the early twentieth century, such as the lives of middle-class women, the complicated connections between individual lived experiences and the big movements and debates of familiar historical narratives, and the often-contradictory range of ideological messages that people were exposed to on a daily basis. The ubiquity, pervasiveness and sheer useful-ness of this apparently insignificant commodity during the period opened doors into people's everyday lives that sometimes offer very different views to those revealed by more conventional historical sources. The cards suggest a population that is vibrant, socially active and consumption-orientated in ways that we would easily recognize now, as well as one that is already fos-silizing its traditions for the purposes of tourism and nationalism. Picture postcards offered Edwardian people a simplified, stereotypical and often idealized view of the world, a fantasy media version of reality of the kind that we are very familiar with now, and that we, like they did, navigate and selectively believe in when it suits us.

Notes

1. 'A Change of Taste', *Irish Independent* (10 May 1907).
2. Niall Murphy, *A Bloomsday Postcard* (Dublin: The Lilliput Press, 2004), 25.
3. Bjarne Rogan, 'An Entangled Object: The Picture Postcard as Souvenir and Collectible, Exchange and Ritual Communication', *Cultural Analysis*, 4/1 (2005), 31–57, 31.
4. Stephen Ferguson, *The Post Office in Ireland, an Illustrated History* (Dublin: Irish Academic Press, 2016), 175–176; Murphy, *A Bloomsday Postcard*, 26.
5. Luke Gibbons, 'John Hinde and the New Nostalgia', in *Transformations in Irish Culture* (Cork: Cork University Press/Field Day, 1996), 37–43.
6. Esther Milne, *Letters, Postcards, Email. Technologies of Presence* (New York, London: Routledge, 2010). Kindle Book.
7. Rogan, 'An Entangled Object', 31–57.

8. Naomi Schor, '*Cartes Postales:* Representing Paris 1900', in Prochaska, David and Jordana Mendelson, eds, *Postcards: Ephemeral Histories of Modernity* (Pennsylvania: Pennsylvania State University Press, 2010), 1–23, 21.
9. Veronica Kelly, 'Beauty and the Market: Actress Postcards and Their Senders in Early Twentieth-Century Australia', *New Theatre Quarterly*, 20/2 (2004), 99–116.

Edwardian Ireland and the picture postcard craze: Responses, debates and anxieties

Edwardian Ireland and modernity

According to 'The Citizen', writing in 1909 in the American magazine *Art and Progress*,

> There was probably never an age so picture-mad as the present. The Citizen has a friend who declares that in a generation or two this will be the only means of communication – that people are forgetting how to read because they are being over-fed by the magazines on pictures, and that they are likewise forgetting how to write because of the picture post-card.[1]

The observations here, and the anxieties associated with them, were made and expressed in many parts of the world in the early twentieth century. An explosion in imagery and in people's appetite for consuming it was a notable feature of the nineteenth and early twentieth centuries. This was apparent in Ireland as elsewhere, and is (and was at the time) seen as a characteristic of modernity. Ireland between 1900 and 1910 was a country in the throes of modernization, despite the fact that many commentators despaired of its backwardness in so many areas, most obviously industrialization, while others, most notably some nationalists and religious leaders, worked hard to protect its people from what they saw as the harmful influences of the modern world.

Especially in the capital, Dublin, whose population was just under 300,000 in 1901, a fondness for shopping, spectacle and leisure was evident that we would easily recognize today. Large and glamorous department stores had begun to appear in the city in the 1840s, and were well established by the beginning of the twentieth century. Spectator sports were becoming very popular and attractions such as Dublin Zoo, the Phoenix Park and the various seaside resorts near the city provided people with places to visit in their free time, facilitated by sophisticated train and tram systems. Large international exhibitions attracted thousands of visitors, the most prominent of these being the Irish International Exhibition of 1907, which was held in Herbert Park in Ballsbridge in Dublin and featured displays of motor cars, electric and gas lighting and machinery, as well as amusements such as a Helter Skelter, a water chute, a crystal maze, a shooting jungle and a cinematograph. Dublin also boasted numerous cafes, bars and restaurants, and several theatres offering a range of fare provided mostly (though not exclusively) by international, often English, touring companies. Cinema was in its infancy, but already popular, with Lumière Cinématographe programmes promoted by the entrepreneur Dan Lowrey in Dublin from 1896, only the year after they were first privately demonstrated in Paris by the Lumières themselves, and two months after their first London screenings.[2] The Irish Animated Photo Company showed 'living pictures' at the Rotunda from 1903, and dedicated, full-time cinemas were established in 1908 in Belfast, and in 1909 in Dublin.[3]

Modernity is not necessarily associated with general prosperity, however, and Dublin, and Ireland generally, was well known for its poverty in the early years of the twentieth century, with many commentators focusing particularly on the primitive nature of both urban and rural housing, very high levels of unemployment and ongoing mass emigration. Dublin had the fifth highest death rate in the world, and in 1911 a third of the city's families were tenement-dwellers, occupying a single room.[4] At least 8 million people are thought to have left the country in the century between 1821 and 1921, and the vast majority did not return: by 1911 around a third of all people born in Ireland were living elsewhere.[5] However, Ireland during this period was very much a country of contrasts, and these bleak figures need to be considered alongside others that suggest that, on average, 'Irish living standards may have compared favourably with much of the rest of Europe … a little below the average for Western Europe as a whole and almost 60 per cent higher than the level for Eastern Europe as a whole.'[6]

As Ireland modernized, the production, importation and/or consumption of images of all kinds accelerated dramatically at every level of society as photography, printing, advertising, transport, communication and literacy developed. Nineteenth-century Irish visual culture included, among many other things, such diverse phenomena as the amateur photographic projects of Anglo-Irish landowners, the importation and widespread popularity of cheap illustrated English crime and romance periodicals and the production and importation of large quantities of Catholic religious statuary and pictures in a range of sizes suitable for wearing, carrying around and installing in homes and churches. Two developments were particularly significant in relation to the picture postcard, that of the photographic *carte-de-visite* as a collectible and exchange item from the 1860s on, and of the magic lantern as a portable tool for group entertainment, education and propaganda.

Cartes-de-visite were small photographs first patented in Paris by Disderi in 1854. They were varnished and mounted on sturdy cardboard, and featured portraits of either private or public individuals. They were the same size and shape as conventional printed visiting cards and were often substituted for them, and in many ways they can be seen as a direct ancestor of the picture postcard, used as they were in social communication and exchange rituals and as collectibles. They were produced by the commercial photographic studios which were being established throughout the country, the best known of which was that set up in 1865 in Sackville Street in Dublin by William Lawrence. Lawrence was not himself a photographer but instead, according to Justin Carville, 'a new breed of photographic capitalist', who saw the commercial potential of the seemingly insatiable desire of modern people for imagery.[7] Lawrence produced not only '*cartes-de-visite* of prominent religious and political figures' but also 'photographic medallions, stereoscopic cards and, by the 1880s, a series of photographically illustrated tourist books published under the title *The Emerald Isle*'.[8] Small wonder, then, that Lawrence later diversified further and became probably the largest and most successful Irish producer of picture postcards in the early twentieth century.

According to Kevin and Emer Rockett, the magic lantern, a system for shining a light through an image (drawn, painted, photographic, printed or multimedia) and projecting it onto a screen for individual or group viewing, is thought to have been 'in widespread use in Ireland from the early eighteenth century':[9]

> Thus, a full two centuries before the advent of cinematography projected moving pictures, audiences could collectively experience through magic lantern shows a great variety of mass-produced visual representations, both 'real' and 'magical'.[10]

The presenters of magic lantern displays often toured on an international circuit, providing shows with added special 'magical' effects as required as well as a spoken commentary that contextualized and made the images more meaningful to their audience. Two important developments in the 1820s made magic lanterns much more usable and consequently more popular, the discovery of limelight as a brilliant light source and the mass production of slides.[11] Companies that produced slides for magic lanterns, such as Lawrence, often reused many of the same images when they later moved into postcard production. During the nineteenth century, magic lantern use became more widespread in both public and private venues, but Irish people also enjoyed other image-based group entertainments such as panoramas, 'immersive large-scale paintings' applied to the inner wall of a circular room, so that the viewer was surrounded by the image, and *tableaux vivants*, 'theatrically posed static representations of paintings, statues and events'.[12] Technologies for viewing apparently moving and three-dimensional imagery, such as the kinetoscope, the mutoscope and the stereoscope, also became available in the late nineteenth century, although these devices were limited to individual viewing. The advent of cinema projection, of course, changed that, opening up a new type of communal entertainment experience, and opportunities for much greater economic exploitation as well as control.

The picture postcard, therefore, did not suddenly appear to innocent eyes. Irish people had been exposed for some time to a wide range of constantly developing visual technologies and the imported and home-produced imagery they displayed, and most were likely to be very visually literate and sophisticated in their understanding of image codes and conventions. People brought to their encounter with postcards a familiarity with existing visual technologies and how they worked, and this influenced their responses to and interaction with them.

The picture postcard

The picture postcard itself was also an international phenomenon, made possible largely by developments in postal organization and regulations as well as by those in printing, photography, literacy, consumption and transport. During the nineteenth century, as Sandra Ferguson has recounted, the speed and frequency of mail delivery increased considerably due to improvements in transport technology, and cheap postal rates were introduced based on weight.[13] The plain postcard, with space for an address and stamp on one side and message on the other, was first issued in Austria in 1869, and in Britain in 1870. By the end of 1871 more than 1,500,000 postcards were being sent weekly through the British mail, and in the decades that followed it became an important communication tool for businesses and government agencies, and for individuals who wished to connect with others without the elaborate formalities that had become associated with letter writing.[14] Concerns were expressed about a resulting decline in literacy (since a postcard, in contrast to a letter, allowed the addition of only a brief message), and about loss of privacy, but economics and convenience overrode these. The Switzerland-based Universal Postal Union (established in 1875) allowed the application of standardized prices, sizes, weights and formats to facilitate speedy and efficient handling and processing.[15]

Developments in printing and photography made possible and encouraged the addition of imagery to postcards, although many were then hand-coloured and embellished, often by home workers.[16] In 1894 the British Post Office relinquished its monopoly and allowed the general public to send privately printed picture postcards with an attached adhesive stamp through the post in the United Kingdom, including Ireland.[17] Publishers saw the commercial potential of this, and companies such as Raphael Tuck and Valentine's, which were already producing other printed products such as greeting cards, now began to diversify into postcards. In 1899, according to the TuckDB Postcards website, 'Tuck issued its first regular Series of Postcards, a group of twelve consecutively numbered chromographic (i.e. colored) views of London'.[18] New companies were also established to specifically supply (and encourage) the demand for postcards. At first, however, individualized communication needed to be squeezed into the available space around the image, as the other side was still retained for the address and stamp only. This meant that there was room to write only 'the briefest and most formal salutation', as one newspaper commentator remarked, unless the sender was gifted with 'calligraphy of microscopic dimensions'.[19]

Then, in 1902, the British Post Office allowed the sending of post-cards with divided backs, one half for the user to write a message and the other for the address and stamp, allowing the image to dominate the front without the necessity of writing over or around it. In subsequent years other postal authorities followed suit, such as France in 1903, Norway in 1905 and the United States in 1907.[20] The result was the development of what Frank Staff in his book *The Picture Postcard and Its Origins* (1966) has called 'a gigantic industry' and 'one of the biggest collecting crazes the world has ever known'.[21] There was such an enormous boom in the production, purchasing, sending and collecting of picture postcards that in 1903 the *Glasgow Evening News* gloomily forecasted that within the next decade Europe would be 'buried beneath picture postcards'.[22] Bjarne Rogan has calculated that in the first two decades of the twentieth century between 200 and 300 billion postcards were produced and sold worldwide.[23]

Picture postcards were mainly produced by commercial companies, but were also sponsored by groups with political and other specific interests to promote. They were bought because of their visual appeal and/or message, and their functionality. They featured an exhaustive variety of images, both black-and-white and coloured, usually accompanied by some sort of text title or caption. These included land-, town- and seascapes; notable buildings; modern forms of transport; celebrities; newsworthy events, particularly 'disasters'; political and sporting figures; attractive females; cute children and animals; 'interesting' foreign people; rural workers and comic and satirical cartoons. Many picture postcard subjects were carried over from other image formats and, indeed, postcard producers drew on practically every form of existing visual tradition, including fine art, comedic entertainment, fantasy, documentary image-making and personal and celebrity portraiture. Many cards also featured similar subjects to the emerging medium of cinema, so that, for instance, *Rough Sea at Dover*, a short film made in 1895, also appears as the title of many later postcard images, and both early film and postcard representations of Irishness tend to feature the Lakes of Killarney, tourists kissing the Blarney Stone, the Giant's Causeway in Antrim and an Irishman called Pat or Paddy often accompanied by a pig.[24]

More or less any subject was possible, although some of the more risqué ones, deemed sexually or politically offensive or socially dangerous, were censored, and, if procured, had to be posted in an envelope. Despite the cheap price of picture postcards, the massive numbers sold meant that their production, distribution and sale generated huge profit, and their subject matter tended to be market driven, with imagery frequently manipulated and recaptioned to make them more appealing to consumers. F. E. Dixon, in his article 'Pioneer Publishers of Dublin Picture Postcards' (1979), singles out Valentine's, a company established in Dundee in Scotland which did a lot of business in Ireland, as particularly 'expert at faking, producing realistic snow scenes or moonlit views by retouching, substituting automobiles for jaunting cars, etc'.[25] However, there is also plenty of evidence of such practices by many other companies.

Postcards could be bought from shops, street traders and/or vending machines in every town and village in Ireland, as well as from railway stations, on ships and at even the most remote tourist spots. Purchasers gave postcards as gifts to others, sent them through the post, or kept them themselves, frequently collecting them in specially designed albums. They were often given, kept or posted as holiday souvenirs, but this was not as dominant a function of postcards as it became later. As the telegraph and telephone were not yet accessible to many people, they were particularly popular as a means of quick, informal communication, similar to texting in the early twenty-first century, and this was facilitated by the frequent and generally very efficient daily postal deliveries of the era[26] (see Figure 1). They were also used to send greetings on special occasions, such as birthdays, Christmas, Easter and Valentine's Day, taking a sizeable share of the market from conventional greeting cards. An advertisement in the *Dundalk Democrat* in December 1903 announced: 'Christmas Picture

Post-Cards – the latest novelty; will be Christmas Card of the future', and urged the reader to 'Take time by the forelock and send one'.[27]

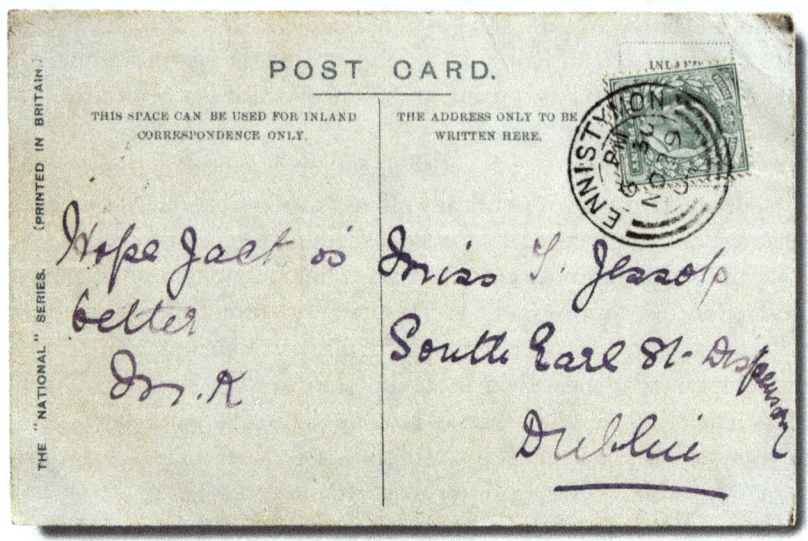

Figure 1. Postcard message sent to Christina Jessop. Christina Jessop's card collection.

Communication by picture postcards could be further personalized by the use of 'real' photographs, often taken by private individuals, printed as a postcard either by using a new type of Kodak camera or by a commercial company that provided such a service, such as Purcell & Company in Patrick Street in Cork or Glass's Studio of Carlisle Road in Londonderry.[28] In 1908 Hely's in Dublin offered to produce postcards from a photograph of 'yourself, your house, [or] your favourite animal', twelve for two shillings and hand-coloured for an extra shilling.[29] Brook Smith of Stephen's Green in Dublin suggested the real photo postcard was an ideal Christmas card: 'Xmas is coming, and with it the desire to see your friends; if that is impossible my Personal Postcards are next best; any photo can be copied.'[30]

As mentioned already, the picture postcard phenomenon was an international one, and big postcard firms in particular, such as Raphael Tuck & Sons, described by the *Freeman's Journal* in 1904 as 'the principal manufacturers of postcards', advertised and sold their products in many countries.[31] Raphael Tuck & Sons was originally based in London, but by 1903 had offices in Paris, Berlin, Montreal and New York.[32] They and other companies also outsourced many aspects of their production, and a great deal of early postcard printing, for instance, was centralized in Germany because of factors such as low labour costs and its long-standing printing tradition and therefore existing infrastructure.[33] Raphael Tuck & Sons was constantly updating its product range, producing novelty variations such as 'Picture Puzzle' cards (1909), which were pre-cut into jigsaws.[34] According to the *Freeman's Journal* in 1906 Tuck's cards varied in size and price from 'the popular card for the poorest market to the elaborate "art portfolio" and "porcelain panels". There are designs in parchment, scroll ... celluloid, alabaster ...'[35] They also came up with some creative marketing techniques, running numerous competitions with substantial cash prizes for those who could produce the largest collections of (Tuck) postcards, and those who came up with the most original ideas about what to do with them.[36] Suggestions included using them to paper a nursery or make a fire screen.[37]

Other companies also did their best to meet the demand for endless novelty. As early as 1893 a postcard was issued which was also a miniature newspaper, 'with four tiny illustrations accompanying a comic tragedy in 33 words, some puzzles, jokes, and prize competitions, an editorial note, and a few advertisements at the bottom'.[38] By 1903 Hold-to-Light and Transparency cards were in circulation, which revealed special visual effects when looked at with a light source behind them. Cards whose imagery and text required heat, a mirror or tilting in order to be visible were also published.[39] In 1904 an Italian company brought out a postcard that could predict the weather (according to the *Cork Examiner*), by changing colour in different atmospheric conditions.[40] In the same year cards also went on sale with attached transparent celluloid gramophone discs so that spoken messages and music could be recorded and sent.[41] Cards of various non-standard shapes, 'freak' postcards as they were called in the *Donegal*

News, such as seashells, fish and animals, or cards which incorporated a series of pull-out views under a flap, became subject to restrictions by the Post Office. Glitter or 'jewelled' cards were also a problem, as the powdered glass or mica was seen as injurious to the health of postal workers[42] (see Figure 2). As a result, they needed to be placed within an envelope for

MISS GRACE LANE.

Figure 2. 'Jewelled' detail on a card. Ellen Duff's card collection.

postage, and senders were charged the letter rate of a penny rather than the postcard rate of a halfpenny. Some cards included text on the back that warned consumers of this. Many postcards sold for Saint Patrick's Day were advertised as having a small packet of shamrock seeds attached, or even sprays of 'real shamrock', both of which could also cause problems in their passage through the mail.[43] The application of real hair and real feathers, often to the heads and hats of actress images, was also tried, as were cards with added scent, pressed flowers, velvet, fur fabric and lace. Despite all these attempts at variety and novelty, postcards remained, as Julia Gillen and Nigel Hall have observed, highly regulated objects, whose 'shape and size were determined by the Post Office', and whose consistent and light-weight but strong construction facilitated their easy handling, sorting and carrying in large quantities.[44] Postcards featuring images of distant places and people, both imported and locally produced, were sold in Ireland and images of Ireland, often produced by non-Irish companies, were sold abroad.[45] Irish people, therefore, including those who had little ability or desire to read the books, magazines and newspapers of the period, were exposed via postcards to a large variety of images, along with the ideas and values they communicated.

Picture postcards in Edwardian Ireland

Dublin-based firms such as Lawrence, Browne & Nolan, Tallon's, Eason's and Hely's were prominent on the Irish market. According to Dixon, Lawrence originally only supplied photographs for other companies to use for postcards, but soon started to produce their own, and Valentine's were actually the first to produce Irish 'view cards', developing such a successful Irish trade that in 1905 they established a Dublin branch.[46] Apart from foreign firms, Dublin companies had competition from a myriad of local producers throughout the country such as Horgan brothers in Youghal, A. H Poole in Waterford, Guy's in Cork and Fergus O'Connor, who started his postcard business in Cork before 1900 and moved to Dublin about 1908. It is difficult to establish the proportion of Irish-produced (either printed, published or commissioned) to imported cards in Ireland during this period, but postcard collections that have survived from the time, as well as advertisements and opinion pieces in newspapers, suggest that there were far more of the latter than the former. Modern collections in Irish museums and libraries have tended to focus on cards featuring Irish national and local subject matter (which may or may not have been produced in Ireland), but this does not necessarily reflect the interests of card purchasers and collectors in early twentieth-century Ireland.

As was the case in other countries, the Irish media frequently commented on the new 'craze', as it was called. The *Cork Examiner* reported in 1904 on 'an enormous increase in the use of pictorial postcards which shows a tendency to displace letters and official postcards'.[47] The following year it cited the opinion of the Postmaster General that a measurable decrease in letter delivery could be attributable to the increase in postcards, of which 734,500,000 had been delivered in the United Kingdom the previous year, an increase of nearly 20 per cent.[48] According to the *Irish Independent*, in 1906 the number of postcards passing through the Irish post alone was estimated at 32,800,000.[49] In May 1907, however, it predicted that the craze was dying out, offering the opinion that 'speaking generally, the picture postcard craze had not specifically harmful results'.[50] This obituary was somewhat premature, however, and the numbers sent through the post continued to increase, albeit at a decreasing rate. During the first decade of the twentieth century in Ireland picture postcards became ubiquitous, almost impossible to avoid, so that for instance a visitor to Killaloe in County Clare in 1907 saw one area of the town so dominated by shops selling them that he thought it could be called 'Pictorial Avenue ... all the doors and windows decorated with comic life, Irish life, country life, town life, high life, low life, and no life'.[51] Hely's in Dublin advertised a selection of 5,000 different varieties of postcard in 1904, but by 1908 J. A. Coleman of Bailieborough in County Cavan claimed that his customers could select from 'tens of thousands', although it is not clear whether this number refers to his total stock of cards or the number of different types he had for sale.[52]

Commentators worried that Irish entrepreneurs were not fully exploiting the business potential of this new phenomenon. According to the *Derry People* in 1904,

It is quite certain that not one-hundredth of the picture pasteboards bought with money earned in Ireland are produced in this country. Our stationers' shops are full of cards with views of Irish scenery and notable buildings and works of art. Nearly all are placed on the market by English firms. English photographers, English lithographers, and English printers reap the benefit, as well as the astute English capitalists who study the public taste and cater for it.[53]

In response, Irish newspapers often went out of their way to praise and promote postcards published in Ireland. The *Anglo-Celt* reported the following in 1904 on postcards produced by J. A. Coleman of Bailieborough:

It always gives us pleasure to record the enterprise of a resident in our towns, go-ahead being unfortunately so rare in Ireland … It is no exaggeration to say that the fifteen (in packet) … for a shilling are far superior to many of the Continental cards we have seen … The man or woman who purchases an imported card while one of Coleman's is to be had is a poor sort of patriot.[54]

Cards with text in the Irish language also received a considerable amount of newspaper coverage, such as those produced by Dawson's in Maynooth featuring the O'Growney Memorial, a monument dedicated to one of the founders of the association for promoting the Irish language, the Gaelic League.[55] Walter Farrell, based at Hereford Road in London, also specialized in 'view' cards with Irish language text, and these were regularly endorsed by the Gaelic League.[56] The use of Irish peat to make postcards was also much praised. The *Freeman's Journal* assured readers that the series published by McGinly and Mackey in Dublin was designed and printed in Ireland, and the paper was manufactured in Ireland, 'whilst the fact that it is made from Irish peat, "each card a bit of the old sod", is a unique souvenir to friends abroad'.[57] The Celbridge Peat Paper Mills in Kildare also produced postcards 'made from Bog of Allen peat'.[58] Companies such as these saw a marketing advantage in their products being identified as distinctively Irish. Sometimes non-Irish companies used misleading names or trademarks to suggest that their products were Irish or made in Ireland, and the Irish Industrial Development Association (IDA) took measures against these, successfully bringing a case for instance against a London-based picture postcard company which wanted to call itself 'Shamrock and Co'.[59] The IDA also took the General Manager of the Great Northern Railway of Ireland to task about his company's use of foreign-printed picture postcards, despite the fact that they were purchased from a Dublin firm. He responded that he hadn't known they were printed abroad and promised that it wouldn't happen again.[60]

Nevertheless Irish newspapers ran numerous advertisements and editorial promotions for non-Irish postcard producers, particularly for Raphael Tuck.[61] This company's productions were described as 'exquisite', 'unique' and 'humorous ... [but] free from the slightest trace of vulgarity'.[62] The *Killarney Echo* conceded that 'The firm's productions are all works of Art, and if Irishmen and women must send to England for their postcards, etc., Messrs Tuck and Sons give the best value we know of.'[63] Newspaper commentators also tended to be impressed by any attractive Irish-themed postcards, regardless of where they were produced, pointing out their potential for promoting tourism to the country. Examples were the various bestselling Irish 'views' published by the London and North Western Railway. 'The sale of the cards have been phenomenal', enthused the *Freeman's Journal*,

> with over five and a quarter million having been purchased up to date ... The new sets, which are specially devoted to Ireland, will, no doubt play a large part in directing tourist traffic to Ireland, whose scenic beauty they depict with artistic skill.[64]

As a writer in the *Kerry Weekly Reporter* stated in relation to the issuing of a new set of Kerry views by the Pictorial Stationary company in London: 'Really artistic view postcards constitute a splendid recommendation to health and holiday resorts, and as they are circulated without cost to the authorities should prove a valuable form of advertisement.'[65]

The picture postcards that circulated in Ireland in the first decade of the twentieth century showed the same breadth and variety of subject matter as elsewhere, and a similar combination of the local and the exotic. In Irish newspapers in 1906, for instance, Raphael Tuck was advertising an eclectic mixture of 'Killarney views, Animal Expressions, some reproductions from "Punch", British Sea-birds, Australian types, Indian Chiefs, and beautiful views from many of the famous places of the world'[66] (see Figure 3). Advertisements from 1907 and 1908 from The Card Company in Belfast give a sense of the exhaustive range of their stock: Dickens characters, copies of famous paintings, 'Wave Series', 'Hands Across the Sea',

Figure 3. *Chief 'Stranger Horse'*, Indian Chiefs – Series 1, Raphael Tuck. From <https:// tuckdbpostcards.org/items/117478>

Irish-built liners, famous men and women, famous cathedrals, humorous life, motoring, 'losers', prehistoric, children, dogs, scenes abroad, cricket, football, Irish views, naval life, variety artistes, famous comedians, actresses 'assorted, coloured, and plain', zoological gardens, and scenes from Irish life which included 'Paddy Leary, Dear Harp, Low-Backed Car, [and] Pat's Courtship'.[67] These perennials competed for attention with more fleetingly topical cards featuring subjects such as the Boer War generals (1902), the Cork International Exhibition (1902), the Entente Cordiale (1904), the Battle of Port Arthur (1904), the visit of Cardinal Vannutelli to Armagh (1904), the Irish Language Procession in Dublin (1905) the Dublin International Exhibition (1907), as well as victorious sporting teams and individuals (see Figure 4).

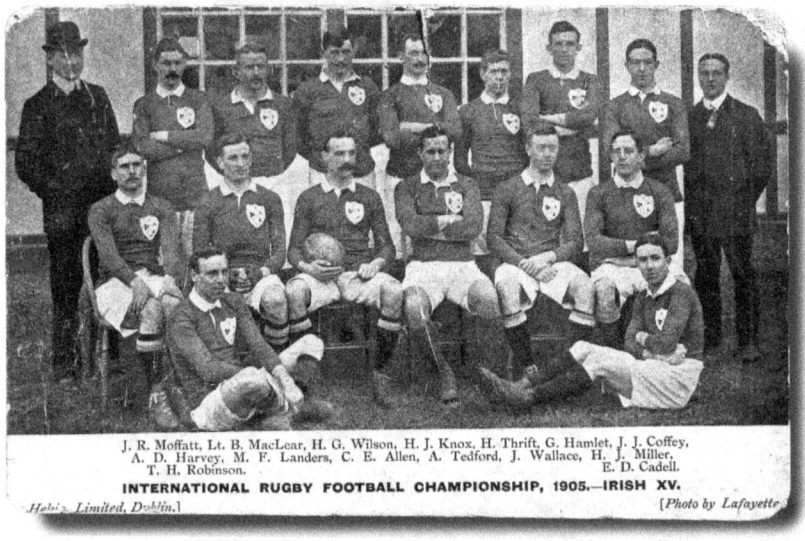

J. R. Moffatt, Lt. B. MacLear, H. G. Wilson, H. J. Knox, H. Thrift, G. Hamlet, J. J. Coffey, A. D. Harvey, M. F. Landers, C. E. Allen, A. Tedford, J. Wallace, H. J. Miller, T. H. Robinson.   E. D. Cadell.

INTERNATIONAL RUGBY FOOTBALL CHAMPIONSHIP, 1905.—IRISH XV.

Hely's Limited, Dublin.]   [Photo by Lafayette.

Figure 4. *International Rugby Football Championship, 1905 – Irish XV*, Hely's, Dublin. Christina Jessop's card collection.

Picture postcards could be seen as entertaining, amusing, emotive, educative, propagandistic, titillating, irritating or offensive, depending on the cards and the viewer. They pictured Ireland to Irish people, as well as bringing the spectacle of the wider world to even the most determined stay-at-homes. They forged and maintained connections between geographically widely separated people and places. Often the exact same cards circulated in North America, Australia and Europe as in Britain and Ireland, as was the case with images of female music-theatre stars who toured internationally, such as Marie Studholme, Maude Fealy, Marie Corelli, Zena and Phyllis Dare and Gertie Millar.[68] These images, many published by the Philco Publishing Company of London and the Rotary Photographic Company in Middlesex, became enormously popular with young Irish women, and Hely's of Dublin regularly advertised 'assorted actresses' in various newspapers. The influence of such imagery on Irish women was commented on in the *Evening Herald* in 1904, in which a writer noted the 'abnormally large' number of 'imitation "Gibson girls" in Dublin', a fad attributed to the popularity of postcards based on the fashionable and idealized 'Gibson girl' image popularized by the American illustrator Charles Dana Gibson (1867–1944).[69] Raphael Tuck also issued a series of photographic images of 'the original Gibson girl', the actress Camille Clifford (see Figure 5). Gibson girl images, like the photographic postcards of languid, carefree and glamorous stars from musical theatre, must have suggested very novel and seductive ways of performing femininity to many young Irish women, especially compared to more conventional Irish Catholic female role models such as the Virgin Mary.

As early as 1903 some commentators were expressing strong reservations about some of the messages communicated by postcard imagery and their social effects. The *Ulster Herald*, for instance complained about the large number of 'silly objectionable cards … sent through the post by young persons'. The writer went on to quote an opinion piece from the periodical *The Irish Rosary*, which railed against the increasing numbers of cards that were

> calculated to appeal to the idle, the silly, the vacuous, and the fabulous mind. They are comic, pseudo-comic, epicene, suggestive, smutty, silly, crude, coarse, and oftentimes outright vulgar. A study of these things make (sic) one amazed at the shallow-wittedness, or even the lack-wittedness, that the purchasers of them will consent to be amused by.[70]

Examples of objectionable subjects were given in a related article in the *Fermanagh Herald*:

> Seaside scenes; bulgy females – elderly and irate – clad in burstingly tight bathing dresses; skinny, frightened-looking men, being tyrannically ill–used by the plump, elderly amazons aforesaid, younger men and women performing dear knows what idiotic pranks, and convulsed with laughter at their own drollery.[71]

Figure 5. *Miss Camille Clifford*, Raphael Tuck. From <https://tuckdbpostcards.org/items/109418>

There were also more specific concerns about issues such as obscenity and the corruption of young people, and the perpetuation of negative Irish stereotypes both in Ireland and abroad, and these will be considered in later chapters. Generally, however, postcard imagery reflected and constructed similar ideas, values and fantasies to those circulating via other media. Anxiety about its possibly deleterious effects on society generally but especially on young people was also not unique to the postcard phenomenon. The magic lantern, popular illustrated literature and early

cinema had all been criticized (and suppressed at times) as media of potential corruption. The postcard was distinctive in that it was very cheap,
and so reached more people than most other visual media; it was also
very portable and could be sent to and received from anywhere in the
world; it provided mass-produced imagery which individuals could then
add to and manipulate as a means of practical communication and/or
personal expression; it could be exchanged as a gift and it could be collected and treasured as a memento or object of aesthetic or other pleasures. Postcards could be kept private (sold and exchanged secretively, kept
in personal albums for individual perusal and posted in envelopes), but
more commonly they were publicly displayed for sale, collected to be
shown to family and friends, and posted with additions and manipulations easily visible to postal workers and anyone else *en route* from sender
to receiver. All these possibilities could provoke anxiety in some early
twentieth-century commentators, and today they make the Edwardian
postcard a complicated object of study, whether in Ireland or elsewhere.
Rogan calls it an 'Entangled Object', entangled, that is, in many different
discourses,

> aesthetics and communication, ritual and symbol, technology and business, play and
> action, imagination and remembrance, desire and materiality, commodity as well as
> subjective experience … There seems to be no end to the perspectives that may be
> applied to the picture postcard.[72]

The chapters that follow will examine picture postcards in Edwardian
Ireland in relation to a selection of discourses, under the broad categories
of collectors and collecting, communication, nationalism, empire, mod-
ernism, revival, travel, emigration, tourism and the lives of women. Such
a study cannot really be comprehensive, and no doubt there are many
other aspects of this fascinating subject which will be teased out by future
scholars.

The emergence and subsequent ubiquity of picture postcards happened within a relatively short timeframe, and their impact on Edwardian
society is difficult to imagine in our present era, when the postcard has a
much reduced presence and function. To get some idea of how prominent
they were, it is worth briefly considering the Irish International Exhibition

in Ballsbridge in Dublin in 1907. Many postcards were published and bought featuring different views of the Exhibition, and special editions were also brought out to celebrate specific events such the visit of Edward VII and Queen Alexandra in July.[73] The venue itself featured its own post office and a large number of stalls selling postcards from a range of companies, including six dedicated postcard stands (with space and facilities for writing) by Tallon's of Dublin, who advertised a 'Stock of About One Million Post Cards', with about 20,000 different varieties.[74] There was also a stage entertainment performed several times a day in September, called *The Living Picture Postcard Album*, which apparently 'elicited unstinted admiration'.[75] This consisted of a stage set which looked like a giant postcard album, whose covers opened and whose pages turned as part of the performance, revealing a series of life-size postcard 'pictures' peopled by actors who first appeared in static poses but then moved to reveal themselves as 'real live figures'.[76] This celebration of postcard collecting via what seems to have been a *tableau vivant* suggests its prominence and embeddedness in the culture of the period, which is the subject of the next chapter. It also positions the picture postcard as one of a range of visual media that were popular at the time, some new and some older, and highlights the ongoing exchanges and referencing that were common between them.

Despite some serious poverty and deprivation, Edwardian Ireland was a country in the throes of modernization, and one of the manifestations of this was its participation in the newly emerged international obsession with buying, sending, receiving and collecting picture postcards. Although the mass production of picture postcards really only began in Britain and Ireland in the late 1890s, the numbers circulating rapidly rose to millions, and they soon became an unavoidable aspect of Irish life. Giant international and smaller Irish companies competed to exploit their profit-making potential, and the Gaelic League and other groups tried to harness the format for nationalist and Irish business interests, but they remained a truly international phenomenon, often the product of specialized processes located in many different countries and then exported and posted all over the world. Like other manifestations of modernity in Edwardian Ireland and elsewhere, the picture postcard generated many anxieties and debates, exacerbated by the fact that it was cheap and ubiquitous enough to be widely accessible even to the young and poor, but its convenience and the appeal of its variety of imagery, constantly updated by canny producers, ensured that it remained an important aspect of Irish popular culture until at least the First World War.

Notes

1. The Citizen, 'Picture Post-Cards', *Art and Progress*, 1/1 (1909), 11–12, 11.
2. Kevin Rockett and Emer Rockett, *Magic Lantern Panorama and Moving Picture Shows in Ireland, 1786–1909* (Dublin: Four Courts Press, 2011), 218.
3. Kevin Rockett, 'Cinema', in S. J. Connolly, ed., *The Oxford Companion to Irish History* (Oxford, New York: Oxford University Press, 2004), 98; Stephanie Rains, *Commodity Culture and Social Class in Dublin 1850–1916* (Dublin: Irish Academic Press, 2010), 183.
4. Mary Daly, *Dublin, The Deposed Capital, a Social and Economic History, 1860–1914* (Cork: Cork University Press, 1984), 276; David Dickson, 'Dublin', in Connolly, ed., *The Oxford Companion*, 168–172, 171; Daniel Mulhall, *A New Day Dawning: A Portrait of Ireland in 1900* (Cork: The Collins Press, 1999), 70.
5. D. H. Akenson, 'Emigration', in Connolly, ed., *The Oxford Companion*, 179; Diarmaid Ferriter, *The Transformation of Ireland 1900–2000* (London: Profile Books, 2005), 44.
6. Kieran A. Kennedy, Thomas Giblin and Deirdre McHugh, *The Economic Development of Ireland in the Twentieth Century* (London and New York: Routledge, 1988), 13.
7. Justin Carville, *Photography and Ireland* (London: Reaktion Books, 2011), 27.
8. Carville, *Photography and Ireland*, 27. Stereoscopic views were 'small twin images taken with a double-lensed camera and viewed through a stereoscope to give an impression of depth'; Vivienne Pollock, 'Photography', in Connolly, ed., *The Oxford Companion*, 464–465, 465.
9. Rockett, Kevin and Emer, *Magic Lantern Panorama*, 17.
10. Rockett, Kevin and Emer, *Magic Lantern Panorama*, 20.
11. Rockett, Kevin and Emer, *Magic Lantern Panorama*, 45.
12. Rockett, Kevin and Emer, *Magic Lantern Panorama*, 12.
13. Sandra Ferguson, ' "A Murmur of Small Voices": On the Picture Postcard in Academic Research', *Archivaria*, 60 (September 2006), 169. <http://journals.sfu.ca/archivar/index.uphp/archivaria/article/view/12520/13654> accessed 19 September 2014.
14. Christopher Browne, *Getting the Message. The Story of the British Post Office* (Stroud, Gloucestershire: Alan Sutton, 1993), 99.

15. Browne, *Getting the Message*, 104.
16. 'Business', *Freemans Journal* (20 June 1904).
17. F. E. Dixon, 'Pioneer Publishers of Dublin Picture Postcards', *Dublin Historical Record*, 32 (1979), 146–147, 146.
18. 'History', TuckDB Postcards website, <https://tuckdbpostcards.org/history> accessed 6 August 2020.
19. *Ballinrobe Chronicle* (22 May 1902).
20. Rogan, 'Entangled Object', 14.
21. Frank Staff, *The Picture Postcard and Its Origins* (London: Lutterworth Press, 1966), 52.
22. Richard Carline, *Pictures in the Post. The Story of the Picture Postcard and Its Place in the History of Popular Art* (London: Gordon Frazer, 1971), 9.
23. Rogan, 'Entangled Object', 31.
24. Rockett, Kevin and Emer, *Magic Lantern Panorama*, 67 and 224.
25. Dixon, 'Pioneer Publishers', 146.
26. Ferguson, *The Post Office in Ireland*, 175–176; Murphy, *A Bloomsday Postcard*, 26.
27. *Dundalk Democrat* (19 December 1903).
28. *Cork Examiner* (3 June 1905); *Donegal News* (26 September 1908); *Cork Examiner* (19 September 1905); 'Portraits on Postcards', *The Derry People* (12 September 1908).
29. *Irish Independent* (23 July 1908).
30. *Irish Independent* (21 November 1908).
31. *Freemans Journal* (28 October 1904).
32. 'History', TuckDB Postcards website.
33. Rogan, 'Entangled Object', 6.
34. *Munster Express* (18 September 1909).
35. *Freemans Journal* (15 December 1906).
36. *Kerry Evening Post* (2 December 1903); 'Our London Correspondent', *Kerry Evening Post* (2 March 1906).
37. *Evening Herald* (15 March 1909).
38. 'A Newspaper on a Post-Card', *Evening Herald* (8 March 1893).
39. Tonie and Valmai Holt, *Picture Postcards of the Golden Age, a Collector's Guide* (London: MacGibbin & Kee, 1971), 129–130.
40. *Irish Examiner* (4 April 1900).
41. *Irish Examiner* (6 February 1905); *Evening Herald* (2 December 1904).
42. *Donegal News* (9 July 1910); *Evening Herald* (6 September 1904).
43. 'They Say That', *Kerry Evening Star* (10 March 1910).
44. Julia Gillen and Nigel Hall, 'The Edwardian Postcard: A Revolutionary Moment in Rapid Multimodal Communications', paper presented at the British Educational Research Association Annual Conference Manchester, 2–5 September 2009, 3.
45. 'New Postcards', *Cork Examiner* (19 October 1905).
46. Dixon, 'Pioneer Publishers', 146.

47. *Cork Examiner* (18 August 1904).

48. *Cork Examiner* (11 August 1905).

49. *Irish Independent* (9 August 1906).

50. 'A Change of Taste', *Irish Independent* (10 May 1907).

51. 'Killaloe Notes', *Nenagh Guardian* (31 August 1907).

52. *Evening Herald* (3 March 1904); *Anglo Celt* (28 November 1908).

53. 'Picture Post Cards', *Derry People* (3 December 1904).

54. *Anglo-Celt* (17 December 1904).

55. *Meath Chronicle* (3 June 1905).

56. *Freemans Journal* (18 August 1904).

57. 'By the Way', *Freemans Journal* (19 December 1905).

58. *Connaught Telegraph* (31 December 1904).

59. 'The Irish Trade Mark. More Misleading Titles', *Cork Examiner* (14 February 1908). The Irish Industrial Development Association (IDA) was an informal grouping that was first established in 1903, and should not be confused with the later Industrial Development Authority (IDA) Ireland which was founded in 1949.

60. *Freemans Journal* (20 July 1908).

61. 'Picture Postcards', *Cork Examiner* (14 July 1900); 'Raphael Tuck's Postcards', *Freemans Journal* (3 September 1904).

62. *Cork Examiner* (15 June 1906); 'Messrs. Raphael Tuck & Sons', *Drogheda Argus and Leinster Journal* (19 November 1904).

63. *KIllarney Echo* (1 June 1907).

64. 'London and North-Western Railway Picture Postcards', *Freemans Journal* (22 December 1906).

65. 'View Post Cards', *Kerry Weekly Reporter* (30 June 1906).

66. *Cork Examiner* (15 June 1906).

67. *Irish Independent* (8 May 1907); *Irish Independent* (11 May 1907); *Sunday Independent* (15 March 1908).

68. Kelly, 'Beauty and the Market', 99–116.

69. 'Reform in Paris', *Evening Herald* (2 November 1904).

70. 'Picture Postcards', *Ulster Herald* (3 October 1903).

71. 'Picture Postcards', *Fermanagh Herald* (3 October 1903).

72. Rogan, 'Entangled Object', 3.

73. *Freemans Journal* (13 July 1907).

74. *Evening Herald* (4 May 1907); *Irish Independent* (6 May 1907).

75. *Freemans Journal* (21 September 1907).

76. *Irish Independent* (14 September 1907).

CHAPTER 2

Collections, collectors and collecting

Postcard collecting

The collecting of picture postcards during the Edwardian period emerged from a range of very diverse collecting practices, and collectors themselves and their motivations also varied considerably. Some saw picture postcards as similar to collectibles such as stamps, coins or cigarette cards, and conferred a higher monetary value on particular examples that were unusual, for instance, or completed a series. The image on the card was important for them, but the postmark could also be significant. Picture postcard collecting, like that of stamps, rocks or butterflies, could also be seen as educational. Children were encouraged to collect as a means of developing their understanding of subjects such as geography, geology and nature, as well as of scientific classification and approaches to understanding the world. Newspapers also reported approvingly on the use of postcard collections in formal education: according to the *Ballinrobe Chronicle* in 1905 picture postcards were playing 'a prominent part' in geography classes in Dutch schools. Collections of cards posted back to schools by teachers travelling abroad proved 'far more attractive to the child's eye than the ordinary woodcut in the book or chart on the wall'.[1] The same article also noted that Surrey County Council rewarded elementary school children with 'view' picture postcards for good attendance and punctuality, and suggested this as a good idea also for Irish National schools. In 1908 the *Cork Examiner* included a report on the use of postcards as an educational aid in schools in Germany, where 'postcards illustrative of natural and political history are to combine instruction with amusement'.[2] Companies made a point of publishing material suitable for this market, such as the Country Press in Kensington which produced several series of 'nature study' cards featuring images of British trees, ferns and grasses.[3] Raphael Tuck's *Birds* series published in 1910 had a similar function, and included information printed on the backs of the cards about the species featured on the front.

Postcard collections could also function to document personal travels or those of friends, so that the postmark and the added written message became important along with the picture. This kind of collecting is related to the printed, and later photographic, 'views' brought home from a Grand Tour or similar adventure by tourists of previous generations. Other popular picture postcard collectibles, such as actress or other celebrity images, were more in the tradition of *cartes-de-visite*, standard-sized studio-taken photographs of private and widely recognized individuals that became a popular middle-class enthusiasm in the 1860s. *Carte-de-visite* albums were often handsomely bound and contained representations of family, friends and well-known local, national or international personages, frequently very elegantly mounted and arranged. The images were often gifted and shared within social groups, and the albums were kept in the parlour to be brought out for the diversion of visitors. Both *carte-de-visite* and postcard albums, and later, family photograph albums, were sold with regularly spaced slots or holders for the display and convenient insertion and removal of images without damaging them.

The compilation, display and enjoyment of *carte-de-visite*, photograph and postcard albums were linked to a wider popular album culture that was well established long before the nineteenth century. The *Album Amicorum* or friendship book was used by male university students from the sixteenth to the eighteenth centuries to record their encounters with other students and professors as they travelled around Europe. Friends contributed greetings, dedications, illustrations and emblems to the album, so that, according to Katie Day Good, it was 'an intrinsically social medium'.[4] The culture of enjoying and sharing albums continued into the nineteenth century, when scrapbooks became very popular particularly with women and girls. Albums sold with blank pages were filled with small mementos that people wanted to save, according to Maurice Rickards 'such items as pressed flowers, paper cuts and silhouettes, dried seaplants, feathers, puzzles, poems, and other natural and graphic ephemera'.[5] They also contained 'scraps', brightly coloured printed paper cut-outs which in the second half of the century were mass-produced specifically for this market. A great deal of nineteenth-century scrap imagery uses similar motifs and styles to later Edwardian postcards, and many of the companies that produced scrap on a large scale, such as Raphael Tuck, Hildesheimer and Davidson Brothers, later became significant producers of picture postcards.[6] Scraps, Rickards claims, were such popular collectibles that they became a 'worldwide cult'.[7]

Katie Day Good compares nineteenth- and early twentieth-century scrapbooks to the modern social media platform Facebook, seeing both 'as sites of *personal media assemblage* and *personal media archives*, a designation that highlights the simultaneously social and archival dimensions of each form'.[8] In both cases users construct 'individualized collections of media fragments both original and appropriated', and 'the flexibility of each format permits friends, family and other contacts to directly inscribe their own artifacts onto other people's pages, provided that they are granted access by the owner'.[9] The primary function of both, she argues, is 'the documentation of friendship', although of course the social sharing of that documentation is also an important aspect of it.[10] Picture postcard albums can be seen as a later, Edwardian, manifestation of scrapbooks, maintaining their social and archival functions. Postcards were often collected in these albums because of their visual appeal, but also because of the people who sent them and the messages they wrote on them. The postcards could also be accompanied by photographs, handwritten verses or other souvenirs that had personal meaning. The compilation of a picture postcard album could therefore be an ongoing construction of a particular personal and social identity which could be savoured privately or displayed and shared with others. By the early twentieth century, this kind of album culture had become very much associated with women, and attracted dismissive comments as a result. However, it was still very much alive, as a quote from the *Irish Independent* from January 1905 suggests: 'The New Year has brought us back the album. It enshrines picture postcards, amateur photos and the literary efforts of unliterary people.'[11]

The picture postcard was certainly remarkable in its flexibility and adaptability, and in its consequent adoption by a wide range of people for many different purposes. This partly explains the unprecedented enthusiasm with which people collected it, which Richard Carline argues in his book *Pictures in the Post. The Story of the Picture Postcard and Its Place in the History of Popular Art* (1971) was 'in full swing throughout the world well before the end of the [nineteenth] century'.[12] According to Klich and Weiss, 'photographic visiting cards, printed advertising cards, hatcheck stubs, tobacco cards, cigar bands, bookplates, postage stamps, and tram tickets – all had their collectors. The postcard eclipsed them all'.[13]

That this was recognized early on is borne out by a report in the *Ballinrobe Chronicle* as early as 1898 which claimed that in Austria and Germany collecting postcards was 'to a certain extent supplanting that of postage stamps'.[14] The first of many international picture postcard exhibitions took place in that same year, in Leipzig, a city which, not coincidentally, was 'a major center of postcard publishing'.[15] Such exhibitions showcased not only postcards but also magazines, clubs, publishers, suppliers of albums and other collecting accessories, as well as collectors themselves and their contact details. Klich and Weiss cite a collection displayed at a Venice exhibition by a Miss Antonini, which contained an impressive 9,000 cards.[16] A promotional and supportive institutional structure of clubs, exhibitions and magazines thus developed which was similar to that associated with philately.[17] Collectors made contact with each other through placing advertisements in specialist journals, but also in the mainstream press, specifying the kinds of cards they would like to collect and exchange. Raphael Tuck also published annually their own *Postcard Exchange Register*, which contained the names of more than 2,000 collectors of Tuck's postcards worldwide who were willing to exchange cards with others.[18]

The Irish weekly *Sunday Independent*, which began publication in 1906, included such advertisements in a column titled 'Our Weekly Levee, chats and replies on matters of interest', alongside short verses, readers' advertisements, queries and responses, information on miscellaneous, legal and medical matters, and a 'missing friends' section. These advertisements were often from readers based in other countries who specifically wanted to collect Irish cards.[19] In 1909 the same newspaper published a joke satirizing this modern obsession (which it called 'the new style') for collecting cards from as many different places as possible:

'No, John, I cannot marry you.'
'Then I start for Japan to-morrow.'
'Make it Afghanistan. I have no postcards from there.'[20]

There seem to have been no Irish-published postcard magazines during the Edwardian period, but British publications were easily available in Irish bookshops and bookstalls and through the post. According to Carline, six journals dedicated to postcard collecting were published in Great Britain during the early years of the century, most of which did not survive past the Golden Age.[21] There were sixteen such publications in France, and several in other European countries, the USA and South America, most of them also short-lived.[22] Tonie and Valmai Holt, writing in their *Picture Postcards of the Golden Age, a Collectors' Guide* in 1971, list the more successful British ones as *Postal Cards and Covers* (started 1901), the *Poster and Postcard Collector* (1903) the *Postcard* and the *Postcard Connoisseur* (both 1904), and the best known and most successful, the monthly *Picture Postcard Magazine of Travel, Philately and Art*, which started in January 1900 at a price of one penny, and finished publication in December 1906.[23] It was, according to its editor, 'the first magazine to combine travel, philately and art through a natural connecting medium, the Picture Postcard'.[24] It carried information on new postcard publishers and publications as well as facilitating exchanges between collectors. The *Picture Postcard Magazine* was favourably reviewed in the *Connaught Telegraph* in July 1900, where it was described as 'neatly got up and well compiled', with 'superb' illustrations, 'Notes on Novelties, Paragraphs for Collectors etc'.[25] Although a substantial proportion of the reviewed edition seems to have been taken up by scenes from the Boer War and 'illustrations of England's defenders in South Africa', nevertheless the writer observed approvingly that 'old Ireland is not forgotten', as it also included illustrations of 'Patrick St. Cork; Reginald's Tower, Waterford; the beautiful Blackwater, Kerry etc.'

King's Bibliography of Irish Pictorial Post Cards, a small publication aimed at collectors of Irish postcards, was published in London in 1903 by Jeremiah King. It was meant to be a first edition, a prelude to a 'second and enlarged edition', but it is unclear whether the latter was ever actually produced. King compiled his information from what he considered the most prominent postcard publishers of Irish-themed cards of the period, Blum & Degen, Stewart & Woolf, Strain, Raphael Tuck, Valentine, Wrench, Guy & Co., Hely's, Lawrence, McCaw, Fergus O'Connor and T. P. O'Halloran, acknowledging however that a 'large number of special view cards of the smaller towns are on sale only locally', and requesting readers and publishers to send in lists of these.[26] King, a historian originally from Kerry and a collector himself of postcards of County Kerry, encouraged other collectors of Irish cards to contact him at his London address.[27]

Postcard magazines supported but also heavily promoted the activity of collecting, something which needed to be done to keep the enormous and complex system of postcard production and distribution profitable. One means by which this was achieved seems to have been flattery: editorials in the *Picture Postcard Magazine* described the postcard collector as a member of 'an artistic, cultured and wealthy class', with a 'love of order and systematic perseverance, a love of beauty and a regard for art', all expressed via the picture postcard.[28] Postcard magazines and newspapers also included competitions and prizes, including those launched by Raphael Tuck as promotions for their own cards. The latter tended to present (Tuck) postcard collecting as a pursuit associated with high culture and art, and their competitions as designed to foster a love of such things.[29] The mentioning of celebrities and royalty as collectors associated the practice with glamour and status: the *Evening Herald* published a piece in 1899 claiming that Queen Victoria was now known to be an 'assiduous collector' of illustrated postcards, and had 'commissioned the Dowager-Duchess Ernestine of Coburg to collect specimens for her on the Continent and send them to Windsor'.[30] In 1907 the *Irish Independent* published a short article titled 'Kaiser buys picture postcards', and in 1908 the *Leinster Express* claimed that the royal princes were also collectors.[31]

Other ways that publishers could encourage the practice of postcard collecting were to continually produce new types of postcards, and to publish cards in series thematically or otherwise related to each other, in the hope that people would feel the need to collect them all. Raphael Tuck published numerous series, and Irish publishers also used this approach. In 1905 for instance Eason's issued a series of photographic postcards of

Rome, which they claimed 'ought to have special attraction for Irish collectors', as they included images of the Irish college in Rome and of Saint Agatha's, where the heart of Daniel O'Connell ('The Great Liberator') was kept.[32] The desire to appeal to as many different groups as possible, while generating more and more collectable series for the serious deltiologist, is shown by the London and North Western Railway Company, which had produced forty eight sets of six cards by 1907, including 'How Royalty travels by Train', 'City of Dublin', 'Lancashire Sea Resorts' and 'Beeston District'. According to the *Irish Independent*, five and a half million of these cards had sold since they began publishing the series a couple of years previously. They were priced at two pence for a set of six cards, or all forty-eight sets for seven shillings and four pence postage free.[33] Other companies published series focusing on the military, on ocean liners, on heraldry and any other subject that could capture the interest of special interest groups as well as the broader collecting public. Cards commemorating specific events, especially sensational ones, could also be attractive to different types of collectors, and Eason's capitalized on this by for instance issuing a series of images of the large Irish Language Procession which took place in Dublin in 1905, featuring 'very faithful reproductions of the chief events of the big display', while Hely's produced a series in the same year called 'The Disastrous Floods at Bray'.[34] Cards with images of sporting events and stars were also very collectable, and regularly published by both these companies as well as many others. Such postcards could be collected not just by postcard collectors, but by people collecting a range of different souvenirs in relation to a particular interest or phenomenon.

Some types of cards were seen as particularly valuable and were sought after by serious collectors. Raphael Tuck tapped into this market by producing 'de luxe', specially printed and limited advance first editions that could only be obtained by subscription.[35] Many cards however became valuable only because of their rarity, frequently due to their having been censored or suppressed. The *Evening Herald* published an article listing some of these in 1904, and it included cards featuring a portrait of the novelist Leo Tolstoy (banned by the Russian Government), cards that poked fun at, or otherwise satirized, various European monarchs (censored by the French government) and cards that bore 'the name of God or Mahomet, any drawing of the Kaaba, or any portrait of a Mahometan woman', forbidden by the Turkish government.[36] A report in the *Evening Herald* in October 1904 from Lyons in France highlighted the status of the postcard as a serious collectible of sufficient potential value to make it worth stealing. Apparently 'thousands of rare and expensive cards' were found in the apartment of a local and seemingly respectable citizen, having been systematically stolen over a period of time from local businesses.[37]

The fact that the picture postcard could be sent through the mail added an extra dimension to its appeal both as a souvenir and a collectible. A postmark identifying the specific time and place of mailing was perceived as adding another layer of authenticity, a 'proof' that the sender had actually visited a specific location or been present for a particular event. As Rogan observes, it also added to the validation of the object itself, the card, especially for collectors coming from the tradition of postal collectibles.[38] Carline quotes one summer visitor to the Rhine in 1900 as observing that 'postcards, to be of value to a collector, should be posted from the place illustrated'. This visitor noticed

> during his trip down the Rhine … that at each stopping place a waiter was sent ashore with a large consignment of cards for the post. He was astonished to learn that they were mostly addressed by the passengers to themselves in order to secure the appropriate postmark.[39]

A special attraction of the Paris Universal Exposition of 1889 had been the opportunity to send a postcard from the top of the newly constructed Eiffel Tower.[40] In 1897 the *Evening Herald* reported that French cards issued in commemoration of the Tsar's visit to Paris could be exchanged for the relatively enormous sum of four shillings each if they bore a postmark of the actual date of the visit.[41] Rogan has also written about the concern of Norwegian tourists of the period to 'have the correct cancellation' and reports of long queues and 'sweating postmasters applying stamps and cancellations as fast as they could' at tourist destinations, especially ports where steamships stopped on the way to North Cape, Norway's northernmost point.[42] He quotes Lausberg as claiming in 1912 that an 'even more "authentic" way of cancelling the cards on the North Cape cruises … was to let the midnight sun burn a hole in them by means of a magnifying glass.'[43] This suggests an elevation of the postmarked picture postcard to something like a relic, where the mark of authenticity is more to do with physical and emotional connections and faith than the stamped official sanction of a government body. No doubt postcards were seen as both officially authenticated, potentially valuable collectibles *and* resonant mementos in 1898, when the funeral of the former Chancellor of the German Empire, Otto von Bismarck, was heading towards his tomb in Friedrichsruh:

> While the procession was wending its way from the Castle to the mausoleum a clamorous multitude surrounded the little post-office at Friedrichsruh bent on dropping into the box numberless postcards illustrated with views of the burial place. Their ambition was to send to their friends and to themselves picture cards bearing the stamp of the date and the hour of Prince Bismarck's funeral. One Berlin dealer, with a keen eye to business, addressed to himself no fewer than 6,000 of these 'historical' documents. In all over 20,000 picture cards were posted at Friedrichsruh in the course of the morning.[44]

Collections and their composition

It is difficult to know what sorts of picture postcards were mostly collected during the Edwardian period, partly because there were so many different types of collectors, all with different preferences. People who have written about Edwardian postcards are generally of the opinion that view cards (cards featuring rural or urban scenes from specific geographical locations) were the commonest and most popular type of picture postcard collectible during that period, and this may be true, especially as publishers increasingly responded to the rapidly growing international tourist industry.[45] However, assumptions about the collections of the early twentieth century may also be biased according to the criteria and values of later collectors, and since many of the original Edwardian collections have been broken up by later collectors in order to make their own new ones, it is impossible to know for sure. The study of Edwardian postcard culture and collections is thus made problematic because the most obvious source materials for such a study, contemporary collections of Edwardian cards, are biased in favour of certain card types.

The early twentieth-century craze for postcard collecting was mostly over by the end of the First World War, and only a few individuals continued to pursue it until the 1960s and 1970s, when it became popular again, although not to anything like the extent it had been previously.[46] This new wave of collectors had very specific ideas about collecting and what was worth collecting, especially in relation to postcards from the early twentieth century. According to the Dublin collector Fred Dixon, writing in 1979,

> collectors tend to specialize: some seek views with trams or other particular vehicles; some prefer architectural subjects; some want 'glamour' or humour, etc. Nearly all study only the picture, but there is scope for research on the other side of the card, in addition to the obvious possibilities of the stamps and postmarks. I refer to the evidence of who printed and who published the postcards.[47]

Personal or other added messages were therefore seen as mostly irrelevant, as were their histories beyond their initial publication and perhaps postage. Collectors were not generally interested in preserving and examining postcards in context as multifaceted artefactual evidence from the past, but in putting together pictures from a variety of sources (and often periods) which contributed to their own particular projects. Old collections were therefore plundered for individual cards that conformed to the rationale of the new collection being created. For instance, the American collector Leonard A. Lauder (b.1933) focused on collecting, at different stages of his life, Japanese and Weiner Werkstatte cards, pictures of New York City buildings and of Miami Beach Art Deco hotel buildings.[48] He later branched out

> to cover diverse interests, whether long-standing or relatively new, in topics as varied as art and design, advertising, vernacular photography, propaganda, architecture, war, social history, political cartoons, aviation, and ethnography.[49]

Although such a list suggests an approach based on an objective pursuit of knowledge, Lauder also stated that different sections of the collection resonated with him at different times of his life, and for different reasons, so that his collecting was also shaped by very personal impulses, and made meaningful primarily in relation to his own life experience.

The British collectors Tonie and Valmai Holt recommended that 'cards may be collected by subject, type (hold-to-light etc), manufacturer, artist, photographer etc.'[50] To this day postcard collectors continue to use a similar approach, and the contemporary Irish writer (and collector) Perry O'Donovan claims that

> almost every deltiologist has a category of interest – transportation systems, communication systems, the work of a particular publisher or artist, animals in postcards, children or toys in postcards, religious or political subjects, and so on – infinite possibilities – ballet postcards, castle postcards, sports cards, the shop-fronts of Ulster ... you name it and someone somewhere is probably specializing in it.[51]

O'Donovan's book *Love from Cork, Postcards of the City and County* (2013) features mainly reproductions of the picture-side of cards from two Irish collectors, John James and Adrian Healy.[52] Quotes from the back of the cards are included in the book, mainly to add some interesting colour to the accompanying text, but the focus is on the individual images as representations of place (many different time periods are included, in no particular order). This bringing together of a number of postcard images of a particular subject or range of subjects is the approach taken in the vast majority of books that focus on postcards. The Irish Postcards Collectors forum on the website CollectIreland.com also organizes cards according to the subject of their imagery, and on the e-commerce website eBay, which has become a very significant source for postcard collectors worldwide in recent years, cards can be most easily searched for according to categories such as subject represented (most commonly a geographic location), artist and publisher. New collections are thus frequently organized around variations and similarities in visual representations, with other connections and references played down, ignored or simply lost altogether. Eugene Thaw, in his essay 'The Art of Collecting' for *The New Criterion*, suggests that this erasure of the original context of an object is essential to 'true' collecting. In contrast to just 'accumulating' things, true collecting involves acquiring objects that have some relation to each other and putting those objects into the kind of order that reflects the collector's response to them. Each true collection achieves personality beyond and apart from the sum of the objects. This personality is definable and has a value in itself. It is lost if the collection is dispersed or mutilated.[53]

Unfortunately, as noted above, the creation of a new collection that 'achieves personality' usually entails the destruction of existing collections and the personalities and other qualities that they expressed, and this is what has happened to many collections from the Edwardian age.

Contemporary museum collections

Scholars and institutions are increasingly taking picture postcards seriously as historically valuable artefacts, and this has resulted in many modern museums putting together card collections which complement and possibly shed light on their other collections. The Linen Hall Library in Belfast, for example, has an important Irish and Local Studies Collection and a comprehensive Northern Ireland Political Collection, as well as an archive of more than 7,000 postcards. According to their website these feature mostly topographical views, images of 'almost every city, town and village in Ireland', alongside some 'humorous and specialty cards'.[54] Individual postcards (from a broad time frame) have been procured from a range of sources and organized into a new collection which provides viewers with 'a sense of what life was like in remote villages and towns over one hundred years ago', as well as information on changing 'architecture, fashion ... transport', 'housing, local industries, sport and leisure'.[55] The museum's collection process, driven by educational and local-historical aims, favours therefore a focus on topographical views and the visual documentation of subjects such as Irish customs, sports and well-known personalities and 'types'.

A similar collection is held in the Cork Public Museum, situated in Fitzgerald's Park in Cork City. Again, the criteria for constructing this collection focussed on cards whose imagery is related to Cork City and county. As a result, from the 631 identifiably pre–First World War cards in this museum that were examined for this book, there is a huge preponderance of view cards featuring the town-, land- and seascapes of the area, mostly photographic imagery but with a sizable proportion of illustration. There are very few comic cards other than those that refer in some way to Cork, such as various images of young men practising their 'Blarney' on young women, usually combined with a representation of Blarney Castle. There are even less actress cards, although Figure 6 features glamorous females also juxtaposed with a conventional view of Blarney castle. There are many showing ships, trains, monuments and buildings, exteriors and interiors, and people involved in activities such as heading to market or kissing the Blarney Stone. There are a very few portraits of notable Cork people, and a small number of generic cards with localized messages superimposed.

Figure 6 *Blarney Castle*, Our Belles, Raphael Tuck. Cork Public Museum archive, post-card collection 23.3 2014.6.518.

The Cork Public Museum collection contains many unposted cards, which can be difficult to date, as well as cards which were posted but whose postmark is indecipherable, often due to the stamp having been removed by stamp collectors. It provides very useful information on the kinds of imagery used to represent the area as well as the main publishers of such cards during the period. Lawrence is the most frequently identified publisher, with over 200 cards, while Valentines and Wrench of London are also well represented, as are the Cork-based firms Guy & Co., Fergus O'Connor and the Irish Pictorial Card Company.[56] There are also numerous cards from many small local publishers, such as E. Carroll Dawson in Bandon, F. McCarthy in Clonakilty, Horgan brothers in Youghal and J. S. Barry in Kinsale. The international character of the postcard industry and the mobility of postcards and postcard imagery is highlighted by the fact that many cards featuring Cork imagery were both sent and received in other countries – for instance a card (publisher unknown) featuring 'Mitchelsown Lower Cork Street' was sent in 1907 from Ansonia Connecticut to another address in the same city, and another published by Macdonald of Buttevant, County Cork and featuring the Barracks in Buttevant, was sent and received in 1910 within Rome, Italy.[57] Cards could also be postally used many years after publication, suggesting a slow turnover for some producers or retailers, or possibly hoarding on the part of buyers. This collection contains a card published by Wrench, a company that went out of business in 1906, which was posted in 1912.[58]

The text additions written on these cards suggest multiple uses, and may or may not clearly relate to the image on the front of the card. Many are obviously written by people travelling, and these often comment on the card's image or the location generally, or on the people or weather, the latter ranging from 'glorious' to a brief and rather dispirited 'still raining'. Leisure activities are mentioned, such as going boating or shooting, attending the Queenstown regatta or seeing the actress Phyllis Dare in the show *The Dairymaids*.[59] One sender bemoans the lack of shopping opportunities in the area: 'I could get nothing for you as there is nothing worth buying down here.' Another, posted in 1904, composes her message in exaggerated stage Irish: 'If I catch ye throwing a wink at Bridget I'll scalp the both of ye begorra it's moighty desprete I'm feeling.' Meetings and travel arrangements are proposed, and there are grumblings about delayed trains and choppy seas. Many cards are communicating family news and enquires and reports of health and well-being to friends and relatives both nearby and far away. One, posted in 1911 and featuring an image of the Carnegie Library and Municipal buildings in Cork, reports on the birth of a 'bonny son'. Another delivers the sad news of the death of a baby. Several communicate birthday, Christmas, New Year's and St Patrick's Day greetings. Some, on the other hand, are clearly being used for business purposes, noting for instance that an order is ready or on the way. A collection such as this therefore provides a window into the casual social interactions of the period, allowing us to listen in on the jokes and empathize with the joys, sorrows and inconveniences of daily life. We can 'hear' the everyday speech of people in a way that is not usually possible with more formal historical documents. However, since the context and connections are largely lost to us, our understanding is necessarily very partial and limited.

Comments added to the cards do, however, offer some insights on the postcard phenomenon itself, and the practice of collecting. One sender hopes the recipient has 'not got a card like this as it's horrible having a lot with the same view on them I think', writing beside an image of Main Street, Clonakilty, Co Cork. Another hopes 'you will like these p.c.s only one more to complete the Cork series'. Many seem to have been writing to less unenthusiastic recipients, judging by comments such as 'You seem to have quite forgotten us', 'Dear Cis, I don't know whether you are living or not …' and 'Dear Mother, I know your aversion to postcards …'. The use of a postcard to postpone the more burdensome task of letter writing is also evident: 'Will commence answering your bombardment of letters tomorrow'.

Most of these comments were written on 'view' cards, as these are by far the most numerous type in this collection, but another recently compiled Irish postcard collection used different collection criteria, and as a result the types of cards it features are more diverse. Niall Murphy put together a collection of postcards posted in or near Dublin in the year 1904 (based on the postmark), the year in which James Joyce's iconic novel about Dublin life, *Ulysses*, was set. Murphy collected more than 1,600 of these postcards, and published images of 252 of them in his book *A Bloomsday*

Postcard (2004).[60] Of the 252 cards reproduced in the book, less than half,
just over 100, are view cards showing scenery, street and waterscapes and
buildings, some of which are paintings of generic picturesque scenes rather
than representations of identified localities. There are around thirty images
of royalty, actresses and other well-known people, and the same number
of comic cards. The rest of the cards feature subjects such as cute-looking
animals, sporting events, Irish 'characters' and scenes of other countries and
peoples, including images of the Russo-Japanese war. There are also several
cards advertising products and businesses, and greetings cards. Although
view cards are still the largest single group, there is a much wider variety
of subject matter in this collection than in the previous ones discussed,
because of the collecting criteria used, and this variety is likely to be more
representative of the actual range of cards bought and sold, or at least
posted, in Ireland during the Edwardian period.

Personal and family collections

Original Irish card collections from the Edwardian era are the richest
sources for a study such as this, although they are not necessarily easy to
come by. The personal collections examined in detail here were, except
for one, put together by women during the early twentieth century, and
they vary in their level of formality, in how 'seriously' they were collected.
The collectors were all Irish and living in urban centres, the women in the
cities of Dublin and Belfast and the town of Ennis in County Clare, and
the man in various towns in Counties Mayo and Galway.

Many commentators during the Edwardian era considered picture
postcard collecting at the time as primarily the preserve of women (or
'young ladies', as they were often referred to, somewhat dismissively), and
later writers have tended to agree with this view. According to Naomi
Schor, postcard collecting was seen as an exception in the normally male-
dominated world of collecting, 'the very example of the feminine collectible', or a 'feminine vice', as it was labelled in 1907 by the prominent
London journalist James Douglas.[61] Rogan similarly states that the picture

postcard craze 'satisfied new leisure habits, like the collecting interests of women – a group which until then had had few opportunities of finding an accepted outlet for such desires'.[62] Carline also argues that in 1900 most collectors were women, who preferred cards featuring 'views, landscapes and works of art', although he claims that this had changed dramatically by 1906, when the men outnumbered the women by five to one, attracted to new types of subject matter such as 'comic cards, actresses and "posed beauties"'.[63] Carline based these conclusions on his analysis of readers' advertisements in the monthly *The Picture Postcard Magazine of Travel, Philately and Art*, published between 1900 and 1906, and the kinds of cards they said they wished to collect. Women, apparently, often stipulated 'views', and stated 'no comics' or 'no fancy cards'. He does say that 'strangely enough' some women did collect actresses, but that men didn't really collect views.[64] However, the readers of (and certainly writers to) such a magazine were more likely to be relatively 'serious' collectors, and may not reflect the preferences of the majority. Certainly there are plenty of both actress and comic cards in the women's collections examined for this book, and Jeremiah King, the previously mentioned author of *King's Bibliography of Irish Pictorial Post Cards*, seems to have been primarily a collector of view cards of County Kerry.

An all-female postcard collectors' club was founded in Paris in 1900, and Miss Antonini's collection of 9,000 cards, exhibited at a Venice exhibition, has already been mentioned.[65] As Peter Gilderdale has also pointed out, Raphael Tuck aimed their postcard competitions mainly at women, so they must have considered this the more significant demographic, or the more susceptible to their marketing.[66] Tuck's third and largest competition, in 1906, was titled 'Home Decoration', and large cash prizes were given for the 'best use of postcards for decorating tables, screens, cupboards, overmantels and other objects'.[67] In 1909 the Dublin-based *Evening Herald* also requested suggestions for the using up of collections of picture postcards, and those published all involved the decoration of parlour, drawing room or nursery fire screens, or their use as nursery wallpaper. Frosted cards were recommended for the fire screens, as they would catch the light when the fire was lit.[68] Such projects are very much the kinds of activities with which middle-class women and girls were encouraged to productively and creatively fill their time, and suggest a comfortable blend of traditional female domesticity and modern postcard collection that may have seemed more reassuring to readers of the *Evening Herald* than the kind of obsession seemingly displayed by the likes of Miss Antonini.

The women's collections examined here are very different to the museum collections looked at earlier. Their collection criteria are uncertain and seem rather haphazard. Aesthetics are probably significant, and family ties, but it is impossible to assess which was more important. They seem to be for private use, intended for personal perusal or viewing by family or friends, but not for public consumption. The cards in them do not seem to be objectively valuable, or even particularly valued, as many carry personal messages often on the front and the back and their imagery is frequently written over or marked in some way. They contain some real photo postcards of private individuals as well as commercially produced imagery. Such collections may have been more likely to survive intact because of their perceived worthlessness, and/or their personal value to the family to which they belong.

The collection of Christina Jessop (1878–1968) (see Figure 7), who was my husband's grandmother, was preserved by her family, which is how I encountered it. It consists of 278 picture postcards sent to her between 1903 and 1908 from her fiancé, relatives, friends and acquaintances. Of these cards, 196 have Irish postmarks, while the remainder were posted in Belgium, Canada, England, France, Germany, Scotland, Switzerland, the United States and Wales. Eighty-three of the cards feature subject matter that is specifically Irish, such as painted images of an Irish peasant and a couple dancing a jig, and illustrated and photographic prints of landscapes, seascapes, townscapes and individual buildings. Non-Irish subjects, the majority of the collection, also include views of places and buildings, images of celebrity actresses and music-theatre stars, children and animals in cute or amusing poses, prints of popular artworks and humorous cartoons. The collection is assembled in an album, but it is not known when this was done, and the cards were taken out and their sequence changed several times since the collection was originally put together, so that their original relationship to each other was not preserved.

Figure 7. Christina Jessop, photograph, photographer unknown. Private collection.

Of the 278 cards in Christina's collection, 120 can be identified as published in England or, less commonly, Scotland. Forty-six were published in Ireland, and twenty-seven in Switzerland, from where her brother Jack sent back many from a holiday in 1907. Fifty-five cards have no publisher identification, or are real photo postcards. The remainder feature the names or logos of publishing firms in Belgium, Canada, France, Germany, the United States and Wales. Most of the big English card publishers of the period are represented in her collection, including Raphael Tuck & Sons (thirty-four cards), Valentine & Sons (seventeen cards), and Siegmund Hildesheimer (nine cards), as well as Bamforth, C. W. Faulkner, Davidson Brothers, Frederick Hartmann and Rotary Photographic.

The majority of her Irish-published cards (twenty-four) are from the Dublin-based Lawrence company. Fergus O'Connor (mostly identifiable only from his Eire go Bragh logo) published six, and Hely's and Eason's published five and three, respectively. There were also cards from J. Tallon, Dublin, A. H. Poole, Waterford, Horgan Brothers in Youghal, and a company set up in 1904 that printed all its inscriptions in the Irish language, Cuideacha na gCártai Posta Gaedhealach (The Irish Postcards Company).[69] Irish companies made valiant attempts to withstand the competition from such giants as Tuck and Valentines, producing distinctively 'Irish' images for the local and foreign market, but the English companies also did this, and many of the 'Irish' views in Christina's collection were published by them.

Christina was a middle-class Catholic woman from Dublin. Her parents had worked in the South Dublin Union workhouse, he as Assistant Master and she as a teacher, and Christina was one of a small but increasing number of Irish girls who completed secondary school, at the Dominican Convent in Eccles Street. In 1900 she became one of the first women in Ireland to qualify as a pharmacist, a job she held in various establishments in Dublin until 1908, when she married and went to live in Queenstown (now Cobh) in County Cork.[70] After her parents died, she lived between 1903 and 1908 with her brother Jack, also a pharmacist, and her sister Rose, a seamstress. Another brother, Charles, emigrated to Canada in 1903 to seek his fortune in the Yukon goldmines. The Jessop siblings lived in an apartment attached to Jack's workplace, the dispensary at 33 South Earl Street, the address to which almost all her postcards were sent, and which was located in one of Dublin's poorer areas near the city centre. Her collection of cards suggests a wide and lively social circle during this period, a group of people positioned socially somewhere between Ireland's poverty-stricken lower classes and its small wealthy upper and upper-middle classes, part of a growing middle or lower-middle class group increasingly able to spend time and money on leisure, consumption and travel.

The next collection I examined was an album, bought from a Dublin antiques dealer, containing about 150 cards exchanged primarily among members of the Green family who were living in Belfast. It appears more neatly organized than Christina's, with cards arranged according to subject matter, which again is very varied, Irish and non-Irish. The range of publishers is also similarly wide, although the names most frequently identified are Raphael Tuck, Rotary and Valentines, with only two from Lawrence. There is a much higher proportion of unposted cards in this collection, making many of them difficult to date, and there are also quite a few cards with postmarks from after the First World War and even later. The amount of unposted cards suggests a greater interest in the collection of specific card types rather than the compiling of mementoes of family and friends. The first section of the album, for instance, is filled primarily with unused cards featuring actresses, mainly the popular British dancer and stage actress Mabel Love (1874–1953), mostly published by the Rotary Photographic Company which was established in London in 1901. There is also a series which reproduces illustrations of glamorously dressed women by the Canadian artist Philip Boileau, dated 1907 and published by the American Chas. Scribner's Sons, bearing titles such as *Those Bewitching Eyes* and *A Passing Shadow*. These cards are also unused. However, as with Christina's album, it is not known when the Green family cards were assembled into the album, nor if they are now in their original positions.

Nevertheless, this album also contains a significant number of cards featuring birthday and Christmas greetings, one of which even looks home-made, as well as real photo postcards of apparently private individuals, suggesting that it fulfilled a range of functions which included the pres-ervation of family mementoes. The Green family, according to the 1901 Irish census, lived in 67 Cavehill Road in Belfast. The father was Michael, a 57-year-old contractor, and his wife was Scottish-born Mary, 45 years old. The census lists seven children of theirs, three boys ranging in age from 17 to 21, and four girls between 6 and 14 years old. The three boys are described as assistant contractors, and the girls as scholars, and all are recorded as literate and Roman Catholic. 67 Cavehill Road was a private, nine-roomed house, classified as second class and occupied only by the Green family, who had no servants.

By 1911 the family had moved to a fourteen-room house in nearby Indiana Avenue, which was classified as first class. An extra daughter, 29 years old, is recorded who must have been away in 1901, but otherwise the family is the same as previously, still with no servants. All the siblings, who now range in age from 17 to 32, are described as single, the girls as scholars, the eldest son as a contractor and another as a civil engineer. Most of the addressed cards are to 'Mrs Green', presumably Michael's wife Mary, or to her daughters Delia, who was 6 in 1901, or Helen, 2 years older. A small number were sent to, or from, a son, William, who was a cadet in Moorepark in Kilworth County Cork around 1916–1917. The actress cards and those featuring images of glamorous women were presumably chosen to appeal to the young girls, Helen and Delia, whose teenage years mostly coincided with the Edwardian era. Even if they were not, the collection and presentation of these cards in the album provides us with a glimpse of the kind of popular culture accessible to such Irish girls during this period.

The third collection consists primarily of cards sent to a young woman, Ellen (Nelly) Duff, who was working as a waitress in Fleming's Restaurant in Dublin, operating from 1 South Great George's Street, a building which has since been demolished. Nearly all the posted cards in her album (which is in the archival collections of the County Library in Portlaoise, County Laois) were addressed to there. The first page bears an inscription in elaborate handwriting 'To Miss E. Duff From a Sincere Friend Xmas 1914'. Despite this, the postmarked cards in Ellen's collection are all dated between 1904 and 1906, and most of them 1905, so she was gifted the album some years after she collected the cards (see Figure 8). A high proportion of the seventy-nine cards in this album were also unposted, and about a third of

Figure 8. Ellen Duff's postcard album.

the collection features images of actresses or unnamed glamorous women. Many of the rest are comic cards, including popular 'write-away' cards (cards that provided the beginning of a phrase that the sender could then complete), and images of Irish 'types', and there are very few views. Rotary is the most frequently identified publisher. The first section of the album is devoted to a series of cards published by Hely's in Dublin featuring wedding and family portraits of the aristocratic Bute and Bellingham families, who were united in 1905 by the much-publicized wedding at Castle Bellingham in County Louth of the fourth Marquis of Bute, John Crichton-Stuart, and Augusta Mary Monica Bellingham, daughter of Sir Alan Bellingham.

In the census of 1901, the 18-year-old Ellen Duff was recorded as staying in a five-roomed first-class building classified as a 'shop and dwelling' at 20 Exchequer Street, just off South Great George's Street. The census lists seven women and two men in this building, with 50-year-old Mary Murphy as head of the household. The occupations of the women were cook, carver and waitress, and one of the men was a carver and the other a waiter. Ellen is listed as a waitress, unmarried and born in Queen's County (now County Laois). None of the occupants had been born in Dublin, but instead in Wexford, Wicklow, Roscommon, Donegal and Queen's County. Apart from the head of the household and two others aged 40 and 27, all were only 18 or 19 years old. All were recorded as Roman Catholic. By 1911 Ellen had moved to Fleming's Restaurant (described as 'dwelling and restaurant') at 1 South Great George's Street, a premises managed by the 31-year-old Elizabeth Middleton. Apart from Elizabeth and Ellen, there are five other women recorded in this first-class five-roomed building, two shop assistants, a waitress, a cook/domestic servant and a kitchen maid/domestic servant, ranging in age from 21 to 40. Ellen is also listed as a waitress. All are recorded as Roman Catholic.

Unlike Christina, who lived with her brother and sister, and the large number of Green family members living together, Ellen seems to have been staying in shared accommodation away from her family home. She may have still had family and friends in Queen's county, as a number of the cards she received were sent from Maryborough, now Portlaoise. One card in the collection was posted in Dublin in 1905 and addressed to Ellen at Ross, Maryborough, Queen's County. She seems to have been attending a wedding at the time, as the writer asks to be remembered to the bride and groom, and reminds her not to forget to bring back some wedding cake. A family of Duffs, a widowed farmer with two brothers and five children (ranging in age from 14 to 22), is recorded as living in Ross, Clondarrig (about four miles from Maryborough) in 1901, and this may have been her family. They all lived in a three-roomed house categorized as third-class, and were recorded as Roman Catholic.

Figure 9. *Miss Olive May*, London, Empire Series. Ellen Duff's card collection.

Ellen's collection is notable for its small number of views, and the predominance of images of glamorous women and comic cards, the sort of cards often dismissed as frivolous, or even disapproved of, by critics. Often the added text on these cards does not seem to relate to the image, but on one, a photograph of the beautiful actress Olive May, the sender writes 'I thought this picture bore some resemblance to you … what do you think?' (see Figure 9). Another bears only the words 'From Herbert' scrawled across the torso and thigh of the dress of a seductively reclining woman, a combination of image and text that can only make the viewer wonder about the relationship between Herbert and Ellen, and how the sending of a card such as this might affect it (see Figure 10). In contrast to the serious-sounding females cited by Carline, specifying their collecting preferences to other readers of *The Picture Postcard Magazine of Travel, Philately and Art*, it seems that actress cards could be both appealing and meaningful to a young woman such as Ellen.

Figure 10. *Untitled*, Musterschutz, Germany. Ellen Duff's card collection.

The fourth collection was put together from cards exchanged by members of the Carmody family in Ennis, County Clare, and it was kept mostly in boxes, not in an album. Ninety of these cards were studied, although again some of these were unposted and therefore difficult to date accurately. The cards feature a mixture of imagery, similar to the other collections – views (just over a third of the sample), actresses, cute children, artwork reproductions, Irish 'types' and comic cards, as well as a number of greetings cards. No one publisher predominates, with several cards each from Raphael Tuck, Rotary, Valentines, Fergus O'Connor and Lawrence, and small numbers from a wide range of other publishers. Most of them

were sent to 25, Mill Street Ennis, or 45 Parnell Street, Ennis. The name
Mill Street was changed to Parnell Street sometime around 1910 or 1911,
and it is unclear if the two addresses refer to the same house. The census
of 1901 records five people at 25 Mill Street, a second-class seven-roomed
building described as a shop: Mary Carmody, a widow and shopkeeper,
her 17-year-old son Michael John and her daughters Irene, 11, and Aileen
Francis, 9, as well as Mary Kelly, a 19-year-old general domestic servant. All
were Roman Catholic. In 1911 the family is recorded under the surname
'Cormody' and living at 45 Parnell Street, a second-class eight-roomed
premises also described as a shop. No servant is listed. Sixty-year old Mary is
still a shopkeeper, but her son Michael John is now the Ennis Town Clerk,
and her daughters, 29-year-old Mary Margaret (May, who must have been
away in 1901) and 19-year-old Eileen (Aileen, also known as 'Ba') are also
listed. Twenty-one-year-old Irene (also known as Erina, Rennie or Rene)
was a student at the time in Southampton in England, and is recorded on
the British census of 1911.

The cards were mainly exchanged between the sisters, May, Eileen
and Rennie, with the occasional one sent to Mrs Carmody, their mother,
and a few to and from their brother, often known as Micko, including
one written in French in 1903 and posted in Paris. The sisters wrote long
messages to each other, and the cards in this respect are often more like
letters, exchanging news of family and friends, enquiring about educational progress ('hope you will be successful at the science exam') and
discussing dress patterns and materials. Most of the cards sent around
1904 and 1905 were addressed to the teenaged Rennie, and they include
many questions about which type of card she preferred ('Hope you will
like this one. Do you prefer views of places?' from Eileen, or 'Is this the
kind of p.c. you want me to send you?' from May) suggesting that she
was collecting cards in a more focused way than the others. Many of the
cards later sent to Rennie went from Ennis to England, as by 1907 she
was in school in Notre Dame convent in Sheffield, and later she attended
a Catholic teacher training college in Southampton, eventually settling
in England.[71]

Apart from these collections, another useful source for Irish postcard
research during this period was a small book published by Brian McCabe

in 2014, *"Dear Miss B" – A Collection of Edwardian Postcards*, based on a collection of twenty-nine cards sent to an Irish woman, Brigid Byrne, who retired to Johnstown Co Kildare and died sometime in the 1940s.[72] These cards were sent mainly to London, when Brigid was living with, and probably working for, Colonel (possibly Luke) Norman and his wife, and also travelling with them and their family, often to continental Europe. Most of the cards were posted between July 1907 and July 1909, sent from Killiney, Dublin and from Kensington, London. Some of these cards at least seem to have been sent from family still living in Ireland, and one bears the text 'best love from all ever your loving sister'. The cards are a mixture of views, including examples from the Irish International Exhibition in Dublin in 1907 and the Franco-British Exhibition in London in 1908, Irish 'types' and greetings cards, three of which are St Patrick's day cards.

An informal collection, kept in boxes rather than an album by a family now living in Cahir, County Tipperary, was also useful. Many of these were sent to a Mayo man, John O'Reilly, and while a considerable number were unused, many were posted to him from America, either New York or Philadelphia, and include comments on the political situation in Ireland as well as news, social arrangements and enquiries and remarks on health and well-being. The cards were addressed to John at a variety of addresses in Counties Mayo and Galway, all draper's shops in Belmullet, Ballina, Ballyhaunis, Tuam and Claremorris. The 1911 census records a Cavan-born John O'Reilly, aged 21, one of three young male draper's assistants in Eaton's draper's shop at 30, Hazelhill (Clare Street) in Ballyhaunis, and he is likely to have been the recipient of these cards. The shop was run by 33-year-old William Eaton, who also lived there with his wife and baby daughter, as did a female dressmaker and a general servant. All were listed as Roman Catholic. There are also cards in this collection addressed to a national school teacher, Bessie Caulfield, living in Inver, Bangor Erris in County Mayo, and cards from her to John, as well as a number to a Nora Browne in Balypierce in Charleville, County Cork. As with Ellen Duff's collections, there are a lot of comic and 'write-away' cards, as well as images of actresses, children, greetings cards, views and real photo cards.

Edwardian postcard collecting emerged from a range of different practices and served different functions, from the careful bringing together of valuable or prestigious examples to the compilation of a set of personal or family mementos. It could be a very serious pursuit involving significant financial investment, or something informal and primarily entertaining, including cards valuable mainly for their aesthetic or souvenir appeal to an individual. Specific magazines, competitions and 'special edition' series targeted the 'serious' collectors, but postcard publishers promoted collecting for everyone, and young women were seen as particularly likely to be consumers. More recent postcard collectors have tended to cannibalize original Edwardian collections in order to form their own, making it difficult to assess which cards were the most popular at the time, and with what sorts of people. Postcard collections can vary considerably in their composition depending on the agenda behind their creation, and this needs to be taken into account when examining Edwardian postcard culture. The collections examined here feature a wide variety of subject matter and commentary, and help to build up a picture of the social interactions of a range of Irish people during the early twentieth century, and of the kinds of mass-produced imagery to which they were exposed. This imagery contributed to their sense of themselves and others, but was also used by them, sometimes unconsciously and other times very deliberately and even creatively, to communicate values, observations and feelings about their world.

Notes

1. *Freeman's Journal* (12 January 1905).
2. *Cork Examiner* (1 April 1908).
3. *Freemans Journal* (18 August 1906).
4. Katie Day Good, 'From Scrapbook to Facebook: A History of Personal Media Assemblage and Archives', *New Media & Society*, 15 (2013), 557–573, 562.
5. Maurice Rickards, *The Encyclopedia of Ephemera, A Guide to the Fragmentary Documents of Everyday Life for the Collector, Curator, and Historian* (New York: Routledge, 2000), 'Scrapbook/album', 285.
6. Peter Gilderdale, *Hands across the Sea: Situating an Edwardian Greetings Postcard Practice* (PhD thesis submitted to the Auckland University of Technology, 2013), 144.
7. Rickards, *The Encyclopedia of Ephemera*, 'Scrap', 285.

8.   Day Good, 'From Scrapbook to Facebook', 557.

9.   Day Good, 'From Scrapbook to Facebook', 559.

10. Day Good, 'From Scrapbook to Facebook', 561.

11. *Irish Independent* (3 January 1905), 7.

12. Carline, *Pictures in the Post*, 64.

13. Linda Klich and Benjamin Weiss, *The Postcard Age, Selections from the Leonard A. Lauder Collection* (London: Thames and Hudson, 2012), 39.

14. *Ballinrobe Chronicle* (30 July 1898).

15. Klich and Weiss, *The Postcard Age*, 41.

16. Klich and Weiss, *The Postcard Age*, 41.

17. There were also philocartical clubs, for people who collected both stamps and postcards. (Holt, *Picture Postcards of the Golden Age*, 145).

18. Holt, *Picture Postcards of the Golden Age*, 145.

19. *Sunday Independent* (12 May 1907; 2 June 1907; 19 January 1908; 18 April 1909).

20. *Sunday Independent* (21 June 1908).

21. Carline, *Pictures in the Post*, 65.

22. Rogan, 'Entangled Object', 20, note 4.

23. Holt, *Picture Postcards of the Golden Age*, 145; Carline, *Pictures in the Post*, 65.

24. Holt, *Picture Postcards of the Golden Age*, 37.

25. *Connaught Telegraph* (14 July 1900).

26. J. King, *King's Bibliography of Irish Pictorial Post Cards* (London: J. King, 1903).

27. King, *King's Bibliography*; *Kerry Evening Star* (18 August 1910).

28. Holt, *Picture Postcards of the Golden Age*, 41; Carline, *Pictures in the Post*, 66.

29. 'Metropolitan Memoranda', *Leinster Express* (2 February 1901); *Kerry News* (26 July 1907).

30. *Evening Herald* (11 July 1899).

31. *Irish Independent* (30 November 1907); *Leinster Express* (29 August 1908).

32. *Irish Examiner* (19 October 1905).

33. *Irish Independent* (17 April 1907).

34. *Irish Independent* (18 March 1905).

35. *Freemans Journal* (3 September 1904).

36. *Evening Herald* (14 November 1904); Holt, *Picture Postcards of the Golden Age*, 157–158.

37. *Evening Herald* (5 October 1904).

38. Rogan, 'Entangled Object', 11.

39. Carline, *Pictures in the Post*, 64.

40. Klich and Weiss, *The Postcard Age*, 23.

41. *Evening Herald* (16 January 1897).

42. Rogan, 'Entangled Object', 11.

43. Rogan, 'Entangled Object', 20, note 6.

44. *Evening Herald* (22 March 1899).

45. Seamus Kearns, 'Collecting Picture Postcards', *Dublin Historical Record*, 54/2 (2001), 139–144, 141; Rogan, 'Entangled Object', 8; Klich and Weiss, *The Postcard Age*, 44; Perry O'Donovan, *Love from Cork, Postcards of the City and County* (Cork: Collins Press, 2013), vii; Gilderdale, *Hands Across the Sea*, 265.

46. A. P. Behan, 'History from Picture Postcards', *Dublin Historical Record*, 46/2 (1993), 129–140, 130; Dixon, 'Pioneer Publishers', 149.

47. Dixon, 'Pioneer Publishers', 149.

48. Klich and Weiss, *The Postcard Age*, 13.

49. Klich and Weiss, *The Postcard Age*, 15.

50. Holt, *Picture Postcards of the Golden Age*, 47.

51. O'Donovan, *Love from Cork*, vii.

52. O'Donovan, *Love from Cork*.

53. E. V. Thaw, 'The Art of Collecting', *The New Criterion*, 36/6 (2012), 1. <https://www.newcriterion.com/issues/2002/12/the-art-of-collecting> accessed 14 August 2020.

54. Linen Hall Library Collection, <http://www.postcardsireland.com/about> accessed 16 August 2020.

55. Linen Hall Library Collection.

56. Fergus O'Connor moved to Dublin some time during the first decade of the twentieth century, but he is still listed in 1907 as a postcard publisher at 2 Dyke Parade in Cork. The Irish Pictorial Card Company suffered a disastrous fire at its premises in Maylor Street in Cork in 1907, and subsequently seems to have gone out of business.

57. Cork Public Museum archive, postcard collection. D17.15.2002.563; D18.12.2003.47.18.

58. Cork Public Museum, D18.12.2003.47.140.

59. Cork Public Museum, D19.3.2004.8.66.

60. Murphy, *A Bloomsday Postcard*.

61. Schor, '*Cartes Postales*', 12.

62. Rogan, 'Entangled Object', 3.

63. Carline, *Pictures in the Post*, 66.

64. Carline, *Pictures in the Post*, 66.

65. Carline, *Pictures in the Post*, 67.

66. Gilderdale, *Hands across the Sea*, 253.

67. Carline, *Pictures in the Post*, 69.

68. *Evening Herald* (15 March 1909).

69. Dixon, 'Pioneer Publishers', 147.

70. Dr Margaret Ó'hÓgartaigh, *Quiet Revolutionaries, Irish Women in Education, Medicine and Sport, 1861–1964* (Dublin: The History Press Ireland, 2011), 220, note 5. Niamh O'Leary, 'Not Just Four Generations in the Profession – But the First Woman Pharmacist Too!', *IPU Review* (February 1993), 38–39.

71. Interview with Rennie's grandniece, Hilda Haugh, May 2015.

72. Brian McCabe, *"Dear Miss B" – A Collection of Edwardian Postcards* (Naas: Kildare County Council; Brian McCabe, 2014).

Postcards: A medium of private and public communication

Postcards were developed initially as a medium for communication and were widely adopted for this purpose very quickly. In the three months following the launch of the first postcard in Austria in 1869 nearly 3 million postcards were sold, and, according to Ferguson, 'by the mid-1870s, most of the Western world was using the half-penny or penny postcard'.[1] Initially, these were without imagery, thin pieces of card of a mostly standard size and format (this varied in different countries), designed to be easily and cheaply sorted and transported, with space for an address and stamp on one side and a short message on the other. They were quick and easy to write and send, allowing little space for the elaborate and often tedious formalities that had become conventionally associated with letter writing. Various images and motifs were soon added to the cards in some countries, but this was hampered by regulations in others. Greeting cards, tourist views and pictures of hotels and restaurants in postcard form began to appear in Germany, Austria and Switzerland in the 1870s and 1880s, and by the early 1890s a wide variety of picture postcards was available in many European countries.[2] The picture postcard industry began to grow in Britain and Ireland after 1894, when the Government relinquished its postcard monopoly and allowed production by private manufacturers. The USA's first official colour postcards were sold at The World's Columbian Exposition in Chicago in 1893, and most restrictions against the private printing of picture postcards were lifted there in 1898.[3]

The addition of imagery to cards further reduced the possible size of any added message, as nothing other than the stamp, name and address was allowed on the non-picture side. As Gillen and Hall have argued, the decision in 1902 by the British Post Office to allow the sending of postcards with divided backs was therefore particularly significant for the development of the picture postcard as a communication tool, in that the imagery and text no longer had to compete for the same restricted space.[4] Now one full side could be devoted to the image, and half of the other was specifically reserved for any added message. These cards however could initially only be sent within Britain and Ireland, but it was not long before most countries allowed them, one of the last being the United States in 1907.

Both plain and picture postcards became indispensable for business communication, in Ireland as elsewhere. The postal service was generally fast and efficient, deliveries were frequent, and since the telephone was still relatively uncommon, the postcard was the best option available for brief messages requiring a relatively quick reply. Potential customers could use it to ask a retailer for a pricelist, a free catalogue, coupon or sample, to respond to promotional competitions or to send in an order, while retailers could notify customers of opening hours or that an order was ready to be collected. Tables in restaurants and cafes could be reserved with a postcard, or jobseekers could send one in response to a job advertisement. The latter, however, sometimes specified 'postcards ignored' or 'apply by letter', suggesting that postcards were still considered inappropriate by some for certain communications, whether due to concerns about privacy, propriety or for some other reason.[5] Increasingly, however, advertisements and notices in newspapers, including job advertisements, stated 'a postcard will suffice'. The addition of imagery to postcards opened up a whole new world of opportunities to companies, allowing them to communicate directly with retailers and customers while publicizing their businesses and products in new, appealing and memorable ways, and they quickly took advantage of this. Trade cards and novelties had been produced for some time and collected for their attractiveness, as postcards would be later, so a wide repertoire of suitable imagery and motifs was already developed.[6]

The postcard 'craze', however, was mainly so-named because of the vast numbers of private individuals who bought picture postcards for personal collection or to send or gift to others, and who adopted them with unprecedented enthusiasm as a medium of communication. As with business use, individuals had used plain postcards to communicate with family and friends, but the addition of imagery added enormously to their appeal. An attractive picture combined with decorative pre-printed text often needed only a short extra sentence from the sender, or even just a signature, to communicate greetings or well wishes to a recipient, and many of the earliest types of picture postcard featured views of scenery, resorts and hotels accompanied by the words 'Gruss Aus' (Greetings from) followed by the name of the place (Figure 11). These cards were tourist mementos, but as Gilderdale has correctly pointed out, they were also, and primarily, greeting cards designed for communication.[7]

Figure 11. *Gruss Aus Flüelen*, Lautz & Jsenbeck, Darmstadt. Christina Jessop's card collection.

Greeting cards for special occasions such as Christmas, New Year, Easter and birthdays had been around for some time, but customized picture postcards partially replaced these, as, not requiring an envelope, they were cheaper to send. In December 1906 the *Irish Independent* reported 'a greater demand than ever for postcards with seasonable greetings', and in 1907 Christmas postcards 'with special greetings printed on them, were to be seen in the sorting office literally by the thousands'.[8] The trend continued in 1908, with the Dublin post office handling an 'immense quantity of postcards from all parts of the world'.[9] Increasing numbers of Irish Christmas postcards were published, often merely featuring images of Irish locations with Christmas greetings superimposed. Some of these were also produced by British companies – Figure 12, for instance, shows a view card of the Sugar Loaf mountain in Glengariff, County Cork, published by Hildesheimer of Manchester and London, with added festive greetings. Hildesheimer was a publisher of Christmas cards from 1876 on, but Raphael Tuck, who began producing Christmas cards in 1871, seems to have been by far the most prominent producer of all Christmas stationary for sale in Ireland, certainly if the promotional pieces in Irish newspapers are a good guide. According to the *Freeman's Journal* in 1906, 'Raphael Tuck is as essential a part of Christmas as Santa Claus himself. The festival would seem as impossible without the one as without the other'.[10] However, most of the major postcard producers published Christmas postcards, most commonly featuring romantic winter scenes or sweet-looking children. Many people also sent Christmas greetings on postcards whose imagery and caption had nothing to do with Christmas, either ignoring or disdaining the increasing trend towards mass-produced festive sentiment. Most Christmas postcards (and postcards featuring Christmas greetings) in the collections I have looked at were posted on Christmas Eve, and post was delivered throughout Ireland on Christmas Day. The author Kate O'Brien, remembering her childhood in early twentieth-century Limerick, recalled a highlight of Christmas Day as the postman's arrival 'intoxicated before one-o'clock, and [he] very certainly did not leave our house without some further cheer'.[11]

Figure 12. *Christmas Greetings, Sugar Loaf Mountain, Glengariff*, Hildesheimer, London & Manchester. Cork Public Museum archive, postcard collection 23.3 2014.6.592.

Publishers also produced postcards tailored for other occasions, as well as multi-purpose greeting postcards with text such as 'Greetings', 'Best Wishes' or, on one of Christina's which was posted from Youghal in 1906, 'Many Happy Days'. Such cards were increasingly produced by Irish companies, with Hely's and Lawrence particularly keen to advertise their versions to the Irish public.[12] Christmas and Easter postcards with Irish emblems and motifs were aimed at customers sending greetings to friends and relatives abroad, and a market also developed for postcards celebrating and sending good wishes on St Patrick's Day.[13] These latter were sent both within and outside Ireland, and sometimes included small packets of shamrock seed (which needed to be put into an envelope), highlighting the material character of the picture postcard and its multiple functions as a gift and memetic device as well as a communication tool, all of which were closely interlinked. St Patrick's Day postcards featured images of emblematic Irish locations such as Killarney and Glendalough and motifs such as shamrocks, 'antique harps', Celtic interlace, and 'hands across the sea', as well as text in the Irish language[14] (see Figure 13). Newspaper advertisements for them included phrases such as 'Patriotic Picture Postcards for St Patrick's Day' and 'every Irishman should buy', appealing to the heightened sense of Irish nationalism of the period and encouraging a semi-public identification with it, although many of these cards, possibly the majority, were not produced in Ireland.[15] Tuck, again, is a name that occurs frequently on such cards, and on postcards generally expressing greetings from Ireland (including those in the Irish language), although there were many other publishers of them in Britain and the United States. Dodson, postcard producers based in Wales who advertised in the *Freemans Journal* in 1906, were careful to address as broad a market as possible by emphasizing that their customers could choose St Patrick's Day postcards which were 'Catholic or Protestant' and therefore 'certain to please'.[16]

Figure 13. *Cead Mile Failte, A Hundred Thousand Welcomes*, Raphael Tuck, From <https://tuckdbpostcards.org/items/53083>

Senders also used a wide variety of picture postcards to send get-well wishes, announce births and even deaths, make appointments, convey congratulations or thanks, or advise that a parcel or letter was received or on the way. Any of these could be scribbled on the back of a scenic view, an actress photograph, an image of a historic building or monument, or of a kitten sitting in a basket. For instance, a card sent in 1907 from Strabane to Ennis, reports that 'dearest Granny died', on the reverse of a photograph of the smiling and glamorous actress Pauline Chase. Sometimes the image on the front of the card is directly referred to by the sender or seems to be relevant in some other way to the added text, but in other cases, as here, it is difficult to escape the idea that the writer just grabbed whatever card was to hand in order to send the message as quickly as possible.

Card publishers also discovered an enthusiastic market for what were called 'write-away' cards, which gave the start of a phrase that the writer could then continue and individualize themselves. Tuck, again, was the major British producer of these, starting around 1900, although there were many others, such as Hildesheimer and Wrench, and they all tended to combine the text, in imitation handwriting, with a comic drawing. Typical examples from the collections I have looked at are 'I am pleased to hear …', 'So sorry I was out …' and 'Please drop in …'. Hely's published their own versions, illustrated by the artist Frank Rigney, one of which can

Figure 14. *Don't Keep me in suspense …*, Hely's Dublin. Ellen Duff's card collection.

be seen in Figure 14. The card features the phrase 'Don't keep me in suspense …' beside a rather darkly comic drawing of a man in the process of being hanged, to which the writer has added: 'Write a line and say what I am to do. If you can possibly come, do. Yours, Bob.' A card in Christina's collection, produced by Tuck and posted in Dublin in 1905, features the words 'I was rather amused …', but in this case the sender has continued the sentence (starting on the front and working round to the back) in the Irish language (see Figure 15).

Figure 15. *I was rather amused …*, Raphael Tuck. Christina Jessop's card collection.

A communications revolution

Messages on early twentieth-century postcards developed a characteristic style. They are typically (although not always) short, informal and, to a reader without contextual knowledge, somewhat cryptic. They may include abbreviated words and modified grammar and punctuation, and their meaning may be enhanced, completed or altered in some way by their combination with the card's pre-printed imagery and/or text. This messaging style is a result of both the public's interactions with the new format and card manufacturers' ongoing responses to this interaction. The picture postcard phenomenon was recognized at the time as something of a revolution in communication, and modern scholars, such as Julia Gillen and Nigel Hall, have also seen it as such.[17] Like all revolutions, it generated anxieties, especially about a possible decline in literacy, and more specifically in the skills of letter writing. As early as 1896 the *Irish Examiner* reproduced a short piece bemoaning the fact that letter writing 'as understood by our fore-fathers' was 'rapidly becoming a lost art'.[18] As the author saw it, fundamental changes were happening in the way people wrote. Letters, when they were written, were now 'curtailed', 'in the style of a postcard or telegram' and even people's handwriting had changed, the 'delicate "Italian hand" once in fashion' having given way to the 'bold, dashing calligraphy characteristic of modern bustle'. An *Evening Herald* article from 1904 also blamed the postcard for a 'decay of epistolary style', commenting rather drily that 'the habit of writing two or three words on the edge of, say, the "Colosseum by Moonlight" or "Tea Planting in Ceylon" will accentuate the brevity of the modern letter-writer, whose geography, however, it will presumably improve'.[19] James Douglas, writing in 1907, saw such brevity as possibly problematic, at least in the eyes of some:

> There are still some ancient purists who regard Postcards as vulgar, fit only for tradesmen. I know ladies who would rather die than send a Postcard to a friend … The Postcard is, indeed, a very curt and unceremonious missive. It contains no endearing prefix or reassuring affix. It begins without a prelude and ends without an envoy. The Picture Postcard carries rudeness to the fullest extremity. There is no room for anything polite.[20]

Several commentators, however, praised the convenience of the postcard, especially in contrast to letters, albeit at times with tongues firmly in cheeks. A writer in the *Dundalk Democrat* in 1903 called it 'an ingenious compromise with your conscience' which saves 'the sickening task of writing letters to your friends':

Consider the convenience of it. If a man is away from home, instead of wasting pre-
cious time inditing a letter to his wife he can fire off a picture postcard, and profit-
ably employ the time saved in playing a game of billiards or telling funny stories.[21]

James Douglas credited the postcard with relieving modern people from
the 'slavery' and 'toil' of exhaustive letter writing, and reports appeared in
newspapers in 1908 of 'up-to-date physicians' prescribing the use of picture postcards rather than letters as a 'rest-cure' for the tired, overstretched
and 'high-strung summer vacationist'.[22] Many people did take advantage
of the small space allowance on a postcard and wrote very little, merely
adding a signature or even a single initial. Others, however, resisted the
restrictions and wrote their message around and over the image, before
continuing around to the back (see Figure 16). There were also periodic
newspaper reports on individuals who made a point of challenging the
physical limitations of the postcard, such as a *Cork Examiner* piece in
1900 on a man who managed to copy the 46,000 words of a novel onto
a postcard.[23] Such novelty acts aside, the postcard was designed for short
messages, and the majority of its users adapted happily to, and indeed exploited, its constraints.

Figure 16 *St Mary's Church, Cork*, Irish Pictorial Card Co, Cork. Cork Public Museum
archive, postcard collection D17.6 2001.28.

Recent commentators have compared the picture postcard communications revolution of the early twentieth century with that of the early twenty-first century in mobile and digital communications technologies, which has also generated social anxieties and debates.[24] As Klich and Weiss have argued,

> nearly every role the postcard played in the decades around 1900 has an analogue in the electronic technologies of the early twenty-first century. Just as today people issue invitations by email, send quick messages by text, or share collections of images on Flickr, a hundred years ago they did the same things using the postcard.[25]

Guy Atkins, in his article 'The Edwardian Social Network', has similarly noted postcards' resemblance to texts and tweets because of their immediacy and informality, their heavy reliance on abbreviations, and their range of uses from reports back from holiday resorts to 'urgent requests for stock, declarations of love, [and] one-liners to celebrate football victories'.[26] Gillen and Hall also point out that the efficient and frequent postal deliveries of the early twentieth century 'enabled the kind of micro-coordination of activities that Ling and Ytrri (2002) identified in connection with the mobile phone'.[27] The multimodal nature of postcard communication also invites comparisons with platforms such as Facebook and Instagram, where imagery can be self-generated, as it often was for real photo postcards, or appropriated from elsewhere and captioned or otherwise combined with text. An overview of the pictorial subject matter of the vast numbers of postcards bought in the early twentieth century also shows similarities to Facebook and Instagram favourites: attractive land, sea and townscapes; cute children and animals; personal photographs; sports stars and celebrities; newsworthy events; items of local or historical significance; plants and flowers; jokes and erotic and pornographic imagery.

Imagery

The pictures on picture postcards were what attracted people to buy, collect and gift them in such huge numbers, and they were also what made the postcard industry such an enormous and profitable one, driven by a constant quest for variety and innovation. Many senders were happy to rely on the picture, or the picture and pre-printed text, rather than compose an appropriate message themselves. Apart from providing inspiration and saving on time and effort, the cards could function as small gifts and demonstrations of personal taste and shared humour in a way that personally written messages were not seen to do. This was often the case with festive and holiday greeting cards, and even when text was added to these it was often perfunctory. Other types of cards sometimes provided so much pre-printed information that they left little opportunity for any possible personal expression on the part of the sender. One example, sent from Galway in 1914 to John O'Reilly, featured a cartoon image of a man in bed snuffing out a candle and the phrases 'I'm just about "Snuffing it"', 'Come at Once' and, on a wall hanging, 'What is home without another'. The message added to the back of this card merely mentions the day and time when the writer will be in, followed by good wishes and a signature.

However, the imagery on many cards, as noted already, bears no obvious relationship to the message on the back. The birth announcement on the back of an image of Carnegie Library and Municipal Buildings in Cork has been mentioned earlier, as has the actress postcard reporting the death of 'dearest Granny'. Another example (of many) in Christina's collection features a coloured illustration of the Bay of Naples, including the volcano Vesuvius spewing fire and volcanic ash into the sky, sent to her in 1905 from Lahinch, County Clare. This card was published by the British company Hildesheimer, although it was printed in Italy. On the back, the sender apologized for her 'neglect', presumably in keeping in touch, said that she had been 'rather bothered' lately, but had a 'splendid time' in London. There is no mention of Italy or Vesuvius or even 'hope you like this'. Annebella Pollen, in 'Sweet Nothings: Suggestive Brighton Postcard Inscriptions' (2009), quotes Frederic Vitoux as claiming that the relationship between the two sides of a picture postcard is 'never gratuitous, even if it sometimes remains ambiguous', but, as with the birth and death announcements, it seems likely that this card was chosen primarily because it was conveniently to hand.[28] Nevertheless, for a modern reader, the image of Naples and Vesuvius *does* inflect the overall meaning of the card, even if the exact way in which it does so remains intriguingly elusive. It leaves us with questions about how, and why, an evocative image of an Italian bay with its erupting volcano ended up being used so casually and seemingly thoughtlessly in Ireland in the early twentieth century. Such questions might direct us to (among other things) histories of international and national modernization, among them developments in mass industrialization, transport and communication, capitalism, tourism and image production, distribution and meaning. The use of this card in this situation therefore highlights, among other things, the increasing complexity of life in early twentieth-century Ireland, its connectedness to international forces, and the myriad ways in which this could impact on the lives of ordinary people.

Many senders, nevertheless, turned the mass-produced and stereotypical imagery of the cards into something more individually meaningful and certainly more personalized by their added messages. Even the well-worn phrase 'Hope you like this P.C. [postcard]' pointed to the image on the front as the deliberate rather than arbitrary result of an act of choice and a desire to please. Travellers contextualized the scenes on the fronts of their cards for their recipients with phrases such as 'was here this morning', 'this is near where we are staying', 'beautiful place – glorious weather so far', or they marked an 'X' to indicate the hotel in which they stayed. Others put a lot of work into helping their correspondent understand their particular travelling experience. Figure 17 shows a photograph of the White Star Line steam ship Majestic, on which Christina's future brother-in-law Diarmuid travelled across the Atlantic back to Ireland in 1905. Not content with merely sending an image of the ship on the sea, he humorously communicated the roughness of the crossing as he experienced it by using spiky uneven script: 'I assure you I am perfectly sober. Never judge a man's condition by his writing.' He heightened the level of convincing detail by including under the image 'Written 13/5/05 on the high seas', and the ship's location, latitude and longitude, on that day, which showed that it was some distance off the coast of Nova Scotia. Thus a mass-produced souvenir image of a ship was transformed into a record of what it felt like to make a specific journey on that ship.

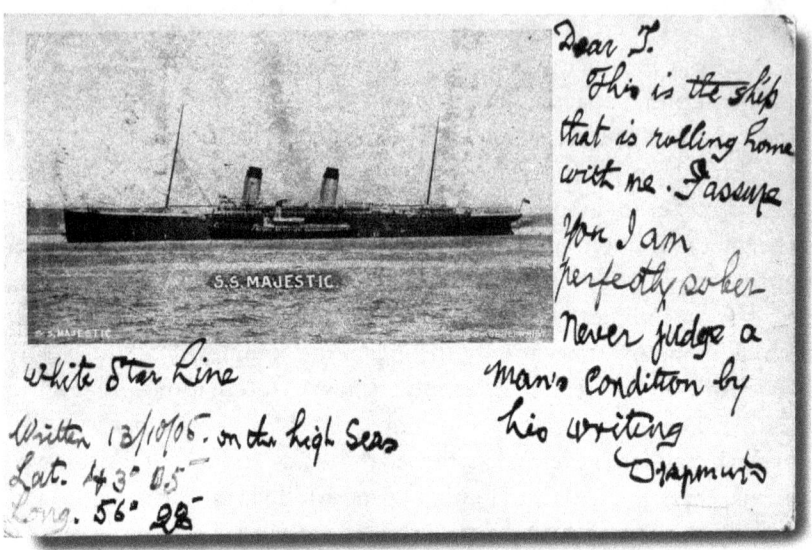

Figure 17 *SS Majestic*, J. Koehler, New York. Christina Jessop's card collection.

Sometimes senders wanted to share a nostalgic memory stirred by the card's image. In 1905, Ellen in Dublin received a black-and-white photographic card of Elphin in County Roscommon, with a large prominent building evident on the right-hand side. On the back her correspondent Lily wrote 'Bring back to memory childhood's happy days (my convent)', thus converting what had been a rather prosaic view card into a personal and evocative statement. Others found personal significance in celebrity images: 'I thought this picture bore some resemblance to you', 'looks like your little nephew' or 'does this remind you of anyone?' 'Serious' cards could be turned into jokes, as in the card in Christina's collection which features a reproduction of a painting by the artist Alma-Talmeda, showing an open-mouthed singer standing by a piano, under which the sender has written 'looks like she is catching flies'. Some of the written comments on picture postcards can be rather startling and open up a whole new angle on their subject. Christina's collection contains a card, again from Diarmuid, sent just after he arrived in America (see Figure 18). It shows the East River and Brooklyn Bridge in New York, and underneath he has written 'Emigration is a curse but it is great fun'. Comments such as this provide us with glimpses into the individuals using these cards, their idiosyncrasies, humour and their sometimes surprising take on the mass media messages with which they were presented. Diarmuid is presumably well aware of the misery of emigration, and even more of the unrelentingly negative discourse surrounding it in Ireland, but on this day in 1905 he was a young man in search of adventure and travelling to New York seemed like a wonderful thing to be able to do.

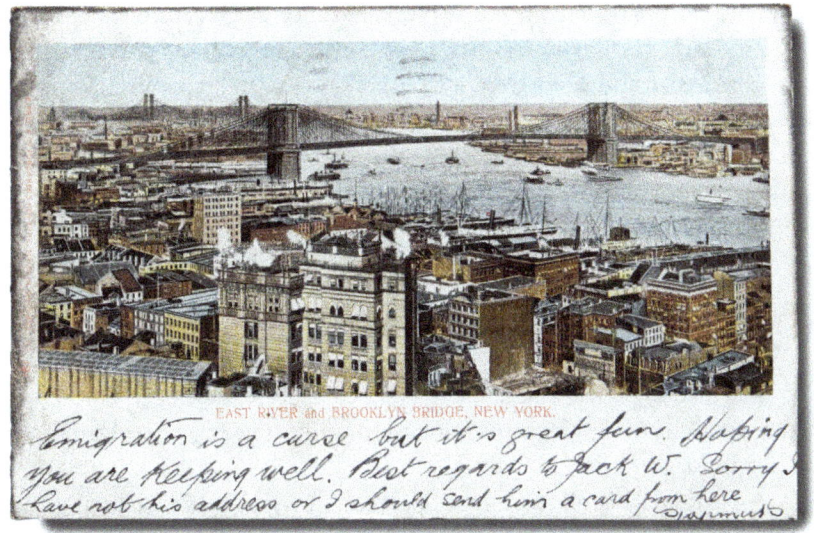

Figure 18. *East River and Brooklyn Bridge New York*, E. Frey, New York. Christina Jessop's card collection.

According to Pollen,

rather than set up an artificial 'either/or' competition between the postcard's two opposing sides, it is preferable to consider the postcard as a double-sided medium with two intersecting opportunities for meaning … The scriptural side reanimates the image side in sometimes unexpected ways.[29]

Gilderdale has shown that the reverse is also the case. In his research on the 'Hands Across the Sea' (HATS) postcard genre in relation to early twentieth-century New Zealand, he examined postcards sent from people who were experiencing separation from their loved ones. He found that whilst handwritten texts on postcards remained primarily stoic, the pre-packaged visual vocabulary on greetings postcards allowed users to send strongly emotional arguments for the maintenance of their relationships without ever having to put these into their own words. Postcards, it seems, gave the Edwardians the option of being both stoic and sentimental.[30]

Thus senders could exploit the pre-printed imagery and text as a relatively low-risk way of expressing their emotions. A card sent to John O'Reilly in 1914, and postmarked from the White Star office in Queenstown, appears to do the same (see Figure 19). The front shows a selection of photographic vignettes: a man and woman embracing and looking sad, a steamship on the sea; a train; and the woman alone, staring into middle distance, with an open box of what appear to be letters beside her. A scroll underneath these images features the motto, 'Absence strengthens Love', and underneath that the verse

> I know I do love thee, yes I do love thee
> And when thou art absent then I am sad
> I envy the bright blue sky above thee
> Whose quiet stars see thee and are so glad.

On the back, in pencil, the sender has written a brief message: 'Good bye old sport', followed by a sentence that looks like 'Having a good trip' and an illegible signature.

A particularly poignant use of postcard imagery was reported in the *Sunday Independent* in 1908, after a 17-year-old girl in London, who had been stealing small amounts of money at work, committed suicide by taking poison. Afterwards, a picture postcard featuring an image of Hawardan Churchyard in Wales was found in her bedroom, and on one of the tombstones she had written 'Let me rest in peace'.[31] Other cases reported in newspapers of the time suggested that the imagery on a postcard could have unexpectedly powerful effects on a recipient. The *Cork Examiner* and the *Sunday Independent* both carried short pieces in 1906 about a gunner in Shoeburyness, in England, who killed himself after he received a postcard from his lover which 'unhinged his mind'.[32] The card featured 'a picture of an open coffin with a woman in it, and underneath was written – "I wouldn't leave my little hut for you"'. A tombstone also depicted on the card bore the initials of the gunner. Both the girl in London and the gunner's lover used postcard imagery to amplify and dramatize the impact of their messages, adding their own text to focus its meaning.

Figure 19. *Absence Strengthens Love*, no publisher/printer named. John O'Reilly/Bessie
Caulfield collection.

Senders could also be careless in their use of postcard imagery, and this is highlighted regularly in the frequent breach-of-promise cases reported during the period, when women brought men to court for seriously misleading them over their marital intentions. A Brixton nurse brought such a case against a man in 1907, and amongst other 'affectionate' letters and postcards presented as evidence was a 'series of comic picture postcards representing "The Cats' Matrimony"'. She obviously took the suggestion implied by these images seriously, as she replied as follows to one which alluded to the cats marrying in Gretna Green, a location associated with irregular or 'runaway' weddings: 'Is it to be a Gretna Green wedding. I hope such a breakdown will not befall us. We will talk about it later on.'[33] Another case which was heard in Coleraine Co Derry in 1909 involved a woman suing a farmer, and one piece of evidence put forward was a postcard she received from the defendant while she was away on a short holiday, 'a picture of a young man and a young woman, and underneath were the words, "Popping the question"'.[34] The *Irish Independent* in 1910 also reported on a case where the counsel for the prosecution claimed that 'the amatory correspondence on both sides was entirely confined to picture postcards, on which the pictures, letterpress, and the few scribbled words all bore on love and lovers' meetings, such as a gentleman kissing a lady and the like'.[35] Although other evidence was also presented in most cases, both lawyers and judges seem to have understood postcard imagery as a form of serious and deliberate communication, even when it was in the form of mass-published playful or humorous cartoons.

Relationship maintenance

The text added to Edwardian postcards sent through the post was often very generic and minimal, to the extent that the modern reader is inclined to wonder why the writers even bothered: 'Hope all is well'; 'Here I am'; 'All fine here'; 'Got here all right'; 'Lovely day. Everything A1'; 'See you soon'. Often there is not even a message, just a name or initial. However, this kind of communication, called 'phatic dialogue' by communication theorists, has an important function, the maintenance of social relationships. According to Victoria Wang, John V. Tucker and Kevin Haines, phatic dialogue describes communication 'which is empty of informative content but serves to engage people with one another in purely social exchange'.[36]

> The purpose of phatic dialogue has been linked to the need for hearing the humming of a machine. The 'machine must be "humming" if we are not to think it has broken down'. The relationship between speakers is affirmed by the act of communication rather than the content of communication.[37]

Barbara Becker and Karen Malcolm noted the prominence of this type of communication in a collection they studied of over 350 postcards sent to a cook in Edinburgh mainly between 1904 and 1908. They noted in particular that cards from a correspondent called Jessie, probably a work colleague,

> were so generic and consistent, using the same formulaic openers and closers 'Another for your collection. I arrived here all safe. We had a nice drive out. Hope you are well. Excuse this hurried postcard. Love Jessie', and saying little else, that this sub-register was called phatic … Jessie's postcards would have served to support the women's friendship … without being required to fulfil the additional requirement of exchanging information, since the women could communicate face-to-face at their place of work. [38]

Rogan has made similar observations about the majority of early twentieth-century postcard messages, although he uses the term 'activity orientated' instead of 'phatic' to describe communication between people whose aim is 'to confirm or mobilize' an existing 'fairly close social relationship'.[39] Activity-orientated communication (as opposed to information-orientated communication) prioritizes the activity of communicating in itself, the getting, or staying, in touch. As he points out, the culturally competent postcard-sender in this context understands that a short, efficiently worded message is what is required, drawing on and confirming shared references, not the delivery of new information.

The term 'phatic technology' has also been used to describe technological systems that function primarily to facilitate phatic dialogue, that
is, 'to establish, develop and maintain personal and social relationships', especially when those relationships 'have been stretched across time-space'.[40]
This term has mostly been applied to modern social media platforms,
but it can also be a useful way of looking at Edwardian picture postcard
communication. Phatic technologies, it is argued, create communities of
users, based on social interactions which are 'removed from the physical',
and the members of such communities 'become dependent on the phatic
technology to fulfil some of their social needs'.[41] Phatic technologies such as
Facebook, Twitter and WhatsApp have become normalized in modern life
(as postcard exchange was in the early twentieth century) to the extent that
individuals who don't use them may be seen as odd or strange.[42] Scholars
have also noted the apparent 'triviality' and volume of 'empty exchanges'
evident on such platforms, similar to the observations made about the
written messages on picture postcards.[43]

A feature of phatic dialogue is that its participants often know each
other and already have a relationship. Most picture postcard users, like the
cook and her friend Jessie mentioned earlier, were not solely reliant on postcard exchanges to maintain their relationship. They also had face-to-face
and letter contact, both of which were far more suitable media than publicly
visible postcards for lengthy explanations or intimate confidences. Postcard
messages therefore are often small fragments of larger, ongoing conversations, and many of them can seem very obscure as a result. Some of the
more evocative but ultimately opaque examples from the collections I have
examined include 'Isn't it sad?'; 'I had a great letter from "Teapot" today';
'What's wrong at the camp?'; 'What are your thoughts on the news?'; 'Who
told you about the lion?' and 'You are horrid', the last simply accompanied
by the brief signature 'Máire'. Although it was probably wise not to provide
too much information for the curious eyes of postal workers, these writers
were not necessarily being deliberately mysterious. There was simply no
need to elaborate for a recipient who was familiar with the references, as
Ellen presumably was when she was asked by one of her correspondents in
1905, 'Don't you think it is lovely weather for Gooseimooning?', or when
another signed off 'From yours as ever (Sponge Cake)'.

Many postcards also feature what Rogan calls 'metatexts on communication', communication which is *about* communication itself.[44] Thus we commonly see 'Thanks for PC', 'Still waiting for your PC (or letter)', 'Hope you can read the writing on this', 'Will send a letter' and 'Why don't you write?' And, as he also observes, even cards bearing no added text except the recipient's name and address were still sending a message:

> No card is totally void of information; after all, they state that the sender is or was alive at the moment of mailing … In the same way, cards sent between collectors, with little or no text, also have this secondary, social function of keeping the network going, as if stating 'I'm still interested in your collecting activity and I'll help you enhance your collection.'[45]

Such cards were not always seen as acceptable, however. One of Christina's correspondents wrote in 1906 'many thanks for p.c. It is a very nice one, but you are horrid not to write on it. I thought you promised me a long letter'. Some senders therefore (like Diarmuid on board the Majestic) put some effort into constructing for their correspondents a sense of where they were and what they were doing as they wrote, often aided by the imagery on the card's front. They announced that they were writing it in the post office, hotel or railway station, or looking at a beautiful view, pictured of course on the other side of the postcard. Christina's brother Charlie, who was in Canada in 1907, sent her a card with a photograph of White Horse in Yukon under which he added 'Coming down Yukon River in a row boat to Dawson'. A friend of her other brother, Jack, on a holiday in Switzerland with him in the same year, wrote the message 'Written on the top of Rochers-de-Naye 6700 feet above the level of Lake Geneva' on the back of an image of a small Alpine church set against a lake and snow-topped mountains. Both men were attempting to convey to Christina a vivid sense of what they were experiencing when they wrote the card she now held in her hand. Others had less exotic realities to communicate, such as a toddler shaking a table or an injured hand, both according to the senders making writing the card difficult, or the woman in Queenstown in 1905 who expressed the hope that the recipient was 'getting over Lent alright' as she herself was 'nearly a corpse from it'. As Milne argues, 'by referring to the "here and now" of corporeality … correspondents strive to collapse the time and distance that separate them' and communicate 'a sense of immediacy, intimacy, and presence'.[46] As with modern communication technologies, users could also construct carefully curated images of themselves and their lives for the consumption of others. Tourists sent home pictures of exotic locations, girls in convent schools sent their families images of their science room and real photo postcards of subjects such as their hockey team, and lovers wrote x's and heart shapes on the back of romantic images of couples and flowers. Picture postcard communication, like communication via any other medium, was only as 'honest' as its users chose to be, and it was of necessity selective in what it could express.

For a modern researcher, the messages on picture postcards are seductive and tantalizing but also often frustrating (not unlike the information yielded by most historical sources). Their great advantage is that they offer unparalleled insights into the casual communication of the period, the language, jokes, viewpoints and day-to-day preoccupations of the millions of people who have left little else in the historical record. As Naomi Schor has memorably expressed it, when reading old postcards, 'one is placed in the position of the voyeur, or better yet the eavesdropper on everyday life':

> From the backs of these cards emerges a murmur of small voices speaking of minor aches and pains, long-awaited engagements, obscure family feuds; reporting on safe arrivals and unexpected delay ... in short, carrying on the millions of minute transactions, the grain of everyday life.[47]

As most eavesdroppers find out, however, the information is often presented in puzzling decontextualized fragments which need to be combined with other sources in order to make sense of them, and even then they may remain tantalizingly obscure.

Postcards: Semi-public communication

Privacy was of course a problem when sending open messages for personal communication, and this issue generated concerns similar to those expressed today about internet privacy settings and data accessibility.

Some of the more enigmatic postcard messages were certainly so for this reason and may be why a pseudonym like 'Sponge Cake' was seen as necessary. The *Evening Herald* carried a report in 1909 of a girl in Wolgast in Germany who decided to investigate whether Post Office officials were reading postcards. She therefore 'sent one to a friend, telling her that Count Zeppelin was expected to arrive there in his airship on Thursday ... On that day no fewer than 300 persons arrived at Wolgast from the surrounding districts to learn that there would be no flight'.[48] Some people wrote their messages upside down, which made casual snooping difficult rather than impossible, or in mirror writing, shorthand or some other form of code (see Figure 20). Those who really wanted to keep a message private paid the extra money and sealed it in an envelope. As is the case now, however, many people seem to have been unconcerned about who saw what they wrote, and had no problem expressing strong political opinions or their annoyance with the behaviour of family members on the back of an open postcard. People also sent through the post their real photo personal postcards of friends and family, including babies and children, without worrying about their possible misuse.

Figure 20. *Patrick's Bridge, Cork*, no publisher/printer named. Cork Public Museum archive, postcard collection D17.11 2002.151.

Indeed, some writers took advantage of the semi-public nature of postcard communication by using it to amplify the impact of insults and character defamations. As early as 1892 the *Kerry Sentinel* published an angry piece about this 'common abuse of the postcard', stating that 'any coward can scrawl an offensive message upon the back ... and for the small outlay of a halfpenny enjoy the luxury of publicly slandering his neighbour, whilst sheltering himself from chastisement by not signing his name'.[49] The specific reason for the writer's fury was probably the fact that the editor of the *Kerry Sentinel* himself had been one of the recipients of one of these slanderous cards. However, many such cards were signed, perhaps foolishly. In 1900 a sergeant in the Royal Constabulary repeatedly demanded the return of items from a young woman he had previously been courting, eventually accusing her on the back of a postcard of being in 'unlawful possession' of them. He was convicted of libel for effectively accusing her publicly of theft.[50] Indeed, a writer in the *Kerry Evening Post* in 1903 noted how 'indirectly beneficial' the postcard had been

> to the members of the Bar, as it has constantly been the origin of actions for libel. The habit of sending libels through the post in this compromising manner is not so common, however, since in several notorious instances it has led to smart sentences for a highly obnoxious class of criminal.[51]

However, a piece in the *Kerry News* suggests it was still common enough in 1907:

> Defamatory postcards are sent around and seem to defy the law as they have now established themselves as a form of abuse and annoyance to the community. No person wishes to be charged before the public of what he is not guilty of, and yet we see the behaviour of both sexes interfered with.[52]

In the same year the *Ulster Herald* reported on a case in Limerick which showed that accusations of postcard slander could misfire and bring ridicule down on the accuser. During the hearing the judge described to the court a 'rather amusing' postcard which was presented to him as evidence:

> There is a gentleman lying in bed, and he has a very big pair of feet, which are exposed. Over his head is a barrel of beer, and this is connected with his mouth by a

tube. There is a note bearing the following lines: – 'I have no pain dear mother, now, / But oh! I am so dry. / Connect me with a brewery, / And leave me there to die.'[53]

The judge claimed to have found this card to be 'one of the most shocking' he had ever seen, although there was 'loud laughter' in court when he read it aloud.

Political statements

Individuals sometimes wrote casual political observations on the backs of cards, but others attempted to use postcards to make a semi-public statement aimed at anyone who saw them. For instance, the official half-penny stamp bearing a portrait of King Edward VII, or of King George V after Edward died in 1910, could be placed upside down in what was interpreted by some as an Irish nationalist gesture. This, however, could also be read as part of the 'Language of Stamps', through which various romantic feelings could be communicated depending on how the stamp was angled.[54] A more obvious and unambiguous postcard statement was sent to Christina from her sister Rose and her new husband Diarmuid from London in 1907 (see Figure 21). The image on the front of the card shows the British Houses of Parliament in Westminster Palace, their imposing, elegant architecture advertising and celebrating the power, sophistication and historical prestige of the institutions at the centre of the British Empire. But the message of the card as published has been significantly undermined by the text written on it: 'A united Parliament, a united people, a united EMPIRE' underneath the image, and written on top: 'All that is written below is SARKASTICK.' This cheeky card was processed and sent, seemingly unhindered, from London to Dublin via that other great symbol of the efficiency, modernity and global reach of the British Empire, the British Post Office, and was undoubtedly seen by many people *en route*. This postcard is a good example of how ordinary people can use mass cultural products for their own purposes, manipulating them so that they can end up communicating something very different to that originally intended.

Figure 21. *London Clock Tower and Houses of Parliament,* London Stereoscopic
Company. Christina Jessop's card collection.

Because they were so easy and cheap to use, postcards were also useful
if a group of people needed to be mobilized to make a statement or protest
or to present a petition, and the issuing of pre-printed and stamped versions could make the process even simpler. The Second Boer War (1883–
1900) in South Africa, fought between British troops and Afrikaaners,
generated quite a few such initiatives, particularly in support of the Boer
side. In 1900, for instance, the publisher T. O'Connor of Dyke Parade in
Cork issued a postcard pre-addressed to 'his Highness the State President
of the South African Republic, S.J.P. Kruger, Consulate-General', at 54,
Faubourg Montmartre, Paris, the address where Kruger was taking refuge
having fled from South Africa.

> On the other side there is a pretty picture of 'Welcome', with the President's bust
> carved in a massive rock. The Boer flag, which is borne by the figures representing
> the welcomers, is to be used for the sender's name, vocation, and address, lines being
> made for that purpose.[55]

The *Cork Examiner* reported in 1901 that postcards were for sale in
Paris pre-addressed 'To his Majesty the Emperor of Russia, Chateau

de Compeigne', as Tsar Nicholas II was visiting France. On the front was

> a picture representing Mr Kruger walking with naked feet and loaded down with a heavy cross. The figure stands out against a background shewing burning farms and houses. The picture forms a frame to a brief appeal to the Czar in favour of peace.[56]

These pro-Boer postcard initiatives seem to have been popular, but the *Irish Independent* was unenthusiastic about another proposal in 1905 to use postcards to thank the American President Theodore Roosevelt for his role in the negotiations which ended the Russo-Japanese war: 'It is suggested that people from all parts should send him an artistic picture postcard bearing a line of thanks ... His secretaries would be driven out of their wits by each morning's post.'[57]

Postcard users were also mobilized in Ireland as part of a 'Mail-in-Irish' campaign launched in 1901 by the Gaelic League, the organization founded in 1893 to promote knowledge and use of the Irish language. The British postal system had a rule that all post must be addressed in English if sent from primarily English-speaking areas, which by the early twentieth century included most of Ireland. The Mail-in-Irish campaign encouraged people instead to write names and addresses in the Irish language and was an attempt to force government recognition of the Irish language as a valid form of communication for all Irish people. Officially, as Gareth W. Dunleavy argues in 'Hyde's Crusade for the Language and the Case of the Embarrassing Packets' (1984), the Post Office maintained 'there was no good reason why a world-respected system for collection, sorting and distribution of mail should be jeopardized for the purpose of saving the language of a miniscule number of Irish monoglots.'[58] However, by 1905 the Dublin Post Office was receiving so much Irish-addressed mail that four junior clerks and telegraphists with 'an adequate knowledge of the language' were taken from their regular duties to translate addresses from Irish to English.[59] Large mailings were still sometimes refused, however, and delayed or incorrect translations caused post to be late.

The only collection I have examined which contains cards addressed and/or written in Irish from this period is that of Christina, who was a member of the Gaelic League. Eight of the cards in Christina's collection have both their messages and addresses written in Irish and three additional cards have her name and address in Irish. Judging by her correspondents' responses Christina also seems to have sent quite a few herself, although these have been lost. Many of those who responded in English to her Irish-language messages were supportive, although one begged her to 'not write in Irish because I never get them till about a week after', and another explained that she would have answered her 'pretty P.C.' earlier, but she had 'not as yet been able to get yr message translated!' (adding an apologetic 'Deplorable ignorance!'). Such responses hint at the level of commitment required to persist with this campaign. Post Office staff seem to have had particular difficulty with Christina's surname, Jessop, which her Irish-language correspondents wrote as Níc Sheosaimh, variously interpreting it as Joseph or Jacobs. Her first name was often abbreviated by her friends from Christina to 'Tiny' (partly also because she was a small woman), which converted to Irish became 'Beagáinín', but was translated back to English by the Post Office translators as 'Little'. Her name could therefore be changed from 'Tiny Jessop' to 'Little Joseph', showing that there was a strong possibility of lost or delayed mail even when it was not refused by the Post Office (see Figure 22).

Figure 22. Postcard message sent to Christina Jessop. Christina Jessop's card collection.

Both the Mail-in-Irish and the pro-Boer campaigns exploited the possibilities of the picture postcard as a political tool. Letters and parcels were also part of the Mail-in-Irish campaign, but the enormous existing popularity of sending and collecting postcards as a leisure activity made the cards ideal for this task, as did the fact that they were inexpensive and easy to buy and send, and possibly not too problematic if they were lost. The Irish-language names and addresses on the backs of these cards made life difficult on a practical level for postal workers and forced a review of the system. Also, however, the messages written in Irish and visible to anyone who handled these cards drew attention to the fact that a significant number of Irish people were determined to communicate in what they considered their native language, in the same way that the earlier postcards addressed to Kruger and the Russian Tzar highlighted the extent of Boer support in the population.

The picture postcard as a medium of mass communication

The picture postcard as published was also a medium of mass communication, and a very effective one. Its imagery, often in colour, was superior in quality, variety and popular appeal to that of most other types of publications, and it could be published quickly in large quantities in response to a particular event. For instance, on Wednesday 24 August 1904 Easons sold postcards of the Dublin Horse Show made from photographs taken the previous day. The *Freeman's Journal* praised these cards as 'quick work which it would be difficult to beat. The photographs are well reproduced, and possess clearness, depth, and definition'.[60] The company continued to issue a new set of Horse Show cards daily for the duration of the show. Picture postcards for sale were exhibited prominently in many public spaces, were handled and examined by various people, and often ended their journeys again on display in albums, on parlour fire screens or as wallpaper. According to a *Cork Examiner* piece in 1908 postcards, in contrast to books, 'find a privileged place in many homes. They are shown with pleasure to visitors; everybody sends and receives them; every other shop window is full of them. Consequently the lessons they convey should command a good deal of favour.'[61] Groups with messages to spread, therefore, whether for social, political or economic reasons, made sure to communicate them via postcards, and for some people it is likely that postcards became a more significant information source than newspapers or magazines, since they required less investment on their part in money, effort and time. This raises interesting parallels with present day consumers who receive their news solely from social media, and related modern criticisms of a media culture of soundbites and opinion bubbles.

An entire journal printed on a postcard was published in Paris in 1903, the *Carte Journal,*

> one side containing the usual space for the name and address, while on the other side is a reproduction of a sketch or photograph illustrating the most interesting event of the day, accompanied by half a dozen brief telegrams giving the world's news ... [It] will be published at a penny, [and] will make its appearance on the boulevards every afternoon about four o'clock.[62]

Postcard publishers however generally contented themselves with a single theme or message per postcard. Cards picturing events as geographically disparate as the Bray floods of 1905 or the 1906 San Francisco earthquake found their way into Irish shops and homes. When Halley's Comet made an appearance in the skies over Europe and America in 1910 the postcard was one of the opportunistic media that covered the story. In Paris, according to the *Donegal News*, not only were many postcards published featuring images of the comet, but many more with illustrations of the end of the world, as the comet was seen by some as a sign from Heaven of an imminent apocalypse.[63]

Postcards were a useful way of spreading opinions and propaganda of all sorts. As John Fraser states in his article 'Propaganda on the Picture Postcard' (1980),

> the propaganda use of the picture postcard was realized very early in the development of the postcard boom. The appeal to patriotism lay behind the production of postcards depicting the head of state, army parades and manoeuvres, ships, leading generals and admirals that were common to all the important countries.[64]

Political messages on postcards were often delivered in the form of cartoons and caricatures, and their numbers could escalate dramatically in response to particular events. For instance, the second notorious trial in 1899 of Alfred Dreyfus, a young French officer who was falsely accused of treason, was estimated to have generated over 6 million postcards during a period of eighteen months.[65] The Boer War also resulted in a vast quantity of opinionated postcards on both sides, the British celebrating the heroism of their commanders and troops, and their opponents (who seem to have been prominent in most European countries including Ireland) criticizing what they saw as British incompetence, cowardice and injustices towards Afrikaaners.[66]

Irish political affairs were also aired on picture postcards. Events such as evictions, images of which could be used to illustrate both the problems with and the need for British government in Ireland, depending on the context, had been the subject of a wide range of visual media for some time. In 1890 Lawrence produced a set of sixty magic lantern slides showing eviction scenes photographed between 1886 and 1890, similar to or possibly the same ones which were publicly projected in Dublin in 1897 by Maud Gonne and other activists in protest against the visit of Queen Victoria.[67] Postcards featuring eviction scenes were later issued by a range of companies, including the London-based Hartmann. Wynne of Loughrea published a card featuring the infamous eviction in 1906 of a merchant Martin Ward from his home and business premises in Loughrea. This eviction, carried out on behalf of the notorious absentee landlord the Marquis of Clanricarde, was widely reported both nationally and internationally, and the postcard enhanced and amplified this reportage, 'vividly reproducing', as it did

> the attack upon Mr. Martin Ward's house and its brave defence. It shows distinctly the manure bags over which Col. Sanderson made so merry, as fortifications of the premises; it depicts the barbed wire fences and the men behind armed with rough and ready weapons.[68]

Postcards during this period promoted a range of different viewpoints. Many celebrated the British Empire and its manifestations in Ireland while others advertised the aspirations of Irish nationalists ranging from home rulers to separatists. Christina received a card in 1906 which can be seen as an innocent-looking call to arms, or perhaps just an encouragement to people to learn about the Irish language and culture. It features text in both the Irish and English languages: 'Éire Gaedealac. Cead Míle Fáilte!

[Gaelic Ireland. A Hundred Thousand Welcomes!] Time you came out of your shell, hope to hear you crow soon' (see Figure 23). On this card, published by Fergus O'Connor, a drawing by William O'Duane of a baby bird emerging from an egg symbolizes the birth of a new Gaelic Ireland, ready to start crowing. The nationalist movement seems to have had considerable faith in the communicative power of postcards. In 1908 the Gaelic League committee resolved to publish a series of propagandist postcards with 'a few lines giving the opinion of some important public men on the Irish language movement'.[69] By this means, the committee believed, 'Gaelic League ideas will … be conveniently and almost unconsciously spread'.

Figure 23. Éire Gaedealac. Cead Míle Fáilte, Fergus O'Connor. Christina Jessop's card collection.

However, many consumers of postcards, and of other print media, had little interest in politics or conventionally 'serious' news stories, and instead gravitated towards more entertaining sensation-driven material. In *The Fourth Estate: Journalism in Twentieth-Century Ireland* (2017), Mark

O'Brien has written about the emergence of 'new journalism' in America in the latter half of the nineteenth century and its significant influence on Britain and Ireland.[70] He quotes T. P. O'Connor to support his claim that, among other things, new journalism resulted in

> a changed definition of what constituted news – 'a rejection of the older view that the press existed primarily to record and disseminate high politics' and the adoption of 'a modern tabloid sensibility'. Out went the emphasis on verbatim parliamentary reportage and page-length leading articles, and in came an emphasis on 'gossip, display advertising, sports news, human interest features, articles aimed at women and children and, above all, fast-breaking stories transmitted by wire agencies'.[71]

Picture postcard culture fitted very well with this new journalism. It could feed consumers' desire, for instance, to know what the people and places featured in news stories actually looked like, as well as the market for fashionable celebrity images, illustrations of the latest dance moves, photographs of football teams and topical jokes. The stories of crime and scandal that were a staple of new journalism also helped sell vast quantities of postcards. For example, the *Cork Examiner* reported in 1903 on a coroner's enquiry into the murder of a woman called Camille Holland four years earlier in 1899, at a remote place called Moat farm near Saffron Walden in England. The spot where the body was discovered attracted tourists and photographers, 'and a brisk trade was done in picture postcards bearing views of the Moat House and the spot at which the men, after many days of search and toil, came upon the body'.[72] Victims, defendants and convicted criminals in sensational cases all had their portraits disseminated via picture postcards. In 1910 in London the American Hawley Crippen was convicted of murdering his wife. He was condemned to death and brought to Pentonville Prison to be hanged. Along the route to the prison, 'hawkers of picture postcards depicting Crippen alongside Le Neve [a young woman with whom he had an affair] in the dock at Bow street met with a ready sale'.[73]

Silly stories from all over the world also manifested themselves in print media which found their way into Ireland, and aspects of them were represented and further perpetuated via picture postcards. In 1907, the *Freemans Journal* carried a piece about a popular craze in France for a game called

Diabolo, which consisted of 'spinning an affair like a large reel on a piece of thick cord, about a yard long, fastened to the end of two bamboo sticks … A young Parisienne the other day caught the diabolo 147 times, and her photo is now selling like wildfire on picture postcards'.[74] Raphael Tuck issued several series of postcards along the theme of Diabolo, featuring celebrities playing it, making it the central focus of jokes and even designing a set of Christmas cards around it.[75]

In 1908 the *Cork Examiner* reported on a story from London about a fox terrier who was thought to have swallowed and, months later, regurgitated a live frog, with the result that portraits of both dog and frog were now available to buy on picture postcards.[76] And in 1909 an article in the *Leinster Express* discussed a photographic postcard of a ghost which had been seen in a disused graveyard in Barnstaple in North Devon:

> An enterprising photographer has succeeded – though nobody knows how or when – in photographing the 'ghost', and is exhibiting it in his window as a picture postcard. The sale of the card is abnormal, and the picture only adds to the mystery. By the side of one of tombs, as if rising from it, is a white apparition, but no form can be seen, whether of a man or a woman. The 'ghost' has a large following of strong believers.[77]

No doubt the issuing of the postcard multiplied the numbers of those believers.

During the Edwardian period, picture postcards were widely adopted as a medium of communication for a range of reasons: they were cheap to buy and send, portable, standardized for easy sorting and transport, had just enough space for a message and address, and had a tremendous visual appeal and variety that was constantly updated. They were used for many different types of personal communications, to the extent that a distinctive postcard writing style emerged, characterized by its brevity and abbreviations. Frequently the imagery and text on the card as published sufficed to communicate the desired message, and also frequently the postcard's picture was completely ignored by the sender, resulting in a shifting and ambiguous relationship between the two sides of a card. Additionally, the published imagery and text could be manipulated by the sender to communicate a modified version of the original message, or even one that completely contradicted it. The majority of picture postcards, because they were sent through the post without envelopes, inevitably resulted in semi-public communications that caused unease among some, but that others exploited, sometimes to make political statements. They could be useful political tools in other ways too, as was shown by the successful Mail-in Irish campaign, which made the most of their disposability to flood the Post-Office and force action on their part. Finally, the picture postcard constituted an effective medium of mass communication for the early twentieth century, filling the niche in the market for large quantities of cheap, quickly produced, attractive imagery with minimal textual information. It could easily travel long distances and reach large numbers of people in many countries at minimal expense to its producer. Postcard imagery also answered the consumer's need to see what people and things looked like as well as providing them with tangible mementos to keep and share with their family and friends.

Notes

1. Ferguson, 'A Murmur of Small Voices', 170.
2. Staff, *The Picture Postcard & Its Origins*, 50–54.
3. Staff, *The Picture Postcard & Its Origins*, 62.
4. Gillen and Hall, 'The Edwardian Postcard', 17.
5. 'Telegraph Appointments', *Cork Examiner* (16 February 1906); 'Vacancies for Three Pupils at Boyne Valley Fruit Industry', *Drogheda Argus and Leinster Journal* (30 July 1904).
6. Rickards, *Encyclopedia of Ephemera*, 'Advertising Novelty', 8–9 and 'Trade card', 334–336.
7. Gilderdale, *Hands Across the Sea*, 251.
8. *Irish Independent* (28 December 1906; 26 December 1907).
9. *Irish Independent* (26 December 1908).
10. *Freemans Journal* (15 December 1906).
11. O'Brien, *Presentation Parlour*, 72–73.
12. *Irish Independent* (12 April 1906; 21 March 1910).
13. *Irish Independent* (30 December 1907).
14. *Irish Independent* (7 March 1910); McCabe, *Dear Miss B.*, 26–27. See Gilderdale, *Hands Across the Sea* for a detailed analysis and discussion of this motif.
15. *Kilkenny People* (9 March 1907).
16. *Freemans Journal* (13 March 1906).

17. Gillen and Hall, 'The Edwardian Postcard', 1.
18. *Cork Examiner* (18 January 1896).
19. *Evening Herald* (23 July 1904).
20. Staff, *The Picture Postcard & Its Origins*, 81.
21. *Dundalk Democrat* (19 December 1903).
22. Staff, *The Picture Postcard & Its Origins*, 79; 'Picture Postcards and the Rest Cure', *Cork Examiner* (10 October 1908); *Irish Independent* (24 September 1908).
23. *Cork Examiner* (26 October 1900).
24. Guy Atkins, 'The Edwardian Social Network', *History Today*, 63/6 (2013), <http://www.historytoday.com/guy-atkins/edwardian-social-network> accessed 14 August 2020; Gilderdale, *Hands across the Sea*; Julia Gillen, 'Writing Edwardian Postcards', *Journal of Sociolinguistics*, 17/4, 488–521 <https://eprints.lancs.ac.uk/id/eprint/65539/1/Writing_Edwardian_Postcards_post_print.pdf > accessed 14 August 2020; Gillen and Hall, 'The Edwardian Postcard'; Klich and Weiss, *The Postcard Age*; Rogan, 'Entangled Object'.
25. Klich and Weiss, *The Postcard Age*, 12.
26. Atkins, 'Edwardian Social Network', 4.
27. Gillen and Hall, 'The Edwardian Postcard', 5.
28. Annebella Pollen, 'Sweet Nothings: Suggestive Brighton Postcard Inscriptions', 2009 <https://cris.brighton.ac.uk/ws/portalfiles/portal/260032/Pollen+-+Photography+and+Culture+article+-+for+repository.pdf> accessed 14 August 2020, 4.
29. Pollen, 'Sweet Nothings', 4.
30. Peter Gilderdale, 'Stoic and Sentimental: The Emotional Work of the Edwardian Greetings Postcard', *Journal of New Zealand Studies*, NS22 (2016), 2–18, 2.
31. *Sunday Independent* (26 July 1908).
32. 'Soldier shoots himself dead', Cork Examiner (18 October 1906); *Sunday Independent* (21 October 1906).
33. *Sunday Independent* (12 May 1907).
34. *Donegal News* (23 January 1909).
35. *Irish Independent* (28 July 1910).
36. Victoria Wang, John V. Tucker and Kevin Haines, 'Phatic Technologies in Modern Society', *Technology in Society*, 34 (2012), 84–93, 85.
37. Wang, Tucker and Haines, 'Phatic Technologies in Modern Society', 85.
38. Barbara Becker and Karen Malcolm, 'Suspended Conversations that Intersect in the Edwardian Postcard', in Nina Norgaard, ed., *Systemic Functional Linguistics in Use* (Odense: Odense Working Papers in Language and Communication, 29, 2008), 175–198, 190.
39. Rogan, 'Entangled Object', 16.
40. Wang, Tucker and Haines, 'Phatic Technologies in Modern Society', 84–85.
41. Wang, Tucker and Haines, 'Phatic Technologies in Modern Society', 92, 85.
42. Wang, Tucker and Haines, 'Phatic Technologies in Modern Society', 86.

43. Wang, Tucker and Haines, 'Phatic Technologies in Modern Society', 85.
44. Rogan, 'Entangled Object', 16.
45. Rogan, 'Entangled Object', 16.
46. Milne, *Letters, Postcards, Email*, loc 421, 1380.
47. Schor, '*Cartes* Postales', 21.
48. *Evening Herald* (14 April 1909).
49. *Kerry Sentinel* (6 January 1892).
50. *Kerry Evening Post* (3 March 1900).
51. *Kerry Evening Post* (2 December 1903).
52. *Kerry News* (20 September 1907).
53. *Ulster Herald* (28 September 1907).
54. Atkins, 'Edwardian Social Network', 9.
55. *Evening Herald* (17 November 1900) T. O'Connor was the father of the postcard publisher Fergus O'Connor.
56. Irish Examiner (16 September 1901).
57. *Irish Independent* (4 September 1905).
58. Gareth W. Dunleavy, 'Hyde's Crusade for the Language and the Case of the Embarrassing Packets', *Studies: An Irish Quarterly Review*, 73 (Spring, 1984), 15.
59. Dunleavy, 'Hyde's Crusade', 17.
60. *Freemans Journal* (25 August 1904).
61. *Irish Examiner* (1 April 1908).
62. *Irish Examiner* (24 October 1903).
63. *Donegal News* (21 May 1910).
64. John Fraser, 'Propaganda on the Picture Postcard', *Oxford Art Journal*, 3/2 (1980), 39–47, 40.
65. Fraser, 'Propaganda on the Picture Postcard', 40.
66. Fraser, 'Propaganda on the Picture Postcard', 40.
67. Cullen Fintan, *Ireland on Show. Art Union and Nationhood* (Surrey: Ashgate, 2012), 97–119.
68. *Irish Independent* (28 July 1906).
69. *Freemans Journal* (4 February 1908).
70. Mark O'Brien, *The Fourth Estate: Journalism in Twentieth-Century Ireland* (Manchester: Manchester University Press, 2017), 4–9.
71. O'Brien, *The Fourth Estate*, 5.
72. *Irish Examiner* (1 May 1903).
73. *Freemans Journal* (24 October 1910).
74. *Freemans Journal* (10 September 1907).
75. TuckDB Postcards website <https://tuckdbpostcards.org/search?utf8=%E2%9C% 93&q=diabolo&commit=> accessed 14 August 2020.
76. *Irish Examiner* (6 March 1908).
77. 'A Ghost's Photograph', *Leinster Express* (22 May 1909).

CHAPTER 4

Irish identity: Empire, modernity and revival

Ireland's official status during the Edwardian era as a province of the United Kingdom of Great Britain and Ireland was reflected in much of the mass-produced imagery and in the captions of the picture postcards circulating throughout the country, as well as the stamps featuring the head of King Edward VII which were attached to their back. However, the cards also reveal the complicated and often-contradictory concepts of Irish identity in circulation at the time, and they contributed significantly to the prevalent discourses of empire, modernity and national revival.

Empire

The British Empire by the end of Victoria's reign was extensive and powerful. According to Steve Humphries, by 1897 it 'spanned about eleven million square miles and boasted a population of over 400 million, only 20 million of whom lived in Britain. This represented a quarter of the land mass of the world and over a quarter of its population'.[1] Enormous resources were put into the maintenance and extension of this empire, and particularly into the military machine required to keep it stable. Cultural products, especially popular entertainments such as music hall, theatre, panoramas, magic lanterns and film, were also important in shaping public opinion and fostering a sense of imperial pride. For instance, at magic lantern shows 'audiences in village halls all over Britain were able to picture the extent of the Empire "on which the sun never set"'.[2] International exhibitions also functioned, among other

things, as showcases for the success of the Empire, and one of the biggest
held during the Edwardian period was the Franco-British exhibition in
London in 1908, which featured a fictional Irish village, Ballymaclinton.

This display was sponsored by a soap company and supported by the
Women's National Health Association headed by the wife of the Irish
viceroy, Lady Aberdeen. The Ballymaclinton exhibit mainly consisted of
charming cottages and pretty, industrious 'colleens' (an anglicization of
cailín, the Irish word for 'girl'), as well as structures such as a round tower, a
Celtic cross and a replica of the Blarney stone (see Figure 24). According to
Annie E. Coombes, the displays in the Franco-British exhibition, including
the Irish Village, confirmed 'the mythology of a British colonial power,
benevolent and paternal, ruling over a peaceful and prosperous but more
importantly, *compliant*, empire'.[3] Vast numbers of picture postcards were
produced in association with international exhibitions, and there are many
Ballymaclinton postcards in the collections examined for this book. The
village had its own on-site post office, from which visitors sent thousands
of cards during the six months of the exhibition.[4]

Figure 24. *Colleens Dancing, Ballymaclinton*, Valentine's. Author's collection.

Picture postcard culture also fostered popular imperialism through the mass production and distribution of images of battles and battleships, the Union flag, soldiers, views of royals, royal residences, ceremonials and rituals, as well as of colonial lands and peoples. The Boer War in particular generated 'series after series of patriotic and imperialistic cards', and generals such as Kitchener and Roberts became recognizable as national celebrities.[5] Such cards were available in Ireland, but Ireland's relationship to the British Empire was complicated and unstable. As a result of the Act of Union of 1800 Ireland had lost its status as a separate kingdom, the Dublin Parliament was dismantled and Irish political representatives were obliged to travel to London to take their seats in the Westminster parliament. Ireland was governed by a civil service based in Dublin Castle and headed by the lord lieutenant, a peer appointed by the ruling British party. Ireland during the Edwardian period could be viewed as a British colony or as a province, part of the colonizing machine itself. As James H. Murphy has pointed out it was even seen by some as a region of 'a greater England', like Yorkshire or Devon and Cornwall.[6] Increasingly, however, many Irish people began to define their Irish identity primarily as not British, especially in some nationalist circles where it became important to resist what was seen as a contaminating tide of English and British culture. Politically, the unionist population in Ireland, a majority in Ulster but a minority elsewhere, supported the status quo. A much smaller but increasingly vocal and active nationalist grouping called for complete independence from Britain, if necessary by the use of violence. However, the political party with the greatest majority in Ireland, the Irish Parliamentary Party led by John Redmond, was committed to the achievement of Home Rule by parliamentary means, and envisioned an Ireland of the future which was self-governing but still within the Empire. And, as is often the case, a large number of people held contradictory views or were politically indifferent.

All shades of opinion were represented on the picture postcards which circulated in Ireland during the Edwardian period, and in the collections examined for this book. British naval power in Ireland was celebrated in numerous images of navy ships, often pictured in Cork harbour against the backdrop of the strategically important British base on Haulbowline Island. Cork harbour was often called Queenstown harbour at the time,

after the town (now called Cobh) that was named in honour of Queen
Victoria. There are also many cards featuring Irish-based barracks and
training camps for the British military, often sent to their families and
girlfriends by young soldiers stationed there, some of these in Ireland but
most in Britain. The camps were located in places such as in the Curragh in
County Kildare, Donard in County Wicklow and Kilworth and Buttevant
in County Cork. The Cork Public Museum collection includes quite a few
examples of such cards, collected by the museum as representations of the
local area, although they also appear in personal collections such as the
Green family postcard album.

Before and during the First World War, Bamforth and Company
of Lancashire were particularly successful in combining photomontage
and quotes from popular songs and hymns to create cards that communicated a sentimental and mournful message which often tied into themes of
popular (Anglican) religiosity and British patriotism. One of the company's
earlier black-and-white productions was sent in 1905 to 15-year-old Rennie
Carmody in Ennis from her sister May in Sheffield (see Figure 25). The
image shows a central seated young female figure with her hand gracefully
shielding her head in a gesture suggesting sadness, juxtaposed with an image
in the top left corner of a uniformed soldier lying on a battlefield. The verse
underneath is titled 'Blue Bell', and recounts how the soldier 'fought and
fell/No thought of fame and glory/Only of his Blue Bell'. We do not know
why May chose this card to send to her sister; most likely she was moved by
the romantic representation of a young soldier's death and the sorrow of his
beloved. Alternatively, in the years leading up to 1905 the British Empire was
involved in conflicts in many parts of the world, and May might have had
a particular interest in these political situations, although there is nothing
to suggest this. Her comment on the back addresses only the appeal and
novelty of the card for her sister's collection: 'Hope you will like this PC.
I shall send you the other coloured ones soon. This is quite a new one.'

Figure 25. *Blue Bell*, Bamforth. Carmody family collection.

Apart from the military presence in the country, postcards circulating in Ireland also celebrated buildings and monuments associated with British institutions and prominent figures, such as Dublin Castle, the Vice Regal Lodge (residence of the lord lieutenant), the equestrian statue of George II in the centre of Stephen's Green and the Albert Memorial in Belfast.[7] Postcards of British royalty were also bought, sent and received in Ireland, especially during royal visits to the country. The (nationalist) *Freemans's Journal* reported enthusiastically in 1907 on Eason's rapid publication of a series of postcards commemorating the visit of Edward VII and Queen Alexandra to the Dublin International Exhibition: 'which will be in great demand by everyone as an interesting souvenir. Their Majesties appear as prominent figures in each view and the members to the Exhibition Council and Committee in attendance can be easily identified.'[8] James H. Murphy in his book *Abject Loyalty* has discussed the warm welcome given by many Irish people to British royals, even by some who held nationalist or, somewhat paradoxically, separatist views.[9] He gives a range of reasons for this, including their celebrity, the glamour of the younger royals and the hope that individual members might be more positive than the government about granting Ireland a degree of self-governance.[10] King Edward VII was particularly well liked in Ireland, because of his genial personality and fondness for horseracing, and because he was (wrongly) thought to be in favour of Home Rule and possibly converting to Catholicism.[11] His popularity in Ireland meant that when he died on 6 May 1910 a Mass was celebrated for him in Dublin's Catholic Pro-Cathedral, attended by the Archbishop of Dublin, William Walsh.[12] On 13 May 1910 John O'Reilly in Belmullet County Mayo received a postcard from a friend in Ballyhaunis who had written on the back: 'King "Ned" is no more. Great loss to Ireland.'

Home rule

By the Edwardian period, a significant number of Irish people, particularly the middle classes, expected and hoped sooner or later to be granted Home Rule. Their optimism is reflected in a message on the back of another postcard sent to John O'Reilly, wishing him 'a happy prosperous New Year 1910, the year of Ireland's independence', and adding the hope that 'when 1911 dawns ... the Home Rule flag will triumphantly wave in Ireland'. Many felt that conditions in Ireland would improve if the Irish population could decide its own policies and frame its own legislation according to its needs. It was unclear exactly what form Home Rule would take, but it was envisioned as most likely to be a limited degree of independence from the United Kingdom which still kept Ireland within the British Empire, 'Nationality within the Empire'.[13] In 1910 the Irish Parliamentary Party held the balance of power in the London parliament which opened up opportunities to push the Liberal government to commit to Home Rule for Ireland. A Bill was passed in 1912 (due to come into effect in 1914) leading to extensive mobilization of a unionist anti-Home Rule movement in Ulster. As Lauren O'Hagan has observed, this resulted in mass rallies and riots and a well-organized propaganda campaign that included the publication of numerous picture postcards.[14] Outside Ulster, particularly in Britain, Home rule was seen by its opponents as a possible threat to the stability of the Empire. Home Rule was shelved in 1914 with the outbreak of the First World War and became irrelevant in the wake of the 1916 uprising and the 1918 election victory of the separatist Sinn Fein party.

Home Rule was a prominent part of the discourse on Ireland for a long time, to the extent that it became the theme of numerous humorous postcards published in Britain. A card with an illustration by the British artist Donald McGill was sent to John O'Reilly in Ballina in 1913 (see Figure 26). It shows a baby with a crown perched crookedly on its head and holding a sceptre and orb, titled 'A Real Home Ruler'. This can be read as a light-hearted joke or as a disparaging comment on the unreasonable demands of the infantile Home Rule movement. According to John Killen in his book *John' Bull's Famous Circus. Ulster History through the Postcard 1905–1985* (1985), McGill supplied many postcard images for the London publisher Joseph Asher, and they frequently ridiculed Home Rule and the Irish situation in general, often using stereotypical images of an Irishman called 'Pat'.[15] Some cards used humour in a more pointed way, designed and distributed to propagate a very specific political message. According to an article titled 'A Political Postcard' published in the *Evening Herald* in 1912,

Figure 26. *A Real Home Ruler*, no publisher/printer named. John O'Reilly/Bessie Caulfield collection.

the picture postcard figured to a much greater extent than usual in yesterday's deliveries from the Post Office to the House of Commons. It was a political postcard
and it came from Belfast. Every member of the Irish Party and of the Labour Party
received in postcard form a variation of the familiar picture which is sold so extensively to British tourists in Dublin representing 'Paddy' driving a pig. In the picture
from Belfast, Mr. Redmond is represented driving a pig, the face of which is supposed
to be that of Mr. Asquith. [the British Prime Minister] There is a milestone with the
words 'To Home Rule' and there is a direction-post pointing to 'Home Rule' and to
'Separation'. There is a neighbour looking over a wall interrogating Mr, Redmond,
and the following dialogue is printed below: – 'Neighbour – Where are you driving
him to? Johnny Redmond – Whist, ye divil, ye, it's Home Rule he thinks we're goin'
to, but its Separation I'm drivin' him to.'

This card clearly put forward the argument that Home Rule was merely a
ruse, and the real aim was total political separation of Ireland from Britain
and the Empire. The *Evening Herald* reporter was not impressed, noting
that 'the picture, though copiously coloured, is neither artistic in execu-
tion, nor striking in idea, and the postcard propaganda does not seem very
promising for conversions to the anti-Home Rule cause'.[16] The anti-Home
Rule movement produced a wide range of picture postcards, including
photographic portraits of its leaders Edward Carson and James Craig and
cartoon images forecasting the economic decline of Ireland if Home Rule
was achieved. Many of these were issued by major mainstream British
card publishers such as Miller and Lang, CW Faulkner, Photochrom
and Valentines, while others were produced by Ulster companies such
as Hurst and the Ulster Publishing Company.[17] An *Irish Independent*
writer took offence at another postcard circulating in Ireland in 1912 'on
which the portrait of his Majesty the King is flanked by photographs of
Sir E. Carson and Mr Bonar Law [the leader of the Conservative oppos-
ition], and which bears the inscription – "One King, one flag, one Fleet,
one Empire"'.[18] Expressing again the faith that so many Irish people had
in the goodwill towards Ireland of the royal family, the author wondered
if the King's permission had been sought before the card was published.

Anti-Home Rule postcards were also issued by separatists who
thought that Home Rule did not go far enough, such as the members of
the Dungannon Club, an organization established in 1905 in Belfast by
Bulmer Hobson and Denis McCullough to promote Irish independence.[19]

The Club produced propaganda in the form of picture postcards and other print material attacking the recruitment of Irish men to the British army and Irish parliamentary representation in Westminster, and promoting the ideas of the emerging Sinn Féin ['Ourselves Alone'] movement. The postcards were advertised in the Dungannon Club magazine *The Republic*.[20] The aim, according to Hobson, was to convince Irish people 'that the governmental system of England – the armed garrison she keeps in the land – will go down as grass before the reaper before the first generation in Ireland that trusts in itself and starts to work out its own salvation, relying on itself alone'.[21] The postcards' black-and-white images were reproduced from illustrations mostly made for magazines, and humour and satire were commonly used as well as representations of relevant historic events such as scenes from the rebellion of 1798. The artists involved were from Ulster, and included the Morrow brothers, Jack and George, Robert Lynd and John P. Campbell.[22]

The Irish rising of 1798 had been extensive and violent. It was led by a group inspired by the French Revolution called the United Irishmen, and its suppression and aftermath resulted in the Act of Union of 1800. Its centenary was celebrated in 1898, and various '98 committees were established to erect commemorative monuments in towns across Ireland (many of which were not erected for some years). As John Turpin has argued, 'the 1798 centenary celebrations which took place throughout the country had a strongly contemporary political dimension. These were not sentimental commemorations of "battles long ago", but a rallying point for resurgent nationalist opinion in the 1890s'.[23] While many of the monuments were promoted by the Irish Parliamentary Party as a means of consolidating and unifying nationalist support, Turpin argues that their heroic representation of armed rebels is more celebratory of violent resistance rather than constitutional methods as a means to independence. They thus expressed and contributed to a growing mood of impatience with constitutional party politics and the goal of Home Rule in Ireland in the early twentieth century. This would feed into the attitudes that resulted in the 1916 Rising, the demise of the Irish Parliamentary Party and the success of Sinn Fein in the 1918 elections. Picture postcards also played an important part in spreading the message of the '98 commemorations and monuments: for instance, 5,000 cards were published in 1905 which featured a photograph of a sketch by the sculptor Oliver Sheppard for a proposed '98 monument in Enniscorthy, County Wexford, where some of the heaviest fighting had taken place. The cards both publicized the project and were an aspect of the fundraising drive. They were advertised in newspapers (according to the *Irish Independent*, every postcard bought helped 'the good work') and they were on sale 'at all stationers'.[24] Sheppard's Enniscorthy statue group represented a priest (the famous rebel-priest Fr Murphy) guiding a young rebel armed with pike and sword, reflecting the increased prestige and intersection of Roman Catholic and nationalist aims in Ireland in the early twentieth century.

The popular picture postcard therefore played an important role in disseminating different and often conflicting ideas about Ireland's relationship to the United Kingdom and the British Empire. Also, it must be remembered that the imagery on postcards could be used in different contexts to make different points. Eviction scenes, for instance, or representations of derelict cottages, could either be presented as critical of British rule in Ireland or as expressive of the ongoing need for it. Similarly, images showing prosperity and development could demonstrate the effectiveness of the imperial system, or the readiness and ability of Irish people to govern themselves. Stereotypically 'Irish' images of turf-carrying peasants, couples dancing jigs and whitewashed thatched cottages could show the distinctiveness of Irish culture, the product of a very different race to the English, and therefore make a case for self-rule. Or they might suggest a more primitive nature and civilization, and therefore the necessity for their submission to a more 'advanced' people. And of course card users could turn an intended published message into something meaning its opposite, as with the card mentioned in the previous chapter which was sent to Christina Jessop from her sister Rose in 1907, which transformed the original celebration of empire into a mocking rejection (see Figure 21).

Figure 27. *Irish Spinning Wheel*, Lawrence. Christina Jessop's card collection.

Modernity

Many Edwardian picture postcards, especially those aimed at the tourist market, show the Irish landscape as wild and untended, with sparsely distributed cottages and ruined castles and churches, and occupied by people engaged in pre-industrial activities such as peasant farmers, turf gatherers, milkmaids and textile spinners. Ireland was constructed in these images as an ancient land unspoiled by modernity, a concept which appealed to tourists but which was also at least partly internalized by many Irish people themselves. The poverty and hardship associated with economically undeveloped rural societies was glossed over in these images, which often feature attractive, smiling barefoot girls cheerfully going about their daily tasks, as in the many examples published by William Lawrence and Fergus O'Connor (see Figure 27).

Photographic images of similar subjects tend to look a lot less picturesque, the cottages more rundown and the people less cheerful, but they still present the idea of a land where time has in many ways stood still. Photographs of Irish villages and small towns on postcards also tend to look rather bleak, with local inhabitants standing in front of uneven rows of ramshackle cottages or stern unadorned terraces and staring curiously into the camera (see Figure 28). The writer Padraig Colum wrote in 1912 that

Figure 28. *Famed Finea*, O'Leary. Christina Jessop's card collection.

the Irish country town is harsh and ugly, for it has been built by people who are still
in the pastoral stage. The street is wide for the movement of herds. Four out of every
five are public-houses. In the depths of these shops, one can see bacon and boots,
reaping machines, and sacks of lime. One might borrow money in such a shop, or
book one's passage to America.[25]

The idea of Ireland as 'still in the pastoral stage', but also wedded to an
older, more magical world view is reinforced by numerous postcard images
of surviving rituals associated with holy wells and shrines, in which Irish
people are shown kneeling and praying in outdoor settings at sites such
as St Brigid's well at Liscannor in County Clare and Gougane Barra in
Cork, the legendary location of an original monastery built by St Finbarr.

However, many picture postcards also represented clear signs of modernization in Irish society, and the postcard itself and the cultures of its
production, distribution and use were further evidence of this. Many commentators also observed these signs, and were uneasy about them. Although
these were much more evident in urban centres, they were also noticeable
in remote rural areas, as the novelist Annie M. P. Smithson observed in relation to 'the bogs and mountains of that bleak corner of Ireland', Donegal,
where she was stationed as a District Nurse before the First World War:

> Alas! even in the mountains of Donegal, the young people are becoming Anglicised.
> English dances are taking the place of the Gaelic; music-hall ditties are sung instead
> of the old Irish songs, and any money the poor foolish girls can scrape together is
> sent off to one of the big English warehouses, which of course supplies them with
> shoddy goods at the dearest prices … The villages are flooded with catalogues from
> all the big English houses.[26]

Smithson is describing aspects of modernization here (the adoption of
fashionable international popular culture and clothing), although she,
as many others in Ireland did, called it 'Anglicisation'. The writer Filson
Young, in his book *Ireland at the Crossroads. An Essay in Explanation*
written in 1904, was much more positive about modernization in Ireland
than Smithson, but he too associated it with what he considered English
thoughts, manners and ideas.[27] He divided Ireland sharply into two, one
with a miserable and one with a smiling aspect, and the latter, he argued,
was the Ireland of the 'trader and the tourist'. Commercially prosperous

Ireland was confined to 'a strip of Ireland's eastern sea-board' and Belfast, due to proximity to English markets and the 'thrift and industry' of the 'descendants of the Scotch and English settlers in Down and Antrim [who] have many of those social qualities ... conspicuously lacking in Irishmen.'[28] Young regarded English people as by nature practical and secular, and England as a place where 'the tide of civilisation runs broad and strong'. He thought Irish people were the opposite: romantic, emotional and spiritual, possessing an 'extraordinary' Celtic psychology, and therefore not very good at being 'civilised'.[29] Young saw himself as critical of England and sympathetic to the problems of Ireland, but his analysis was very much influenced by concepts of essentialist racial characteristics that were popular at the time.

In the late nineteenth and early twentieth centuries Irish people were often categorized as descendants of the Celtic 'race', a concept about which modern scholars are sceptical, but which then could provide a convincing premise for many very different theories about abilities and character traits.[30] According to Barra Ó Donnabháin 'Celt' was originally a general term used in Ancient Greece and Rome to describe 'exotic foreigners to the north'. It fell out of use after the fall of the Roman Empire but resurfaced during the Renaissance.[31] In British colonial discourses of the eighteenth and nineteenth centuries it became used to distinguish colonized, 'primitive' groups, or 'races', particularly in Wales and Ireland, from the 'civilised' Germanic, Anglo-Saxon colonizers, in order to justify colonization. Late Victorian interest in the Celts was cultivated by writers such as the French historian of religion Ernest Rénan, who was originally from Brittany (considered one of the Celtic regions), and the English poet and critic, Matthew Arnold.[32] The concept of the 'impulsive, imaginative, child-like and mystical Celt' was developed and contrasted with the 'enterprising, self-reliant, self-controlled and libertarian Saxon'.[33] Based on this model, Saxons were destined to be rulers, and Celts to be ruled.

Somewhat paradoxically, this essentially British imperial (and negative) construct was appropriated and internalized by Irish cultural nationalists as a means of developing a positive sense of a distinct Irish identity. Writers like the poet William Butler Yeats whose book *The Celtic Twilight* was published in 1893, developed the idea of a noble Irish Celtic past, which could provide a template for a national cultural revival. According to the proponents of Celticism, remnants of this Celtic past could still be found in the folklore, traditions, material culture and language of people located in the West – of Europe, of Britain and of Ireland. They provided a refuge from the frustrations and materialism of the modern world, a sort of mysterious Celtic otherworld which was a place of myth, legend and magic, where time stood still or moved very slowly, and which was therefore never penetrated by modernity. Such ideas about Ireland appealed to many, and they were perpetuated by postcard images of untamed beautiful landscapes, mysterious ruined buildings and idealized peasants.

The Yeatsian view of Ireland tended to see true Celtic Irishness in ancient Irish myths telling of noble and heroic deeds, and in the rustic lives of contemporary 'unspoiled' peasants, what Joep Leerssen calls an emphasis on 'past and peasant'.[34] It therefore did not easily incorporate a modern and pragmatic middle class in search of material betterment, nor indeed the urban classes generally. However, vast numbers of postcard images also show the busy city streets of Edwardian Dublin, Belfast and Cork with substantial and sophisticated buildings, shops and department stores, electric trams emblazoned with large advertisements for the latest consumer goods and crowds of people dressed in fashionable clothing. Raphael Tuck's photographic images of urban Ireland are particularly notable in the way that they often feature slightly blurred moving figures from a relatively low viewpoint, giving the viewer the sense of actually experiencing the fast pace and busyness of the modern city (see Figure 29). Postcards also show the newly developed suburbs of these cites, expanding due to improved transport links with the centres, and the railway stations and trains of Ireland's countywide railway system, as well as the increasingly popular novelty of the motor car.

Figure 29. *Dublin, Grafton Street*, Raphael Tuck. From <https://tuckdbpostcards.org/items/98966>

There is also a great deal of evidence of the power and material presence of the Roman Catholic church in Ireland, photographs of new churches, newly decorated church interiors, convents, seminaries and church-owned hospitals, schools and workhouses, as well as portraits of various Irish bishops and other clergy. The Roman Catholic church would not usually be considered an example of modernity, and in many ways it was not, but its enormous post-Famine extension and consolidation in Ireland had only been possible because of its embrace of the latest developments in mass production, transport and communication. These also facilitated close connections between the Irish Church, the Vatican in Rome and its other branches around the world, resulting in a very efficient and modern system of international cooperation, standardization and control. The Catholic Church has also been seen by writers such as Tom Inglis as a vehicle of modernity in post-Famine Ireland, providing education and opportunities for enhancing social status to the upwardly mobile middle classes.[35] Catholicism in Irish society functioned as an identity marker, an important means of distinguishing Irish from English identity, but it also fostered typically Victorian values such as respectability, responsibility, thrift, the importance of family and the subservient role of women.

The Cake-Walk

Figure 30. The Cake Walk, no publisher/printer named. Ellen Duff's card collection.

Picture postcard culture itself was also a product of modernity, made possible by developments in image creation, consumer choice, literacy, mass production, transport and communication, and its extensive existence throughout Ireland during this period is evidence that Irish people were interacting with their world in very modern ways. The cards themselves provided opportunities for distraction, novelty and consumption, and taken as a whole, the comments written on them convey a very modern sense of restless activity and movement, of people constantly leaving and arriving, meeting, visiting, collecting each other and travelling on journeys within and outside the country. The short, quickly written notes state or suggest

that the writers are in a hurry or busy, and they also demand (quick) responses, asking the recipient to write, 'why don't you write?', 'send me the
news', 'have you given up sending letters and cards?' or 'are you too busy
to write?'. They reveal a relentless round of social engagements planned
and reported on: theatre, visits to the seaside, trips abroad, social visits
to friends and family, *feiseanna* (traditional Irish festivals revived by the
Gaelic League), concerts, theatrical performances, fancy dress parties and
sporting events. They also show a fascination with novelty, with cards
showing current celebrities and clothes fashions and new dancing trends
such as the cake walk (see Figure 30), and there is a message on one card,
sent in 1907 to Bessie Caulfield in Belmullet, County Mayo speculating on
the possibility of transmitting kisses by wireless telegraphy. *The Lincolnshire
Echo* observed in 1903 that the postcard expressed 'the spirit of the age –
brevity and speed', but it can also be seen as an expression of the entirety
of the Edwardian era, positive and negative, with all its contradictions,
and especially in Ireland.[36]

Revival and Irish national identity

Yet there was also a strong and broadly popular movement, not necessarily anti-Empire or anti-modernity (although for some it certainly was),
in favour of resisting the external influences on Irish society and instead
cultivating a distinctive Irish cultural identity. In 1892 Douglas Hyde delivered an important and influential speech on this to the Irish National
Literary Society in Dublin called 'The Necessity for De-Anglicising
Ireland'. English culture, he argued

> if we give it the least chance, or show it the smallest quarter – will overwhelm us
> like a flood, and we shall find ourselves toiling painfully behind the English at each
> step following the same fashions, only six months behind the English ones; reading
> the same books, only months behind them; taking up the same fads, after they have
> become stale there, following them in our dress, literature, music, games, and ideas,
> only a long time after them and a vast way behind ... I would earnestly appeal to

everyone ... to set his face against this constant running to England for our books, literature, music, games, fashions, and ideas.[37]

Historian Joseph Lee argues, however, that (as with Smithson)

> what Hyde mistook for anglicization – the proliferation of government boards, the diffusion of popular literature, the growth of mass consumption – simply reflected the administrative and cultural requirements of mass society, developments occurring more or less simultaneously in all European countries, without in the least involving their 'anglicisation'.[38]

Nevertheless, Hyde's speech and the positive reception it received was a significant factor in the establishment of the Gaelic League the following year, and also influenced opinion-formers such as D. P. Moran, the editor of the weekly newspaper the *Leader* (founded 1900) and strong advocate of the concept of an 'Irish Ireland'. Moran

> contended that the primary issue facing Ireland was not the continuation of English rule, but rather the dominance of English culture ... [which] threatened the survival of the indigenous language, music, and literature; hampered the development of a self-sufficient Irish economy; and generally degraded the national character.[39]

W. B. Yeats was also in agreement on this point, and argued in a lecture given in 1900 that the worst of English culture, and not the best, made its way into Ireland: the 'materialism of England and its vulgarity are surging up about us ... It is not Shakespeare England sends us, but musical farces, not Keats and Shelley, but *Titbits* (sic).'[40]

In response, the Gaelic League developed and supported Irish alternatives to imported culture, such as social events and competitions centred on traditional Irish pastimes and entertainment, and many commentators have noted the revitalizing effects that these had on social life in Irish towns and villages.[41] It also promoted a '*Déanta in Éirinn* (Made-in-Ireland)' campaign, designed to encourage people to buy only Irish goods if possible, thus hoping to improve both Irish culture and the economy. The League became very widespread and influential, and although it never succeeded in its primary aim of making Irish an everyday language for most people in Ireland, it gave it a new dignity and status as an important marker of Irish identity, and helped make Irishness itself something that people were more likely to be proud of. Similarly, the Gaelic Athletic Association, formed in 1885, focused on replacing English games such as soccer, cricket and tennis with Gaelic football, hurling and handball. Mary Colum in her memoir *Life and the Dream* also recalled the revivalist influence on clothing fashions in pre–First World War Dublin:

> In those days there were many men in Dublin who returned to the wearing of Gaelic kilts, which differed from the familiar Scots kilts by being plain saffron or green in colour; sometimes the kilt would be saffron and the brath green, fastened to the shoulder of the jacket with a Tara broach of silver or copper.[42]

In 1903 St Patrick's Day became an official public holiday, and in 1912 William Dawson commented in his essay 'My Dublin Year' that many of the Dublin street signs had been changed from English to Irish names.[43] The increased recognition of the importance of a distinct Irish identity is also reflected in the large number of people who began to use Irish instead of English versions of their name, even though many of them would not necessarily have been able to hold a conversation in Irish. This can be seen by comparing the Irish census of 1901 with that of 1911. Christina Jessop's brother-in-law, for instance, is recorded as Jeremiah O'Leary in 1901, but as Díarmuid O'Laoghaire in 1911, with her sister Rose recorded as Rós, and their children as Rós, Díarmuid and Áine. Between the years 1903 and 1908, many of Christina's correspondents signed off with the Irish version of their name, for example, Maighréad (Margaret), Máire (Mary) and Seán or Seaghain (Jack) (sometimes on the back of images of glamorous English music-hall performers). The optimistic sense of regeneration and renewal that was generated by (and fed back into) these developments was expressed on the postcard featuring the image of the hatching bird already mentioned in Chapter 3 (see Figure 23).

However, the evangelistic rhetoric of some individuals associated with various Irish Ireland movements sounds extreme to modern ears, and may have also been somewhat off-putting to contemporaries. In 1884, the year the Gaelic Athletic Association was founded, its patron the Catholic Archbishop Croke of Cashel famously stated that 'England's accents, the vicious literature, her music, her dances, and her manifold mannerisms' were 'alien' to Ireland, as were 'the men and women who first imported and still continue to patronise them'.[44] Arthur Clery, writing in 1919, also noted the 'all-or-nothing' approach of many Irish Irelanders

> among Irish Irelanders it became no venial matter to eat apples from an un-Irish tree. For the battle for any one point was looked upon as the battle for all. This was the strength of the new movement. It would tolerate no harpists clothed in English shoddy, or cricketers studying Irish, or hurlers singing music-hall songs. No one has ever yet ventured to waltz at an Irish college.[45]

'Irish Irelanders', he went on to argue, 'were usually temperate, often total abstainers, always earnest, self-sacrificing, of high character'.[46] He also remarked on the polarizing effect of such strict attitudes in Irish society in the early twentieth century, as did Dawson, who observed that the influence of the League in Dublin, for instance, ran 'in a parallel stream to the broad river of Dublin life. It does not really mingle with it. It does not imbue your theatres, your concerts, your literature. It seems aloof from its surroundings'.[47]

As a result many people developed a dislike for 'Irish Irelanders', or simply saw them as irrelevant curiosities with unreasonable objections to many of the pleasures of the modern world. C. S. Andrews in *Dublin Made Me*, his account of growing up in early twentieth-century Dublin, remembers his family and neighbours as immersed in pursuits such as soccer, cricket and English comics, and 'Irish-Irelanders were looked on as a joke'.[48] He recalled what he considered a 'typical Gaelic Leaguer' of the period, Ewart Wilson:

> He always wore Irish tweeds and bought nothing that was not of Irish manufacture. He neither drank nor smoked … because alcohol and tobacco contributed to the British revenues. His principal recreation was going for long walks on Sundays to the Pine Forest, Glen na Smol and Glencree … He was totally anti-British.[49]

James Joyce also constructed a rather judgemental and single-minded Irish-Ireland character in his portrait of Miss Ivors in 'The Dead', based apparently on a woman he knew. Miss Ivors accuses Gabriel Conroy of being a 'West Briton' because he writes for *The Daily Express*, holidays abroad rather than in the Aran Islands, and does not want to learn Irish.[50]

IN THE TUNNEL.

Figure 31. *In the Tunnel*, Bamforth. Christina Jessop's card collection.

However, Christina Jessop's postcard collection in particular suggests that some Irish Irelanders, at least, were both dedicated to the revival of Irish culture *and* excited about the pleasures and novelties of modernity, including imported modernity. She herself was clearly committed to the Gaelic League, took an active part in initiatives such as the 'Mail-in-Irish' campaign and, based on cards sent to her, was capable of carrying out a great deal of her personal correspondence via the medium of the Irish language. As a member of the Keating branch of the Gaelic League, and the Gaelic League Amateur Dramatic Society, she appeared in October 1901 in the Gaiety Theatre in Dublin in *Casadh on tSúgáin* (the Twisting of the Rope), by Douglas Hyde, the first Irish language play to be publicly performed in the modern era. Yet she seems to have treasured and enjoyed many cards featuring the celebrities of British Musical Theatre, as well as cheeky joke postcards, some of which could be seen as similar to the kind condemned in 1903 by the *Ulster Herald* and *The Irish Rosary*[51] (see Figure 31).

Irish caricatures

For their part, Irish Irelanders developed a term of abuse for Irish people that they considered as too English in their aims and mannerisms: *Seóinín*, or 'Shoneen'. Clery defines a Seóinín as 'a person who seeks to ingratiate himself or herself with the enemies of Ireland, or who pretends to a social position above that which is normally his'.[52] Shoneen mockery was encouraged by the Gaelic League, as evidenced by an advertisement in the *Westmeath Examiner* in 1905 for the Tullamore Feis, where a competition prize in the art section was offered for designing a 'set of six postcards ridiculing the Shoneen and his ways'.[53]

The League was, on the other hand, very critical of other types of Irish caricatures which were popular both in Ireland and abroad. It was clear that, despite the recent careful cultivation of national pride, many people, both Irish and non-Irish, were still happy to buy, and profit from, what the League and others saw as offensively negative, 'stage-Irish' postcard caricatures of Ireland and the Irish. These often featured motifs such as a silly-looking Irish 'Biddy', or, more commonly, a wild-looking, drunken and foolish 'Paddy', accompanied by a pig, a widely used stereotype (see Figure 32). As Joseph P. Finnan points out,

> John Redmond himself, a dignified member of the British parliament for nearly thirty years who looked as much at home in a top-hat as any British political leader, could not escape this stereotype. Fully one-third of the portrayals of him for the period from 1910 to 1918 showed him in this 'Paddy' identity, often with pig in tow. One cartoon even displayed Redmond himself as a pig.[54]

Figure 32. *Good Luck to Yez*, Raphael Tuck. From <https://tuckdbpostcards.org/items/49446>

Such caricatures had a long history, originating during the twelfth-century Norman conquest of Ireland when Gerald of Wales character-ized Irish people in his writings as violent, savage and uncivilized, and had hardened through subsequent centuries of strife between Britain and Ireland.[55] Lionel Pilkington has noted the presence of Irish stereotypes in sixteenth-century British and Irish theatre, citing as an example the character of Macmorris in Shakespeare's *Henry V* (1599), who is presented as 'innately belligerent, volatile, [and] spoiling for a fight'.[56] Michael De Nie argues in his book *The Eternal Paddy: Irish Identity and the British Press, 1798–1882* (2004), that this 'wild Irish' image was combined in the seventeenth and eighteenth centuries with depictions of the Irishman as 'a bumbling drunkard or fool', and in the nineteenth century both of these were 'blended with popular theories about race and character' that scientifically 'proved' the Irish people's natural inferiority and inability to rule themselves.[57]

The concept of the Irish as racially 'different' was regularly reinforced during the nineteenth and early twentieth centuries by British politicians, writers and comic artists as a means of explaining repeated Irish acts of re-sistance to anglicization. As L. Perry Curtis has shown, such ideas inspired the images of violent, ape-like Irishman, dark and heavy-jawed, that became a staple of popular British periodicals such as *Punch*.[58] De Nie argues that attitudes towards Catholicism and class also fed into Irish stereotypes, in that the Irish were seen as religiously subservient peasants, ignorant and economically backward, and content to live with their livestock in abject poverty and muck.[59] Hence the frequent depiction of 'Paddy' (and/or 'Biddy') with a pig. Pilkington also argues that sentimentalized con-structions of the Catholic Irishman as a harmless fool who, despite other failings, was essentially loyal and deferential to the gentry served to allay fears about the threat of nationalist violence and insurrection. He gives as an example of this the title character in Dion Boucicault's very popular play *The Shaughraun*, which was first performed in New York in 1874.[60] Colonialism, empire building, migration and modern developments in communications, transport and commerce ensured that these stereotypes were transmitted throughout the world, and they were expressed in a range of popular media.

In 1903 the Inchicore Workingmen's Club branch of the Gaelic League in Dublin appointed subcommittees to pressurize local shopkeepers to remove from their windows 'pictorial postcards ridiculing the Irish character'.[61] In 1905 the *Kerryman* reported that in Killarney 'degrading and insulting' postcards were exhibited in many shop windows, showing 'a gross and disgusting caricature of the Irishman'.[62] A year later, these images were still in evidence, and a writer in the 'Sinn Fein notes' section of the paper criticized 'the universal scattering by Irish traders of these English made scurrilities', while also attributing them to a deliberate plan by the English to defame the Irish, a not unusual conclusion at the time: 'It is time that this buffoonery should cease and Irishmen realize that these man monkey monstrosities are the false creations of the foul English mind expressly made to belittle the Irish in the world's eye.'[63] Certainly non-Irish publishers were responsible for many such cards, and Raphael Tuck, for instance, issued a postcard series in 1908/1909 titled *Irish Jokes from Punch*, where the theme throughout was Irish naivety and stupidity. Such cards were certainly not *only* produced by English companies, however. The Dublin-based Lawrence company, for example, was responsible for many of them. *The Spoiled Child* (Figure 33) shows a Lawrence-published card sent from Killarney to London in 1907, and features a cartoonish illustration of an Irish woman with a pig in her arms, with a thatched cottage and a group of children at its door behind her. The accompanying text under the image reads: 'Biddy – Bedad he's more bother to me than me own ten.' On the back the sender has entered into the spirit of the joke, writing 'Sure everything here is grand entirely especially the pigs'.

The problem was also reported in other Irish towns, to the extent that a letter of complaint, signed 'An American Citizen', was sent to the *Irish Independent* in 1908, referring to

the picture postcard type, which wants to show us what an Irish courtship looks like: the colleen is invariably represented in her bare feet. I have seen others, representing a half drunken Irishman embracing a pig, and still a crowd surrounded the window and smiled at the glaring affront.[64]

Figure 33. *The Spoiled Child*, Lawrence. Author's collection.

In America itself, to which millions of Irish people had emigrated during
the nineteenth century, determined measures were taken to combat these
images, which were especially publicly visible around Saint Patrick's Day
when parades were held in various cities. The protest campaigns seem
to have been primarily spearheaded by the Irish Catholic organization,

the Ancient Order of Hibernians (AOH), which was concerned to perpetuate an image of Irish-American Catholics that was sober and respectable. An address by John T. Keating to a meeting in 1907 of the AOH in Chicago, reportedly attended by 500 people, particularly objected to popular representations which gave Irish people ape-like features, stating that they were 'a libel on the Irish physiognomy'. He added that his ancestors 'were as comely as any race of people under the sun, and the Irish women of today are noted for their facial charms'.[65] According to the *Limerick Leader*, resolutions asking for government action against these postcards were sent to President Theodore Roosevelt, 'who expressed sympathy with the members of the Celtic race', with the result that a law was passed banning them from travelling through the American mail.[66] Another Irish-American group, the United Irish League, organized a boycott of offending shops, and 'with one exception all the merchants in the main business streets heeded the boycott warning of the league and removed the caricatures from their show windows'.[67]

Despite these actions, however, the problem resurfaced in 1908, when the Irish-American Union in Chicago called for further boycotting and police action. The *Cork Examiner* quoted from 'the leading Catholic paper, published under the official sanction of Archbishop Quigley':

> One of the insulting caricatures … represents St Patrick astride of a pig, a mitre upon his head, a clay pipe in his mouth. Other insults represent monkey-faced Irishmen astride of fat porkers, of course with clay pipe accompaniment … Fancy the shameless audacity of men who could put out a picture postal card portraying St. Patrick doing the Salome dance![68]

The 'Salome dance' presumably refers to both Oscar Wilde's notorious banned play, first published in French in 1891, as well as to the salacious 'Dance of the Seven Veils' regularly performed by the entertainer Maud Allan since its premiere in 1906 as part of her show *Vision of Salomé* in Vienna. The connection of either to Saint Patrick would have been seen as deeply offensive to many Irish Catholics. The newspaper again called for a boycott, citing the consumer power of the 1,150,000 'upright, influential' Irish-American Catholics living in Chicago. Clearly, however, boycotting and banning could only have a limited effect, as the 'Paddy and his Pig' imagery was too appealing to consumers. In Ireland it could be combated to an extent by denouncing the selling and buying of such postcards as flagrant 'shoneenism', an increasingly powerful insult as the popular mood became more nationalist.[69] To this was added the determination announced in the *Kerryman* in 1906, to replace the offensive caricatures with 'healthy, clean, Irish-made cards', an approach very much in line with that of the Gaelic League.[70]

Considering the level of newspaper outrage at these images, it is worth noting that the Irish media could be surprisingly unsympathetic when it reported on the perpetuation of negative postcard stereotypes of other groups, as the *Cork Examiner* did in 1906:

> In Milwaukee, which is the centre of the German population of the Republic, there is a fierce indignation over certain picture postcards which represent Hans as unusually fat and prodigiously bibulous. Still, small voices have been heard declaring that the offending representations are true to fact, but the Milwaukee Germans are convinced that they are being libelled.[71]

The media debates in the early twentieth century about 'Stage Irish' postcard imagery reflect the sensitivity felt by many Irish people at the time to the way Irishness was perceived, and the complete indifference of many others. That this war of images was fought at the level of the humble postcard suggests that it was recognized during this period as a potentially powerful and convincing medium, its very cheapness and ephemerality broadening its reach to people who were not necessarily receptive to other media messages.

Obscene postcards

Attempts to replace long-held negative Irish stereotypes with more positive ones were arguably mainly of concern to Irish people, but worries about obscene imagery on postcards surfaced wherever postcards were available, although attitudes to obscenity, and concepts of it, varied in different cultures. In Ireland, commentators were coy about defining it, even as they vigorously denounced it. A report in the *Cork Examiner* in 1906 of a case brought before the local magistrates illustrates this well. The defendant, Ernest Rosehill, was brought before the court to explain why cards seized from his shop at 10, Grand Parade in Cork should not be destroyed, and during the proceedings his defence solicitor attempted to define the term 'obscenity' using Nutall's dictionary. He was, however, immediately silenced by the presiding magistrate, who declared: 'There is no need of defining indecency for us, or obscenity either.'[72] Yet Rosehill was tried, and convicted, on the grounds that he exhibited obscene postcards for sale. According to Laurence O'Toole in his book *Pornocopia: Porn, Sex, Technology and Desire* (1999),

> Like erotica and porn, 'obscenity' and 'indecency' depend upon subjective evaluation for definition. The difference is that both obscenity and indecency are 'bad objects', which the law seeks to locate for juridical attention. In Britain, 'indecency' is mostly a lesser crime. Indecency creates a feeling of disgust where one really oughtn't to be exposed to it … Whereas obscenity more seriously threatens to 'deprave and corrupt' (Lord Justice Cockburn, 1888) Obscenity, it is suggested, has the potential to change the way someone behaves, even make a monster of him or her, and so shouldn't be allowed.[73]

O'Toole also adds that 'What obscenity might actually look like is pretty much determined by what the customs or police officer, censor, prosecutor, judge or jury sees in a text or an image, and what they choose to object to', and this situation was no different in the Edwardian period. Whether a particular postcard was regarded as obscene, indecent or immoral seems to have been decided based mainly on common-sense judgements passed by local magistrates who examined and discussed each card brought to their attention, usually by concerned citizens or groups such as the Ancient Order of Hibernians or the Young Men's Catholic Society. An official announcement by the Postmaster General in 1904 did not clarify matters, merely stating that

> by the provisions of the Post Office Protection Act 1884, any person who sends by post a postal packet (which term includes a postcard), having thereon any words, marks, or designs of an indecent, obscene, or grossly offensive character, is guilty of a misdemeanour, and is liable to be fined or imprisoned for twelve months.[74]

Decisions at local level were influenced by pressure groups, by social norms in relation to what was usually seen as acceptable, as well as by concepts of art. The Rosehill case in 1906 was partly defended on the grounds that the defendant was a 'stranger', not long settled in Cork, and

> in other countries people were not so particular as here in regards to pictures and postcards, and his client judged by the standard of other places and not by the standard of Cork. In other countries he had seen cards flaunted in the shop windows as bad as, if not worse than, those that were now sought to be condemned.[75]

Rosehill was also prosecuted for a similar offence in 1908, and this trial generated discussions among the magistrates and solicitors on the 'mixed bathing' represented on some of the cards, whether this was acceptable behaviour in Ireland (it was, in the nearby seaside town of Youghal, apparently), and the appropriate attire for it in places where it was acceptable. The defending solicitor also drew a comparison between some of the offending cards and art images, asking the Head Constable, who had seized the cards in question, what he 'would think if he went to the National Gallery and saw the Velasquez for which the State paid £7,000 or £8,000'.[76] The Velasquez painting referred to was probably the *Rokeby Venus*, a mid-seventeenth-century nude purchased in 1906 for the National Gallery in London, and indeed Raphael Tuck issued a set of picture postcards in France titled *Salon 1902*, one of which, based on a painting by Bouche-Leclercq, looks like a homage to Velasquez' *Venus* (Figure 34).[77]

However, the Cork magistrates were not convinced that there was a valid comparison to be made, and Rosehill was again convicted. Lisa Z. Sigel, in her study of pornography in Britain during the Victorian and Edwardian eras, has discussed similar cases where art was brought in as a respectable precedent by the counsel for the defendant:

> Repeatedly, vendors argued that the origins of the representation should matter and that postcards could not be judged indecent or obscene if they came from 'works of art'. The authorities disagreed. When asked whether a photograph of the Venus de Medici [sic] equalled other nude representations, the chief constable of Manchester replied, 'No, but I suggest that all the circumstances should be taken into consideration; the photograph of nude women under certain circumstances may be all right,

but if it is placed in the windows and sold to youths and sold on the streets, then I say it is not for the good of the community, and you should take all the circumstances into consideration when you decide.' The issue of the individual viewer's place in society defined the meaning of the object as indecent, obscene, or pornographic.[78]

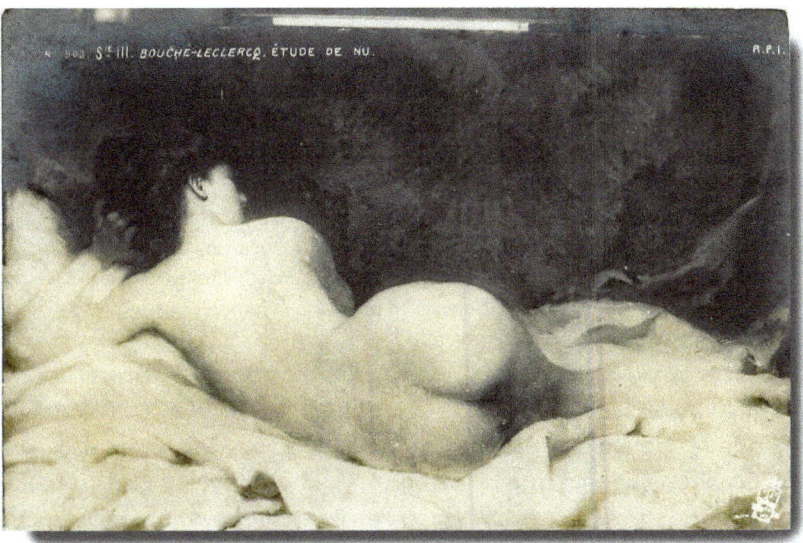

Figure 34. *Etude de Nude*, Raphael Tuck. From <https://tuckdbpostcards.org/items/136876>

Thus the severity of the offence, or even the judgement of whether it was an offence at all, depended significantly on the audience exposed to the postcard, and on officials' assessment of the susceptibility of that audience to corruption. The reporting of such cases allowed public declarations of, but also challenges to, Irish mores and values. However, the vagueness of the language used in many of these discussions and judgements must have hampered rational decision-making, and is well illustrated by the statement of one prosecutor when faced with three problematic cards: 'The first two cards are corrupting and disgusting, but the third is mere filth.'[79]

The Drogheda branch of the Gaelic League was warned about 'indecent' postcards in 1903, when an address by a Fr. Finnegan informed them of the presence in local shop windows of cards 'that should bring the blush of shame to the face of any Irish maiden'.[80] The priest attributed the display of these cards to 'shoneenism', as he and many other commentators saw them as a potentially contaminating force coming from outside Ireland, often described as from 'strangers', England or, also frequently, France or 'the Continent'.[81] This fear of external contamination of a native Irish purity is a constant theme in denunciations of offensive postcards, as in 1906 when a magistrate announced that he fined a shopkeeper for displaying them because he was 'determined to keep the windows of Dublin clean'.[82] The *Irish Independent*, reporting on the case, fully approved, adding that

> numerous prosecutions for offences of this sort have in recent years taken place in England, and it is apparently from that country that the objectionable cards have found their way into Ireland. On this point we are strictly Protectionist, and would gladly see an absolutely prohibitive tariff put on such imports.[83]

The main concern expressed was that such images would corrupt the youth of Ireland, particularly girls. As stated in the *Anglo Celt* 'The circulation or interchange of such postcards does incalculable damage, especially when they get into the hands of callow youth and girls ignorant of the world's ways.'[84] A *Cork Examiner* editorial on the 1906 Rosehill case stated that the police involved deserved 'the commendation of every decent and clean-minded citizen' as 'we do not know of anything more calculated to deprave the youth of any community than that indecent or obscene pictures could be procured or purchased'. Referring to the images as evidence of a 'moral cancer', the writer finishes, somewhat smugly, with a claim that 'the code of proprieties which exists on the Continent is, happily, not applicable in this country'.[85] Magistrates at the Queenstown Petty Sessions in 1908 were told of the circulation of indecent postcards in Queenstown which were 'imported from other lands' and that, as a result, 'there was grave danger that the purity of our young people's lives may become tarnished, and that which we prized as a great treasure might be lost'.[86] Fr Philip O'Doherty, addressing a large Gaelic League meeting in County Donegal in 1907, communicated essentially the same message, framing it dramatically within a historical metanarrative:

> [the Irish] had withstood the Confiscations, they had defeated the sword of Cromwell, they had survived the perfidy of William. Every page of their history was a page of

blood, but at the same time a page of glory, for they had kept the pearl of purity. It was in his opinion the duty of the Gaelic League and of Irishmen as a whole … to use their every endeavour to stem that horrible traffic [in picture postcards] … Was that purity that they so dearly cherished to go down before the foul, filthy things of England?[87]

There must have been a demand for such postcards, or they would not have been stocked and displayed in defiance of such campaigns, and many of those that caused so much worry seem to have generated mostly amusement among the wider population. At Athlone petty sessions in 1909

Sergeant Wilson, who prosecuted, said his attention was attracted to the display window of the defendant's shop by a number of young factory girls laughing around it. He examined the postcards on view, which he considered very indecent, and purchased the one produced, which was abominable, and which was exposed for sale in the window. The defendant laughed at it, and said it was not at all indecent.[88]

According to Sigel, pornography was revolutionized by the development of the simple postcard.[89] Before the 1880s, 'high prices, low literacy rates, class-specific cultural referents, unequal patterns of state repression, and production and distribution patterns restricted the dispersal of pornography in British society'.[90] The people represented in pornographic imagery were usually excluded from using these representations, and this was seen as an 'accepted aspect of privilege'.[91] However, postcard viewing required very little investment of time or money, no specialized viewing apparatus or skills, and a low level of verbal literacy and cultural education. Picture postcards communicated via visuals as well as words and were widely and easily available, including in mainstream sales outlets alongside non-sexual material.[92]

Obscene postcards mingled with other types of postcards in the shops and streets of working-class neighbourhoods. Men, women, boys and girls, the native and the foreign, all sold – and were caught selling – indecent picture postcards … these cards could be found throughout the British Isles and across the Atlantic world in Belfast, Liverpool, London, Manchester, Bristol, Glasgow, Montreal, Yarmouth, Dublin, and Paris.[93]

This sudden increase in accessibility, especially to the working classes and to women, children and foreigners, caused widespread social anxieties about corruption and obscenity. Authorities 'believed that the expanded audience for pornography and its social repositioning fundamentally disrupted an intrinsic moral order'.[94] The expanded audience themselves, however, despite being subjected to vigilant policing and relentless campaigning in the cause of moral purity, often responded with indifference, like the laughing young Irish factory girls encountered by Sergeant Wilson.

Discussions about picture postcards in Ireland in the first decade of the twentieth century bring us right to the heart of some of the many tensions and anxieties of that period in relation to nationalism, internationalism and modernity. As a medium, and despite its low status, the postcard was clearly taken seriously as a transmitter of values and concepts, so much so that various influential groups as well as newspaper commentators had no reservations about advocating and resorting to censorship, boycotting and criminal prosecution in order to limit and control what it communicated. Newspaper coverage of the postcard phenomenon reveals clearly some of the divisions in Irish society at the time, between those who worked hard to construct a culturally protected, Catholic and respectable Irish identity, and those who really didn't care about such concepts; between focused, idealistic nationalists, pragmatic capitalist entrepreneurs, and consumers who had their own particular aims and preferences, often unrecognized or dismissed. Reports and discussions on picture postcards reveal a major fear of many of those who were focused on a particular ideal vision of Ireland, the fear of the popular and its power to fuel resistance. This was frequently expressed as a worry about the tide of popular culture coming in to Ireland from abroad, as in Hyde's 'De-Anglicisation' speech of 1892, but really it seems to have been at least as much a fear of popular opinion and taste within Ireland. Left to themselves, callow Irish youths and shop girls were in danger of cheerfully welcoming the seductive tide of foreign culture, and indeed were already doing so. Yeats was not the only one to recognize that Ireland was 'like soft wax' during these years, and picture postcards came to be seen by many as one of those forces which could significantly determine the form into which it would harden.[95]

Notes

1. Steve Humphries, *Victorian Britain Through the Magic Lantern* (London: Sidgwick & Jackson, 1989), 160.
2. Humphries, *Magic Lantern*, 160.
3. Annie E. Coombes, 'The Franco-British Exhibition', in Jane Beckett and Deborah Cherry, eds, *The Edwardian Era* (London: Barbicon Gallery and Oxford: Phaidon, 1987), 166.
4. *Irish Independent* (19 October 1908).
5. Editor of the *Picture Postcard Magazine*, quoted in Holt, *Picture Postcards of the Golden Age*, 80.
6. James H. Murphy, *Abject Loyalty: Nationalism and Monarchy in Ireland during the Reign of Queen Victoria* (Washington, DC: Catholic University of America Press, 2001), xiii.
7. A controversial monument erected in 1758 and blown up in 1937.
8. *Freemans Journal* (13 July 1907). According to Senia Paseta, the *Freeman's Journal* was Redmondite and represented middle-class nationalism. Senia Paseta, *Before the Revolution: Nationalism, Social Change and Ireland's Catholic Elite, 1879–1922* (Cork: Cork University Press, 1999), 39.
9. Murphy, *Abject Loyalty*, xxvi.
10. Murphy, *Abject Loyalty*, xxviii.
11. Murphy, *Abject Loyalty*, xxviii, 295.
12. Murphy, *Abject Loyalty*, 299.
13. Paseta, *Before the Revolution*, 131.
14. Lauren Alex O'Hagan, '"Home Rule Is Rome Rule": Exploring anti-Home Rule Postcards in Edwardian Ireland', *Visual Studies*, 2020, <https://doi.org/10.1080/1472586X.2020.1779612>.
15. John Killen, *John Bull's Famous Circus. Ulster History through the Postcard 1905–1985* (Dublin: The O'Brien Press, 1985), 109.
16. *Evening Herald*, 'a Political Postcard' (23 October 1912).
17. Killen, *John Bull's Famous Circus*, 16, 49.
18. *Irish Independent* (26 April 1912).
19. Killen, *John Bull's Famous Circus*, 19.
20. Killen, *John Bull's Famous Circus*, 151.
21. Killen, *John Bull's Famous Circus*, 20–23.
22. Killen, *John Bull's Famous Circus*, 24–29.
23. John Turpin, '1798, 1898 & the Political Implications of Sheppard's Monuments', *History Ireland*, 6/2 (1998), 44–48, 45.

24. Turpin, *1798, 1898*, 47; *Irish Independent* (7 September 1905).

25. Padraig Colum, *My Irish Year* (New York: James Pott & Co., 1912), 9.

26. Annie M. P. Smithson, 'Christmas in Donegal', *The Irish Monthly*, 54/642 (1926), 633–641, 635–636.

27. Filson Young, *Ireland at the Crossroads. An Essay in Explanation* (London: Grant Richards, 1904), 20.

28. Young, *Ireland at the Crossroads*, 19, 21.

29. Young, *Ireland at the Crossroads*, 4, 5, 35.

30. See for instance Simon James, *The Atlantic Celts: Ancient People or Modern Invention?* (London: British Museum Press, 1999).

31. Barra Ó Donnabháin, 'An Appalling Vista: The Celts and the Archaeology of Later Prehistoric Ireland', in Angela Desmond, Gina Johnson and Margaret McCarthy, eds, *New Agendas in Irish Prehistory: Papers in Commemoration of Liz Anderson* (Dublin: Wordwell, 2000), 189–196, 191.

32. Ian Bradley, *Celtic Christianity: Making Myths and Chasing Dreams* (Edinburgh: Edinburgh University Press, 1999), 120.

33. Ó Donnabháin, 'An Appalling Vista', 192.

34. Joep Leerssen, *Remembrance and Imagination: Patterns in the Historical and Literary Representation of Ireland in the Nineteenth Century* (Cork: Cork University Press, 1996), 225.

35. Tom Inglis, *Moral Monopoly: Rise and Fall of the Catholic Church in Modern Ireland: Rise and Fall of the Catholic Church in Modern Ireland* (Dublin: University College Dublin, 1998), 129–158.

36. Carline, *Pictures in the Post*, 57.

37. Douglas Hyde, 'The Necessity for De-Anglicising Ireland', 1892, <https://www.thefuture.ie/wp-content/uploads/1892/11/1892-11-25-The-Necessity-for-De-Anglicising-Ireland.pdf> accessed 19 April 2014, 3–4.

38. Joseph Lee, *The Modernisation of Irish Society 1848–1918: From the Great Famine to Independent Ireland* (Dublin: Gill and Macmillan, 1973 and 1989), 140.

39. Frank A. Biletz, 'Women and Irish-Ireland: The Domestic Nationalism of Mary Butler', *New Hibernia Review*, 6 (Spring 2002), 59–72, 61.

40. P. J. Mathews, '"Doing Something Irish": From Thomas Moore to Riverdance', UCD scholarcast, Series 1 (Spring 2008), 2–11, 7. <http://www.ucd.ie/scholarcast/transcripts/Doing_Something_Irish.pdf> accessed 15 October 2014.

41. Arthur Clery, 'The Gaelic League', *Studies: An Irish Quarterly Review*, 8/31 (1919), 398–408, 404.

42. Mary Colum, *Life and the Dream, Memories of a Literary Life in Europe and America* (Garden City, New York: Doubleday & Company, 1947), 105.

43. William Dawson, 'My Dublin Year', *Studies: An Irish Quarterly Review*, 1/4 (1912), 694–708, 695.

44. Kevin Rockett, 'Disguising Dependence: Separatism and Foreign Mass Culture', *Circa*, 49 (January–February 1990), 20–25, 22.

45. Arthur Clery, *Dublin Essays* (Dublin and London: Maunsel, 1919), 132.

46. Clery, *Dublin Essays*, 134.

47. Dawson, 'My Dublin Year', 706.

48. C. S. Andrews, *Dublin Made Me*, Kindle edition (Dublin: Lilliput Press, 2001), 'Childhood'.

49. Andrews, *Dublin Made Me*, 'Boyhood'.

50. James Joyce, *Dubliners* (New York: B.W. Huebsch, 1917), 240–243.

51. 'Picture Postcards', *Ulster Herald* (3 October 1903).

52. Clery, *Dublin Essays*, 137.

53. *Westmeath Examiner* (29 April 1905).

54. Joseph P. Finnan, 'Punch's Portrayal of Redmond, Carson and the Irish Question, 1910–18', *Irish Historical Studies*, 33/132 (2003), 424–451, 427–428. He also argues that 'this portrayal was not confined to the pages of *Punch*, and in fact appeared frequently in many British publications of the time. Depictions of Redmond accoutred as a stereotypical "Paddy", complete with accompanying pig, surfaced in the *Daily Graphic*, the *Pall Mall Gazette*, the *Westminster Gazette* and *Reynolds's Newspaper*' (428).

55. Michael De Nie, *The Eternal Paddy: Irish Identity and the British Press, 1798–1882* (Madison: University of Wisconsin Press, 2004), 136.

56. Lionel Pilkington, *Theatre and Ireland* (Basingstoke: Palgrave Macmillan, 2010), 10–15.

57. de Nie, *The Eternal Paddy*, 175.

58. L. Perry Curtis Jr., *Apes and Angels: The Irishman in Victorian Caricature* (Washington, D.C and London: Smithsonian Institution, 1997).

59. de Nie, *The Eternal Paddy*, 414.

60. Pilkington, *Theatre and Ireland*, 19.

61. 'The Gaelic League', *Evening Herald* (17 October 1903).

62. ' "Clear Air" notes', *Kerryman* (2 September 1905).

63. 'Sinn Fein notes. Killarney', *Kerryman* (13 October 1906).

64. 'Insulting Postcards', *Irish Independent* (9 April 1908).

65. 'A.O.H. and Postcard Caricatures', *Anglo-Celt* (6 April 1907).

66. ' "Irish" Postcards', *Limerick Leader* (24 April 1907).

67. ' "Irish" Postcards', *Limerick Leader* (24 April 1907).

68. *Cork Examiner* (7 April 1909).

69. *Connacht Tribune* (31 July 1909).

70. 'Sinn Fein notes. Killarney', *Kerryman* (13 October 1906).

71. 'Notes and Comments', *Irish Examiner* (2 April 1906).

72. *Cork Examiner* (12 December 1906).

73. Laurence O'Toole, *Pornocopia: Porn, Sex, Technology and Desire* (London: Serpent's Tail, 1999), 7.

74. 'Notes', *Fermanagh Herald* (17 December 1904).

75. *Cork Examiner* (12 December 1906).

76. 'Indecent Postcards', *Cork Examiner* (20 June 1908).

77. TuckDB Postcards website <https://tuckdbpostcards.org/items/136876> accessed 15 August 2020.

78. Lisa Z. Sigel, *Governing Pleasures: Pornography and Social Change in England, 1815–1914* (New Brunswick, New Jersey and London: Rutgers University Press, 2002), 150–151.

79. 'More Indecent Postcards', *Freemans Journal* (16 April 1908). There was a lack of legal clarity throughout Britain as well as Ireland in relation to terms such as 'obscenity' and 'indecency' in the early twentieth century, as shown in David J., Cox, Kim Stevenson, Candida Harris and Judith Rowbotham, *Public Indecency in England 1857–1960 'A Serious and Growing Evil'* (London and New York: Routledge, 2015), 44–64.

80. 'Gaelic League in Drogheda', *Drogheda Argus and Leinster Journal* (10 October 1903).

81. In Britain, according to Carline, 'unrespectable cards of scantily dressed women' … 'were generally described as "French". English tourists, we are told in October 1900, were shocked in the arcades of the Rue de Rivoli'. Carline, *Pictures in the Post*, 68.

82. 'Indecent Pictures. Mr Drury's Strong Comments', *Freemans Journal* (25 January 1906).

83. 'Clean Windows', *Irish Independent* (25 January 1906).

84. 'Latton Notes', *Anglo-Celt* (16 June 1906).

85. *Cork Examiner* (12 December 1906).

86. 'Indecent Postcards in Queenstown', *Cork Examiner* (19 June 1908).

87. 'A Hosting of the Gael', *Donegal News* (3 August 1907).

88. 'Indecent Postcards', *Freemans Journal* (13 October 1909).

89. Sigel, *Governing Pleasures*, 119.

90. Sigel, *Governing Pleasures*, 120.

91. Sigel, *Governing Pleasures*, 120.

92. Sigel, *Governing Pleasures*, 121.

93. Sigel, *Governing Pleasures*, 122.

94. Sigel, *Governing Pleasures*, 120.

95. W. B. Yeats, *Autobiographies* (London: Macmillan, 1966), 199.

CHAPTER 5

Ireland and the wider world: Travel, emigration and tourism

Even in the early twentieth century, when picture postcards were frequently used for everyday communication between people who lived near each other, they were also closely associated with travel. Added text on postcards from the period often concerns travel arrangements, the imagery was frequently chosen to represent places where people travelled to, or sometimes the means by which they did so (such as pictures of ships and trains), and the cards could be used to maintain communication across geographical distances. Developments in transport meant that people at all economic levels could travel more, faster and further than previously, and this was the case in Ireland too. People travelled to visit relatives or friends, for holidays, for work or in pursuit of better life opportunities. While emigration from Ireland had slowed down since the post-Famine years it was nevertheless still very significant, and, as in other countries, there was also migration from rural to urban areas as well as increased leisure travel.

Emigration

Emigration was considered by many to be the defining, and determining, feature of Irish life in the early twentieth century. The French writer on Ireland Louis Paul-Dubois described it in 1907 as an 'Exodus': 'The Exodus of the Irish from Ireland; the Exodus which, during the last sixty years, has torn from her no less than 5,300,000 of her children; which, even now, draws away from her about one per cent of her population in each succeeding year.'[1] The Irish population is estimated to have been over 8 million before the Famine in 1841, declining to about 6.5 million by 1851, and by more than another million by 1871.[2] The decline slowed but continued into the twentieth century. According to Thomas E. Jordan, the '1901 census, published in 1903, placed the population of Ireland at 4,458,775 persons; this was 54.54 per cent of the population in 1841, and represented a decline of 5.23 per cent over the preceding decade'.[3]

Mass emigration from European countries was not unusual in the late nineteenth and early twentieth centuries. Daniel Mulhall in his book *A New Day Dawning. A Portrait of Ireland in 1900* (1999) makes the point that 25 million Europeans emigrated between 1870 and 1900, but nevertheless

> Ireland's emigration rate remained higher than anywhere else in Europe. Ireland was a demographic oddity at a time when the continent's population, substantial emigration notwithstanding, was climbing at an impressive rate due to advances in medicine and sanitation.[4]

Paul-Dubois also pointed out that in the century from 1801 to 1901 England, Wales and Scotland almost trebled their populations.[5] David Fitzpatrick has argued that this 'unique decline of Ireland's population for nearly a century after the Famine was mainly caused by structural emigration which removed up to half of each generation from the country'.[6] Emigration, according to him, was the 'key to Ireland's unusual and remarkably stable demographic system between 1870 and 1914', the safety valve which reduced the 'surplus of young people competing for survival in Ireland's congested markets of marriage and employment'.[7]

Most Irish emigrants in the late nineteenth and early twentieth centuries left for the United States, and most of the rest went to England and Wales. Other destinations were Canada, Scotland, Australia and New Zealand. There was also seasonal migration, as many young men resident in Ireland spent part of the year working abroad. This was particularly the case in the west of Ireland in counties such as Donegal, from where they usually travelled to Scotland. According to Fitzpatrick 'short-distance migration in search of urban employment' was also a characteristic of both Leinster and Ulster.[8] Ellen Duff, whose postcard collection is one of the ones examined in this book, could be considered an example of this, as she was from Queen's County (now County Laois) but found employment in Dublin as a waitress. Similarly, according to the Irish census of 1901, none of the other eight people with whom she lived in Exchequer Street in Dublin were born there, but instead came from Wexford, Wicklow, Roscommon, Donegal and, like herself, from Queen's County.[9] Christina Jessop's fiancé Jack Wilson was from Queenstown, but worked as a pharmacist in Belfast until 1907 or 1908, when he returned permanently to Queenstown. Such travelling in search of better work opportunities became more and more a feature of modern societies.

Social effects of migration and emigration

The social effects of such a high level of population mobility were considerable. Jordan argues that emigration of 'the many changes in Victorian Ireland … matched evolving nationalism in its long-range implications'.[10] The vast majority of those who emigrated from Ireland were young and unmarried, which left a concentration of old people and children behind and made emigration even more attractive to the remaining young. This was especially the case in poorer rural districts with already depleted populations and opportunities, which suffered the most from both foreign and short-distance emigration and migration. As Paul-Dubois argued, 'Emigration engenders emigration. The more the peasants emigrate, the more is social life destroyed in the country districts; hence a fresh reason for emigrating.'[11] The American writer Plummer Flippen Jones, in his travelogue *Shamrockland: A Ramble through Ireland* (1908), described those left behind as 'disheartened' because of the 'immense loss of population and the consequent stagnation in business and agriculture'.[12] The Irish writer Robert Lynd also noted in 1910 that emigration had 'drained the country to an unnatural degree of the young men and women of the marrying age, and those who remain are … frequently unable to marry until all the exuberance of life has gone out of them'.[13] According to Fitzpatrick, by 1911 'over a quarter of 50-year old women as well as men had never married, a fact which placed Ireland very high in the European celibacy league-table'.[14]

Jordan argues that the 'proximity of England and Scotland meant that an Irish emigrant's contact with kith and kin, and visitation, could be maintained'.[15] America, however, was another matter, and many people eventually lost contact with their families due to emigration. Nevertheless, by the early twentieth century, developments in communication and transport meant that it became easier to maintain connection, and to an extent a transatlantic 'imagined community' of Irish people developed. Printed material such as newspapers and books contributed to this, and letters and postcards, as well as the increased flow of travellers between the two countries. America began to be seen in Ireland as a 'land of promise', as Paul-Dubois noted, a view encouraged by the apparent affluence of American visitors and returned emigrants and by accounts of unimaginable opportunities and success.[16] This, as many commentators observed, encouraged further voluntary emigration, and those in America often helped siblings and other relatives to follow them. Paul-Dubois felt that, for the Irish, America had

> become their second native land, and emigration one of their customs … Children are brought up with the idea of probably becoming emigrants; trained to regard life 'in the country' as a transitory matter, merely a period of waiting until the time shall come for them to begin life 'over there'. Ireland, according to the proverb, is 'a Purgatory, where the Irish must suffer in patience before going to America'. To go to America no longer conveys the same idea of exile or expatriation. One may be as much at home in New Ireland as in the 'old country'.[17]

Emigration also provided a regular revenue stream. Irish-Americans, according to Fitzpatrick, sent their families in Ireland at least a million pounds annually, a 'stream of gold' which 'enabled Irish families to extend their reciprocal obligations effortlessly across oceans, so relieving tensions within Irish households while maintaining a modified version of the conventional kinship network'.[18]

Postcards and emigration

The discourse of emigration is evident in the postcard culture of Edwardian Ireland. Popular postcard imagery often tended towards representing the country as a beautiful empty landscape dotted with small isolated cottages and picturesque ruins, and sparsely populated by old peasant folk. Jones wrote that he considered Ireland 'one of the most entrancingly beautiful countries upon earth', and although elsewhere in his book he made it clear that he recognized the tragedy of emigration for Irish society, he also suggested that the country's resultant relative emptiness made it more visually attractive to visitors: 'The depopulation of the country has but served to increase its beauty; for all the old landmarks remain – castle, tower, bridge and cross – and the little farms that were formerly diligently worked with the spade are now covered over with a sward of green.'[19] The idea of the Irish landscape as a beautiful expression of loss and melancholy had a strong appeal for visitors, but also helped shape the self-image of Irish people (at home and abroad) and how they related to their place of origin. The text added to postcard representations of Ireland often emphasized the sense of nostalgia associated with the country with phrases such as 'dear old Ireland' and 'the old country'. St Patrick's Day cards, which were commonly used to connect with relatives and friends living in other countries, featured captions such as 'Greetings from Ould Ireland', and shamrocks were often added to them, small material tokens of the landscape itself. Similarly, the peat postcards printed by McCaw, Stevenson and Orr and issued by Macginty and Mackey in Belfast were captioned, in Celtic-style lettering, 'A Bit of Old Ireland'. Ireland was 'old' in the sense that it had a long history, but old too in contrast to the 'new' country, America, for which its young were leaving, and arguably also 'old', used so often on these sentimental cards, suggested the idea of being spent, finished, a picturesque relic of a brave but sad and disappearing past.

Some of the postcards in the collections examined were designed to explicitly express the sadness of leave-taking, of travelling far away from one's loved ones. Gilderdale for instance, links the 'patterns of twentieth century emigration that left many families separated by the seas' to the development and popularity of the Hands Across the Sea postcard genre, where a motif of clasped hands, often superimposed over imagery such as ships, waves and flags, was combined with the caption 'hands across the sea'. Gilderdale was writing about New Zealand, but this statement applies more generally, and there are examples of such cards in the collections examined, such as the Rotary-published card seen in Figure 35. This was sent from Dublin as a New Year greeting card for 1910 to Rennie Carmody in England.[20] Another, from the Cork Public Museum collection shows clasped hands with a globe as the background, the hands spanning the Atlantic Ocean, and the text 'A Hearty Handshake from Fermoy' followed by 'Tho' oceans may our hands divide, Our hearts dwell ever side by side'. The name 'Fermoy' looks like it was added separately, as if the card (published by Valentine's) was designed as a generic design which could then be made geographically specific by the addition of a desired place name.

Figure 35. *Hands across the Sea, 1910*, Rotary. Carmody family collection.

Brigid Byrne's collection contains two cards posted in 1908 which feature the clasped hand motif, but in these cases it is paired with St Patrick's day greetings, one of which bears the text, in both the Irish and English languages, 'my thoughts are with the loved ones who are far from home this Patrick's Day'.[21] Cards could represent leave-taking and distance from loved ones in a range of ways. One (discussed already in Chapter 3), sent to John O'Reilly from Queenstown and stamped by a White Star Line agent, is captioned 'Absence strengthens Love' (Figure 19). It includes the clasped hands motif as well as a train, a ship on the sea, one image of a couple embracing and another of the woman sitting alone looking sad, and a short verse. Another is postmarked from New York in 1914 with the following verse, titled 'Wishing for you', printed instead of an image on the front:

> This town's all right – I like it fine!
> But still I wish a friend of mine
> Were here to make my joy complete
> By walking with me down each street.

Another, from the Cobh Museum collection and published by Hely's of Dublin features the caption 'The Green Shores of Erin' over an image drawn by John Carey of a young man and an embracing couple on the deck of a ship, the young man, standing beside piles of luggage, holding a shillelagh and waving his hat towards the shore (see Figure 36).

Although some manufacturers clearly felt it worth their while to produce cards dealing specifically with the theme of emigration, there are not large numbers of these in the collections I have examined. Most commonly people used view, comic or other cards and added their own text expressing their feelings, and although they might mention loneliness it is often not clear if this is due to emigration or for some other reason. Many of the cards sent to John O'Reilly were postmarked from New York or Philadelphia, and some speak of loneliness. On one, for instance, sent in 1911, the sender asks for news of Ballyhaunis and adds 'I was very lonely leaving all the boys' on the back of an illustration of a man standing on a woman's skirt and pulling it off, revealing her underwear. The card's punning caption is 'On the Outskirts of New York', and, unless the author is expressing sarcasm, its sauciness seems to contrast with the emotion expressed in the comment on the back. Real photo cards could also be used to keep relatives up-to-date on family members. For instance, in 1913 Bessie Caulfield in Ballina was sent a real photo card from R. Caulfield in Pittsburg which shows a group of workers standing in a shop, on the back of which is written 'this shows about 2/3 of Store. My sister Kathrine in centre aisle. Very best wishes to your mother'.

Figure 36. *The Green Shores of Erin*, Hely's, Dublin. Cobh Museum collection.

Christina Jessop received a series of cards in 1907 and 1908 from her brother Charley, a former clerk in Guinness's brewery, who had emigrated to the United States in 1903 when he was 22. An older brother, William, was already living in Canada since 1892, and never returned to live in Ireland. Charley also settled eventually in Canada, in Vancouver, where he died in

1974 at the age of 93. In 1907 and 1908 Charley sent postcards to Christina from Skagway and St Michael in Nome, Alaska and from White Horse and Dawson in the (then) Yukon Territory in Canada, where he seems to have been working in the mining industry.[22] In the 1890s the area around the Klondike river in Yukon Territory was the focus of a stampede of tens of thousands of hopeful prospectors from all over the world in search of gold. Dawson City developed where the Klondike flows into the Yukon river, and became a supply centre for the wider mining area.[23] The prospectors had a long and difficult journey to get to the gold fields and a high proportion had to turn back or even lost their lives along the way.[24] Also, as Michael James Brand has argued in his thesis *Transience in Dawson City, Yukon, during the Klondike Gold Rush* (2003), by the time many of them arrived all the claims were staked and they missed out on 'the opportunity to own a mine, although most came north with this in mind. When their hopes were not fulfilled, they mined for wages or found employment elsewhere'.[25] This goldrush tailed off after 1899, although new prospectors continued to arrive until around 1910.[26] By 1907–1908, when Charley sent his postcards from Dawson to his sister in Ireland, individual mining there had been replaced by large-scale corporations, and it is possible that he was working for one of the latter.[27]

Charley's postcards to Christina do not include extensive messages nor expressions of personal feelings, relying instead on a few explanatory words written over or around the imagery. Nevertheless the cards, all photographic images, seem to have been carefully chosen to economically convey a sense of where he was and what he was doing. His first card, an image of Muir Glacier in Alaska, was sent in May 1907 from Skagway, which was on the most frequently travelled route from America (Seattle or San Francisco) to the Klondike. It features the short message 'Going to Dawson. Charley'[28] (see Figure 37). The second was postmarked a week later from White Horse in Yukon (represented on the front of the card), which was also on this route, and bears only the message 'Going down Yukon river in a row boat to Dawson. Chas'. By 18 June he was in Dawson city, from where his next card was sent, with a picture of a mining (sluicing) scene and the added message '25 miles from Dawson. Chas'. However, his next card, sent in September, is postmarked from St Michael in Nome, Alaska, and shows an image of a mining settlement overwritten with a few words which are mainly indecipherable, other than references to winter digging and sluicing on Cleary Creek. Nome also became the focus of a gold rush in 1899, although it is unlikely that there would have been many new opportunities there by 1907, and significantly, another card sent from Charley on the same day in September says 'Waiting for steamer for Seattle. Hoping all are well. Chas.' His last card, sent in July 1908, is again postmarked from Dawson, and features an image of Grand Forks, a settlement which grew up within the gold fields themselves.

Figure 37. *Muir Glacier Alaska. Area 354 Square Miles of Ice*, Adolph Selige, St Louis-Leipzig. Christina Jessop's card collection.

Figure 38. *An Eskimo Woman Catching Tom Cod through the Ice, Behring Sea*, B. B. Dobbs, Nome, Alaska. Christina Jessop's card collection.

Picture postcards allowed Charley to convey to his sister a sense of the harsh, sub-Arctic landscape in which he travelled, and presumably worked, as well as of some of the people who inhabited it. His cards include an image of an indigenous woman fishing through a hole in the ice (see Figure 38) as well as one showing some of the new transient population in the area, a group of miners working near Dawson (see Figure 39). These images, accompanied by his brief but very specific explanatory messages, construct his journey as an exciting adventure through a land which must have appeared exotic to Christina. They do not however provide any evidence of his response to it. No opinions or feeling are expressed, and yet his new life must have been shockingly different to his previous one in Dublin, and to that of Christina. Perhaps he also sent more expansive letters which have not survived, or else he was unable or unwilling to communicate his reactions to this very different environment across the distances of space and time which now separated them. Charley's last card to his sister suggests a loosening of the connection between their lives. He posted it from Dawson on 8 July 1908, adding only the message 'Hoping all are well. Chas 8th July 1908', and it arrived in Dublin on 6 August. He had addressed it to Miss C. Jessop, 33, South Earl Street in Dublin, but it was redirected to Mrs Wilson, 18, The Beach, Queenstown in County Cork, her new home since she had married Jack Wilson on 23 June.

Figure 39. *Sluicing Scene, No. 255 Lower Dominion, Creek, Y.T.*, Zaccarelli's Book Store, Dawson, Y.T. Christina Jessop's card collection.

Picture postcards facilitated a more spontaneous and less laboured connection with distant loved ones than letter writing, and their imagery added extra layers of meaning which could interact with the added text in a variety of ways. The small space allowed for writing meant that strong emotions could be expressed in a few words hidden on the back of a joke card, or they could be avoided altogether, as with Charley's cards.

Tourism

By 1900, tourism was a well-developed industry in Ireland. Irish tourism providers competed with those in other countries to attract visitors from abroad, and individual places in Ireland competed against each other for visitors from both Ireland and elsewhere, especially neighbouring Britain. According to Dan Breen and Tom Spalding, Thomas Cooke, the nineteenth-century pioneer of package holidays, helped promote Ireland as a destination in Britain, and later America, beginning excursions to Ireland in 1849 and 'by 1888 able to offer tours throughout Ireland by rail, steamer and coach'.[29] Cooke set up his first Irish office in Dublin in 1874 and by 1900 the company had offices in Belfast, Cork and Queenstown. Irish railway companies offered healthy competition, however, running their own excursions and developing tourist infrastructure (including hotels) along their rail routes.

In 1906, the popular London-published *Black's Guide to Ireland* claimed that Ireland offered 'the English holiday-maker of slender means the most attractive facilities for travelling to be found in Western Europe'.[30] Commentators and travel writers generally agreed that excellent hotels 'containing all modern conveniences and comforts' could be found in major Irish cities and tourist areas such as Killarney, and that accommodation and facilities in general had improved considerably in the last fifty years, although in some areas they still remained very unreliable, with bathrooms 'few and primitive beyond belief' and 'oil lamps or even … old-fashioned tallow candles' the only source of lighting.[31]

Nevertheless, by 1906 travelling to and around Ireland was a much easier and more pleasant experience than previously.[32] The railway system was well developed, and railway companies sold a range of different ticket types to appeal to and encourage potential tourists, such as combination tickets which included sea passages or reduced rates into certain attractions, and Circular Tour tickets which enabled visits to a number of locations within a certain period of time. Where railways had not been developed a range of horse-drawn vehicles with varying levels of speed and comfort could be booked for road travel, such as a public 'long car', or a coach, waggonette, charabanc or 'outside car'.[33] The motor car was also beginning to make an impact in Ireland, as evidenced by the postcard shown in Figure 40, which was posted in 1906 and shows a group of tourists sitting in a car near the Cork/Kerry border in the southwest of Ireland, outside what looks like a traditional thatched cottage which is also a refreshment stop. The 1906 edition of *Murray's Handbook* recommended motoring as a mode of travelling around the country, advising that 'the motorist who exercises both [courtesy and consideration for others] will have no difficulty in travelling through Ireland in all its highways and byways'.[34]

Figure 40. *Tunnel Cottage, Glengarriff, Co. Cork*, Lawrence. Cork Public Museum archive, postcard collection 14.3.1997.54.

Motor spirit can be had almost everywhere. Repair and fitting shops will be found in all the large and most of the moderate-sized towns. Garages have been specially built at some of the best hotels, but coach-houses or other suitable covering will be found available in all towns. The general rule is not to charge for motor accommodation.[35]

Cycling was also popular and well supported with good facilities, and indeed the image in Figure 40 also shows two small figures cycling along the road in the background. Boats were also a useful and pleasant way to access some areas as rivers and harbours often had frequent steamer crossings.[36] In Cork harbour, for instance, there were regular steamers from Cork City to the harbour towns of Queenstown, Aghada and Crosshaven several times every day.[37] This improved infrastructure also encouraged Irish people to view and explore their own country as tourists, and the comments added to picture postcards from the period indicate that they did so. For instance, Christina Jessop received a card from her Dublin friend Máire in 1905 in which the latter told her of 'exploring the "Marble City" [Kilkenny] en route' to the seaside town of Tramore, and of 'doing' Waterford City. A postcard from Christina's fiancé Jack in Belfast described a visit from his father, who lived in Queenstown, and appears to have made a point of viewing all the local tourist attractions while he stayed with his son: 'Father is enjoying himself well – he has seen almost everything about here – and Saturday we were at Blackhead and yesterday we had a lovely day at Portrush & the [Giant's] Causeway.'

Tourists sought out certain 'attractions' for a range of reasons. The origins of modern mass tourism have been traced to a variety of practices, including mediaeval pilgrimages to sacred places and objects, the nineteenth-century romantic quest for solitude and solace in nature, and the pursuit of improved health which for thousands of years inspired trips to locations such as hot springs and mountainous and coastal bathing areas. In Edwardian Ireland the several picture postcards sent from, and featuring images of, the sulphur wells and baths in Lisdoonvarna and the hydro on Saint Ann's Hill in Shandon in Cork suggest the enduring popularity of 'health' tourism, although its most obvious manifestation at this stage was the extremely popular seaside holiday. The saucy seaside postcard was to become a cliché in later years, but even in the early twentieth century it offered plenty of scope for both risqué visual jokes and sexually suggestive imagery. Even mainstream postcard publishers such as Raphael Tuck made the most of the seaside genre, as can be seen in Figure 41, a Tuck card sold in Britain in 1903, and one of a set of six titled 'Seaside glamour, the morning dip'. 'Peeping Toms' and their scantily dressed targets were the staples of such series. Edwardian society offered very few public spaces as socially liminal as the beach, where crowds of people of different classes and genders were allowed to appear and view others in various stages of undress.

Figure 41. *Seaside glamour, the morning dip*, Raphael Tuck. From <https:// tuckdbpostcards.org/items/121735/pictures/326822>

The practices and interests of seventeenth- and eighteenth-century aristocrats on their Grand Tours through Europe are also seen as having established habits of seeking out and viewing certain attractions which persisted in modern mass tourism. For instance, while wild and beautiful scenery held a strong appeal for most tourists to Ireland, William H. A. Williams, in *Creating Irish Tourism: The First Century, 1750–1850* (2010), also argues that the well established habits of the Grand Tour would have made it difficult for most visitors to ignore urban Ireland. Public buildings, churches and cathedrals, bridges, charitable institutions, prisons, schools, military barracks and the like were among the sights tourists were supposed to notice.[38]

He also points out that in Ireland,

as in England, the big house and its surrounding gardens and parklands were among the first tourist attractions ... As Irish tourism grew, the country drew British visitors for whom the habit of exploring country houses had become part of their touring culture.[39]

Similarly, specific routes became popular because of particular associations, and a tourist infrastructure was developed around them. For instance, in the early twentieth century many operators offered tours along the coastal 'Prince of Wales' route from Cork to Killarney via Bantry, Glengarriff and Kenmare. The Cork, Bandon and South Coast Railway issued circular tickets for it and organized coach and car connections, and tourists could stay in modern, comfortable hotels such as Roche's Royal and the Eccles Hotel in Glengarriff and the Great Southern, Lake and Graham's New Hotel in Killarney. While the scenic attractions of this journey were undeniable, it at least partly became the best-known and most developed route from Cork to Killarney because the Prince of Wales, later King Edward VII, had travelled it in 1858, and it was thereafter associated with his name, celebrity and social status, and advertised as 'pre-eminently the route selected by distinguished visitors to Killarney'.[40] Blarney Castle, a fifteenth-century derelict tower house near Cork City, attracted visitors in the eighteenth century because of the ornamental landscaping of its grounds and its views of the surrounding countryside, but sometime in the late eighteenth or early nineteenth century it became better known for a stone in its upper wall which conferred extra verbal powers on those who kissed it, giving rise to what Williams has called 'one of the most peculiar of all tourist rituals'.[41] Due to a range of factors, including a popular verse written by Father Prout (Francis Mahony) in 1835 which celebrated the effectiveness of the stone, easy access to Blarney from nearby Cork City especially after the arrival of the railway in 1849, canny marketing and entrepreneurial exploitation by locals and tourism providers and some creative legend construction, Blarney Castle became by the early twentieth century one of Ireland's most must-see sights, a status it retains to this day.[42] *Murray's Handbook* of 1906 claimed that thousands visited it annually, attracted not so much by 'the charming scenery in which it is placed, as the reputation it has gained for bestowing powers of flattery and soft speeches, "full of guile and blandishments and uncontrollable in its sway over credulity"'.[43] Picture postcards did their bit to perpetuate the fame of Blarney and its 'Stone of Eloquence', and numerous examples exist in the collections examined.

According to Berghoff and Korte, tourists 'did not travel on untrodden paths. They went to see sights pre-defined for them … including a pre-definition of the appropriate response to the sight'.[44] Dean MacCannell, in *The Tourist. A New Theory of the Leisure Class* (1989), has defined a tourist attraction as a sight that travellers to an area are socially obliged to visit, stating that 'no one is exempt from the obligation to go sightseeing except the local person'.[45] He traces the development of tourist attractions *as* attractions through successive phases of 'sight sacralisation', which include authentication, naming, framing and elevation, mechanical reproduction and social reproduction.[46] The phase of mechanical reproduction, he claims, involves

> the creation of prints, photographs, models or effigies of the object which are themselves valued and displayed. It is the mechanical reproduction phase of sacralization that is most responsible for setting the tourist in motion on his journey to find the true objects.[47]

Picture postcards can be seen as part of this phase of sight sacralization, both the products and agents of further tourism. Picture postcards in Edwardian Ireland functioned as what MacCannell calls 'markers', pieces of information about a tourist site similar to 'guidebooks, informational tablets, slide shows, travelogues, souvenir matchbooks etc.'[48] Williams shows how literary associations can also act as markers: for instance, 'the ruins of Kilcolman Castle in County Cork, no more picturesque than those of many other abandoned Irish tower houses, could boast as its marker its connection to Edmund Spencer, author of The Faerie Queen.'[49]

Quoting the claim of John Urry and Jonas Larsen that the tourist gaze 'cannot be left to chance. People have to learn how, when and where to "gaze"', he also observes that

> in Ireland writers produced accounts and guide books. Publishers issued collections of prints of manor houses and scenic spots. Poets memorialized castles and glens ... the obelisk at Celbridge in County Meath, commemorating the Battle of the Boyne and the victory of Protestant King Billy over Catholic James II, once attracted a good deal of tourist attention, in spite of the fact that, apart from the monument, there was nothing to see but some pleasant rural scenery.[50]

Picture postcards bore titles and explanatory text that helped viewers and visitors link specific historical, literary or other associations to particular attractions. There are numerous examples of postcards in the collections examined which perform this function for sights whose significance might otherwise be unclear, such as the relatively unremarkable black-and-white postcard representation of trees posted in 1904 from Youghal to London and titled 'Youghal. Raleigh's Yew Trees under which he smoked his first pipe'.[51] Images of tourist attractions were reproduced on millions of postcards, and indeed no tourist attraction could be considered as such without its image having been reproduced on a card, to the extent that James Douglas grumbled in 1907 that it was 'impossible to gaze upon a ruin without finding a Picture Postcard of it at your elbow.'[52]

Because of their mobility and the enormous numbers circulated, picture postcards became one of the most important tourist markers, in MacConnell's sense of the term, in the early twentieth century. Tourism providers were very aware of this and from early on in its development the postcard was used extensively by hotel owners and transport companies to promote their services. Picture postcards, however, also played important roles in other aspects of the tourist experience, to the extent that some commentators felt that the writing and sending of postcards had become the tourist's main, or even only, purpose. Carline quotes a journalist describing his visit to the mountains of Switzerland in 1900:

> Recently I went up the Rigi with a large party. Directly we arrived at the summit, everybody made a rush for the hotel and fought for the postcards. Five minutes afterwards, everybody was writing for dear life. I believe that the entire party had

come up, not for the sake of the experience or the scenery, but to write postcards and post them on the summit.[53]

Carline also presents some advice from a letter published in the *Picture Postcard Magazine* in October 1900 which mocks (or provides evidence of) the rather perfunctory nature of this tourist ritual:

> Hard-pressed tourists were given some useful hints by Mrs. Montague Fowler, following her recent trip down the Nile. 'To the tired traveller, the picture postcard is an undiluted blessing ... Most hotels are provided with a postcard stall; a couple of minutes suffice for writing the address, a few words and your signature.' To help those using postcards, she offers a sample text, which she herself had frequently used with success.
>
> 'Arrived here safely. Charming scenery (see view above), M.F.'[54]

Many indeed wrote even less than this, but others sent long chatty messages about what they were doing and seeing and where they were staying, whether the weather was good or bad, whether their journey had been rough or smooth, and enquiries about well-being, such as 'Hope you are all in the pink'. Like Mrs Montague Fowler, they often added to or commented on the image on the front of the card in order to more effectively communicate their message. A postcard sent from Cork to Oxford, England in 1904 and showing a picture of *Macroom. The River and Carrigdrohid Castle* features the added text 'We went over this old bridge yesterday'.[55] Another sent from Cork to Kingstown (now Dun Laoghaire, Dublin) in 1902 has a picture of the Cork International Exhibition site, with an added X and the words 'Water Chute where I enjoyed myself and was nearly drowned!'[56] (see Figure 42).

Postcards were also used to make or fine-tune practical travel arrangements: people notified each other of departures, arrivals and their whereabouts, and suggested times and places to meet. Perhaps one of their most important functions in relation to tourism however was as souvenirs. Apart from being posted, they could be gifted to friends and family, or taken home, placed in albums and treasured and displayed for their associations and memories. As Williams has argued, souvenirs, 'help to justify a journey, making tourists feel that they have indeed been somewhere different and seen extraordinary things'.[57]

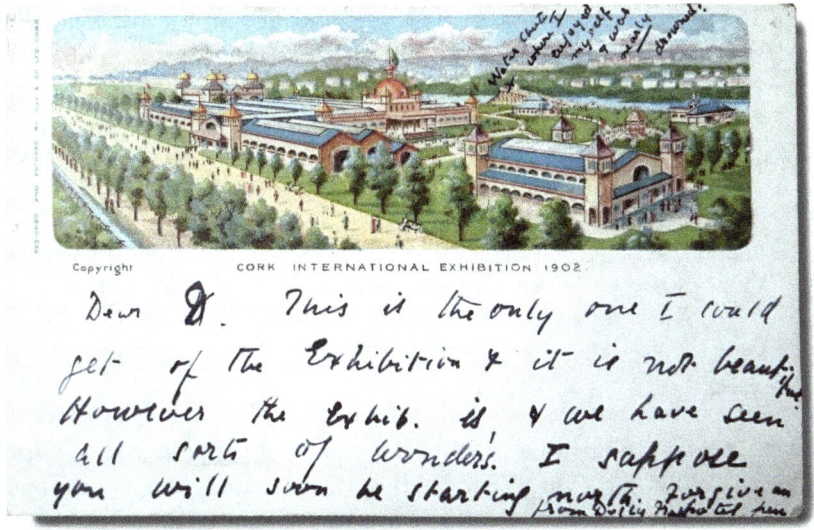

Figure 42. *Cork International Exhibition 1902*, Guy, Cork. Cork Public Museum archive, postcard collection 17.12.2002.321.

The tourist postcard image of Ireland

Many different Irelands, some contradictory, were constructed via post-card imagery, largely because of the many different motives behind their production as well as the different audiences at which they were aimed. Tourist cards often relied on promoting the country's picturesque scenery and such imagery was very popular with consumers in the early twentieth century. Visitors to Ireland had long been attracted by its scenic beauty, and indeed Williams claims that 'Ireland was in the forefront of the development of the scenic pleasure tour' in the century between 1750 and 1850, and that by 1800 'the Lakes of Killarney, the Giant's Causeway and the Glens of Wicklow' had become internationally recognized tourist sites.[58]

The aristocratic travellers of the seventeenth and early eighteenth centuries visited big estate houses with their carefully landscaped grounds, and they enjoyed viewing and collecting classically inspired drawings, prints and paintings of such subjects. However, by the middle of the eighteenth century

> touring became increasingly oriented toward nature and motivated by what the new Romantic Age called 'the sublime' and 'the picturesque'. These changes in interest and aesthetics were accompanied by a significant shift in the status of 'the touring public'. While the aristocracy had dominated the Grand Tour, the participation of the upper-middle class characterized the picturesque pleasure tour.[59]

On the picturesque pleasure tour, travellers went in search of specific landscapes that fulfilled a set of criteria categorized as 'picturesque', a term which initially, in the early eighteenth century, meant 'like a picture' but later became classified as an aesthetic category, adding to the existing categories proposed by Edmund Burke in his essay *A Philosophical Inquiry into the Origin of our Ideas of the Sublime and the Beautiful* (1757).[60] The picturesque, according to Julian Treuherz, was characterized by 'asymmetry, irregularity and uneven texture', different to the 'balance, harmony and smoothness' associated with beauty, but also to the dark drama of the sublime.[61] Williams argues that it had a sense of melancholy and decay that 'did not loom large on the sublime scale, and in order to appreciate it, travellers tended to borrow "from a sentimentalized sublime"'.[62] Guidebooks instructed tourists on how to judge a landscape as picturesque, and Irish scenery was found to be particularly well qualified. According to Williams, 'by the time of the Great Famine, the picturesque had so defined Ireland that even some of those who came to observe the crisis and/or to minister to its victims were drawn to Ireland's scenic landscapes'.[63] In 1864, a writer in the *Times* claimed that

> there is nothing in these isles more beautiful and more picturesque than the south and west of Ireland. They who know the fair portions of Europe still find in Ireland that which they have seen nowhere else, and which has charms all its own. One might suppose the island just risen from the sea ... and the spirit of light and order beginning its work; such is the infinite confusion of surge and beach, bay, headland, river, lake, grass, of land and sea, sunshine in showers, and rainbow over all.[64]

The writer predicted a sharp rise in tourism to Ireland, and consequent prosperity for the country. Ireland's identity (and value) as a picturesque tourist destination was therefore well established long before the emergence of the picture postcard.

The promotion of Ireland as primarily a country of beautiful landscapes continued into the early twentieth century, and indeed is still a central focus of tourist marketing today. By the Edwardian era, mass tourism was well established, and the appetite for viewing and representing natural, beautiful scenery was undiminished. *Murray's Handbook* of 1906 devoted a large section of its introduction to the scenery of Ireland, providing an overview of the 'scenic merit' of its headlands, estuaries, lakes, mountains, mountain passes, rivers, caverns and peat-bogs, while detailing and recommending specific examples in the main text of the book.[65] And numerous postcards from the period featured images of the country's well-known natural attractions, particularly the areas in the south of the country around the lakes of Killarney and the Beara peninsula, the rugged coasts of the west of Ireland, the Giant's Causeway in Antrim, and Glendalough, Powerscourt and Avoca in Wicklow, but also innumerable other less well-known sites. Raphael Tuck published many such images as part of its popular 'Picturesque Counties' series. *Lower Lake, Glendalough*, posted to Christina Jessop in 1906, is typical of many of them. Based on a painting by the landscape artist Edgar Longstaffe and one of a set of six cards representing County Wicklow scenes, it shows a smooth gleaming lake surrounded by steep mountains, with cattle on a stony shore in the foreground (see Figure 43). The evening sky with its purple clouds gathering over looming darker purple mountaintops conveys the melancholy of a dying day, while the sparsity of evidence of human society – the three cattle in the foreground and three tiny houses in the distance – suggests the loneliness of the place. This image was reused on several sets of cards from Tuck, sometimes with different finishes and framing, as were several others that were similar in composition and tone. Angela Mehegan found a similar frequency of representations of empty or near-empty landscapes in her study of rail travel posters from the same period, and argued that they 'fed into Irish national preoccupations with reclaiming the integrity of the precolonial past', appealing to the nineteenth-century traveller's fondness for the sublime and the picturesque and presenting a 'foil to the industrialized cities of England; unspoilt, remote and unpopulated', while at the same time avoiding images of inhabitants that might suggest conflict to the English tourist.[66]

Figure 43. *Lower Lake, Glendalough*, Raphael Tuck. Christina Jessop's card collection.

Apart from certain types of scenery, the picturesque, as Williams explains, inspired a taste for

> the rough, the ruined, the exotic … As the travelling public learned to visually organize landscapes, it found that satisfying 'views' could be formed around a jagged rocky outcropping, a ruined abbey, a rustic bridge, a shepherd's hovel, a crumbling tower house, or a group of colorful peasants.[67]

Such motifs were still very much a staple of postcard imagery in the early twentieth century. Ruined, ivy-covered castles, abbeys and churches were a common theme and occur frequently in the collections examined. A card published by Max Ettlinger and Company of London and New York shows the derelict silhouette of Kilcrea Abbey in County

Cork set against a glowing evening sky, its romantic appeal underscored by a short verse from Byron: 'Proudly majestic frowns thy vaulted hall/ Scowling defiance on the blasts of fate.'[68] Muckross Abbey near Killarney was a favourite in Raphael Tuck's Irish-themed collections, and it too was sometimes represented silhouetted against a vivid sunset, as in Figure 44, which also includes a lone, pensive-looking figure sitting in the foreground. Tuck's set of postcards titled *The Emerald Isle, Picturesque Castles* (listed in their 1908/1909 catalogue) featured coloured reproductions of six different Irish castles only one of which, Lismore Castle in County Waterford, was not in ruins.[69] Such cards, some of which were also issued as St Patrick's Day cards, emphasized the pervasive presence of the past in Ireland and communicated a sense of nostalgia and melancholy.

Figure 44. *Muckross Abbey Killarney*, Raphael Tuck. From <https://tuckdbpostcards. org/items/116224>

The thatched cottage, a common motif in late eighteenth- and early nineteenth-century paintings of Ireland, was also a popular inclusion in Irish postcard imagery, performing, according to Brian P. Kennedy, several

functions as 'a symbol of Irish rural life, fitting in visually with the landscape, satisfying the demands of the picturesque and symbolizing cosy
domesticity'.[70] Postcard representations of thatched cottages varied, but
were often idealized: many were illustrated as picturesquely semi-derelict,
almost indistinguishable from their natural surrounds (see Figure 45), while
others were orderly, neat and pretty, nestling comfortably into the folds of
the land, or, as in the many images from the Ballymaclinton Irish Village
in the Franco-British exhibition of 1908, forming an attractive backdrop
to groups of industrious, smiling Irish colleens. The first type of image
suggested the closeness of Irish life to nature and older, more 'primitive'
ways of living, while the tidiness and cosiness of the latter could be seen
as a demonstration of how civilized Irish life had/could become, given the
right circumstances.

Figure 45. *An Irish Homestead, Bray*, Raphael Tuck. From <https://tuckdbpostcards.
org/items/85240>

Tourists to Ireland, as elsewhere, went in search of what they thought
of as exotic, and in Ireland they looked for signs of a typical and distinctive
Irishness, an exoticism unique to Ireland. Irish people also sought this

out in their own country. Representations of some Irish landscapes and sites, such as the mountains, bogs and winding roads of Connaught, the basalt formations of the Giant's Causeway in Antrim, Blarney castle and its stone-kissing ritual and the Lakes of Killarney, were so well known and so much associated with Ireland they often functioned as visual synecdoches for the whole country. They therefore formed the backbone of the 'Irish' postcard sets issued by companies such as Raphael Tuck. Ruined castles and abbeys, thatched cottages and round towers were also seen as 'typically Irish' features of the countryside, but, based on postcard imagery and the comments added by senders, visitors were also interested in objects such as jaunting cars and the traditional large-hooded woollen cloaks still worn by women in some areas of West Cork. They were attracted too to scenes such as traditional fairs, markets and holy wells. The postcard collection in the Cork Public Museum includes many representations of the Coal Quay market in Cork, also called 'Paddy's Market', an outdoor city market where crowds of shawled women negotiated sales and socialized. Similarly, images of the shrine to St Finbarr at Gougane Barra, usually showing groups of people (some traditionally shawled, others fashionably dressed) kneeling on the ground and praying, must have appealed to many, as they too are common in the collections examined, and were published by several companies both Irish and British. Similar but less well-known religious sites also featured on many cards: Figure 46, for instance, shows a card published by Hartmann of London and posted in 1906, featuring a colourized photograph of a man and two shawled women kneeling at a holy well in Aghada, east County Cork. The shrine includes a tree hung with a statue of the Virgin Mary as well as many pieces of cloth and other small objects, placed there as votive offerings by pilgrims. Such images emphasized the continuity in Ireland of ancient traditions and beliefs, and would have appealed to tourists who were in search of an exotic-seeming 'other'.

Figure 46. *Holy Well, Aghada*, no printer/publisher named. Cork Public Museum
archive, postcard collection 18.9 2002.818.

Postcard images purporting to portray 'Irish life' similarly emphasized
the picturesque, the traditional and the exotic. Raphael Tuck published
several series of postcards titled *Irish Life*, showing various Irish people,
mostly traditionally costumed, barefoot peasants, situated in idyllic rural
settings and engaged in pre-industrial pursuits such as turf cutting and
carrying, spinning yarn, collecting seaweed, fishing, milking cows, churning
milk, feeding pigs, going to market and bartering. Images of individuals or
groups performing Irish jigs, again in rural settings, are also common. Many
similar cards were produced by other British companies such as Valentines
and by Irish publishers such as Lawrence. Occasionally modern leisure is
included as an example of 'Irish life', as on a card titled *The Pleasure Trip*
in a Tuck series *Irish Peasant Life* which first appeared around 1910.[71] This
shows passengers in modern dress being driven in an outside car along a
winding road, against a dramatic backdrop of lake and mountains. Also
occasionally an urban image is categorized as 'Irish life', as in those showing
village or market scenes. One example titled *Irish Life – A Street Seller*, published by Valentines and posted in 1913, shows a shawled woman arranging
items on a cloth-covered table in a street (Figure 47). The woman looks like

a traditional Irish 'type' and the objects she is selling appear to be mainly crucifixes, 'holy pictures' and rosary beads, religious artefacts associated with Catholicism, another major signifier of Irishness. However, these religious items were mass-produced in vast numbers during this period, many in the Saint Sulpice area of Paris, and exported all over the world, so this image, despite its superficial presentation of a traditional, distinctive Irishness, also testifies to the openness of Irish society in the early twentieth century to modern and international influences.

Figure 47. *Irish Life – A Street Seller*, Valentine's. Cork Public Museum archive, postcard collection 18.11 2003.42.8.

Mostly, however, 'Irish Life' was presented as rural and pre-industrial, and Irish people in such images were shown as if they existed independently of time, modernity and external influences. In the Tuck postcard series *British Character Studies*, Ireland is represented only by *An Irish Peasant*, based on a painting by Henri Pitcher of a ruddy-faced man standing in front of a bare mountain landscape. The series also contains images of *An English Rustic*, *A Cornish Fisherman*, *A Scotch Laird*, *An English Squire* and *A Chelsea Pensioner* (shown reading a newspaper), reserving both complexity of social class and modernity only for the English British.[72] Irish 'character' seems to have been evident in some settings more than others: one writer, for instance, who sent a card from Bantry to England in 1905 claimed to be 'Having a good time … studying Irish character. Yesterday a cattle and horse fair, the day before a pig fair'.[73] The Irish peasant, both male and female, was a popular motif on cards published by a range of British and Irish publishers, but possibly even more popular was the Irish 'colleen', generally shown as an attractive young woman, again usually barefoot and engaged in rural pursuits. Lawrence and Fergus O'Connor in particular issued many of these, often based on illustrations by John Carey or L. Anthony, and featuring young women effortlessly and charmingly carrying turf, a basket or a milking stool, or prettily spinning yarn in the sunshine outside a cottage door. Ellen Duff, the young waitress whose collection is one of those examined here, must have been fond of such images, as she kept several examples, as did Rennie Carmody in Ennis. A typical example shows a smiling girl carrying a large basket of turf against a backdrop of bog, lake and mountain and bears the text *Bringing home the Turf* (see Figure 48). These images idealized and emphasized the charm of Irish rural life and people, while playing down the hardship associated with the kinds of lifestyles they portray.

Bringing home the Turf.

Figure 48. *Bringing home the turf*, Fergus O'Connor. Carmody family collection.

They must have seemed as exotic to Ellen, who spent her days working in a Dublin city centre restaurant, as they would have to visitors from outside Ireland. Indeed it is difficult to see how any of the people whose picture postcard collections are examined in this book, such as Christina the pharmacist, Rennie the student, Bessie the teacher or John the draper's assistant, could have identified with the 'Irish life' and people portrayed on many of these cards, and how they could have related to them as anything but 'other'. Modern and urban Ireland did of course feature frequently on Edwardian postcards, but almost never on cards or in series titled *Irish Life* or *Irish Types*, which were mainly confined to the stereotypical and rural exotic. Postcard images of advertisement-covered trams on busy Irish city streets or of fashionable couples strolling along the promenades of Queenstown or Bray were popular and common, but were never titled 'Irish life', and both tourists and locals would probably have been confused if they were.

Irish publishers were just as complicit as foreign ones in promoting this idea of true Irishness as located in the rural and the premodern, and for a range of reasons. For one thing, it was a popular vision that sold well, since tourists, who were often from the urban middle classes themselves, visited locations to see signs of difference from their own lives, not the same sort of people and activities as they could have viewed at home. Nationalist discourse, as discussed in Chapter 4, was also a factor, since nationalism promoted the idea of Ireland as distinctive and different in particular from its heavily industrialized and urbanized neighbour, thereby identifying rural areas and traditional pursuits, along with the people engaged in them, as the purest and most authentic examples of Irishness.

It was however a small step from picturesque 'types' to the kind of crude postcard stereotypes discussed in Chapter 4. Robert Lynd, in his book *Rambles in Ireland* (1912), noted that in Cork, 'outside the best bookshop in the city … you will see a great display of coloured picture postcards with a gallery of colleens and pigs and all the other pseudo-Irish paraphernalia'.[74] He then added,

> I have heard it said that it is not the people of Cork who are to blame for the pervasiveness of these idiocies, but the multitude of tourists who include Cork in their tour to Killarney. I myself saw a tourist in the hotel where we stayed addressing at least fifty of these pig postcards during a wet hour in the afternoon. What visitors to Ireland find to attract them in these intolerable colleens with head on one side and arms akimbo, who exchange fatuities about kisses with turnip-faced young men in tail-coats, is a mystery to the mere Irishman.[75]

Tourists arrived in Ireland conditioned to expect such stereotypes, both on postcards and in reality. Annoying and even offensive as they were to Irish people such as Lynd, they were nevertheless an important aspect of the Irish brand abroad. A short passage from the popular *Black's Guide to*

Ireland of 1906 shows the sort of advice that visitors to the country were given before they arrived:

> The Irish peasant, especially in the west, is as incapable of measuring distances as he is of telling his right hand from his left; both are equally impossible for him. Never, therefore ask, 'How far is it?' but if hard driven for some information, ask *what time* the journey will take. For most Pats go to market and the fair, many go to church, and some nowadays, even in Donegal, catch a train.

Figure 49. *The Passive Resister*, Lawrence. Cork Public Museum archive, postcard collection 19.5 2004.21.47.

It is hardly surprising, therefore that cards such as that shown in Figure 49, humorously portraying the foolish ineptitude of the Irish peasant, were bought and sent by tourists because they thought they captured some essence of real Irishness.

While the Irish peasantry were commonly represented on Edwardian postcards as an aspect of Ireland's rural picturesqueness, the middle classes more often appeared as spectators or consumers of scenic landscapes. According to Justin Carville, landscape painting in Ireland in the eighteenth and nineteenth centuries 'had traditionally been preoccupied with the representation of ownership and agrarian labour', and therefore included landowners and peasants but not the middle classes, who 'literally remained out of sight'.[76] By the early twentieth century, however, 'mass produced tourist imagery, particularly photographic views and picture postcards, brought the middle and ascending classes for the first time into the sphere of visual representation of the natural world'.[77]

> The middle-class tourist became an essential figure in representations of tourism throughout the late 19th and early 20th century. Picture postcards and tourist photographs did not just represent the picturesque view but also the tourist presence in the landscape during the act of visual consumption of the natural world around them.[78]

Figure 50, a card posted in 1905, shows a distanced view of tourists examining and enjoying the natural rock formations of the Bridges of Ross in county Clare. Such imagery reveals the tourist spectacle *as* a spectacle, a product both constructed and promoted via the postcard.

The idyllic or picturesque tourist vision could of course be complicated or undermined by picture postcards published for other purposes. For various reasons publishers, usually local and catering to specific markets (such as soldiers wanting to send cards home showing where they were staying), issued numerous images of dreary looking barracks and military training camps, unprepossessing buildings such as the agricultural station in Clonakilty in County Cork, and schools, presbyteries and convents designed for functionality rather than aesthetic appeal. Photographic postcards of small Irish towns, villages and cottages were seldom as picturesque as those derived from paintings, even if, as in the Raphael Tuck postcard shown in Figure 51, they included the conventional motifs of thatched roof and pig.

Figure 50. *Natural Bridge of Ross*, Lawrence. Christina Jessop's card collection.

Figure 51. *Co Cork, Glengariffe Farmyard*, Raphael Tuck. From <https://tuckdbpostcards.org/items/83384>

Similarly, comments added to cards by senders could undo a lot of the work done by tourism promoters. One correspondent, for instance, wrote on a card sent from Skibbereen to London: 'I've been trying to find you something nice in the way of post cards but it's impossible … PS This is such a half starved part of the globe.' Another remarked in 1909 on a card sent from Bandon to Newton Abbott in Devonshire: 'Splendid weather and fine scenery, but people look poor and miserable.'[79]

Images have always presented a visual argument rather than a faithful reflection of the world, but the picture postcard brought this to a whole new level. Mass production and international distribution meant that publishers could manipulate and combine images and their titles at will in order to satisfy the relentless demands of the market while keeping costs down. The same images were reissued over and over again on new postcards, with different titles and sometimes as different places, in a range of media or combined with other images in different frames. The fact that they were titled and on postcards officially issued by well-known publishers, and that the imagery was often photographic, gave them some authority and suggested veracity, even if the result was sometimes bizarre, as in the colourized photograph of Lower Bridge, Enniskerry, County Wicklow with a large Brown Bear in the foreground (see Figure 52). Brown Bears became extinct in Ireland over 2,000 years ago, but this one looks rather unconvincing anyway as it is made from a piece of fur material stuck to the front of the card. The postcard was published by F. von Bardeleben, New York and Germany, and was sent through the post in Shokan, New York in 1907. Von Berdeleben seems to have issued many postcard images of Ireland, mostly plain colourized photographs, including one of the same Enniskerry scene without the bear, and another with what looks like a Polar Bear, created from white fur, walking across the stream.

Figure 52. *Lower Bridge, Enniskerry, Co Wicklow*, F. von Bardeleben, New York and
Germany. Author's collection

Postcard representations therefore could easily lose any real connection
to what was being represented and take on lives of their own, constructing
an alternative fantasy version of the world. As with modern memes, the possibilities for the creation of new combinations of pictures and words, and
therefore meanings, were infinite. The card shown in Figure 53, *Our Local*

Express, Skibbereen to Ballydehob and Schull, was posted from Skibbereen in Cork to Dorchester in England in 1905, and could be interpreted as a humorous comment on the crowded and primitive train system in West Cork. However, the card, which was published by the Cynicus company of Fyfe, was only one of several issued for different locations throughout Britain and Ireland, all of which were identical except for the place names. There are numerous examples of cards like this in the collections examined, usually generic cartoon tourist cards with the names of specific locations added separately.

Figure 53. *Our Local Express Skibbereen to Ballydehob and Schull*, Cynicus, Fife. Cork Public Museum archive, postcard collection 19.8 2004.41.028.

The image of Ireland constructed by picture postcards during the Edwardian era was therefore complex and often very loosely related to the way people actually experienced the country, especially those who lived there. Even the production of photographic imagery of actual Irish locations distorted the representation of Ireland, because of the large concentration of examples from a limited number of very popular locations. There were probably people, for instance, who thought that Ireland consisted of

Killarney, and that Killarney consisted of six specific locations (the usual number of cards in a series published by Raphael Tuck). According to Urry and Larsen, 'instead of seeing photographs as reflections or distortions of a pre-existing world, they can be understood as a technology of world making'.[80] The same can be said of picture postcards, which is why tourism providers and other groups worked hard to control the image of Ireland they constructed. This was made impossible however by the mobility and susceptibility to manipulation of mass-produced imagery and text, by the industry's endless quest for profit and novelty, by the often-contradictory agendas of different publishers, and by the newly empowered audience of consumers who could now react to and comment on the cards themselves.

Postcards and the Irish worldview

Just as visitors to Ireland arrived with preconceived ideas about the country constructed partly through the widespread availability of mass-produced images, so Irish people similarly developed their understanding of the world beyond Ireland. There had been such an explosion in photographic and postcard imagery that by the early twentieth century it would have been almost impossible to visit any reasonably well-known tourist site without having seen an image of it beforehand. As James Douglas noted in 1907,

> nobody need fear that there is any spot on the earth which is not depicted on this wonderful oblong. The photographer has photographed everything between the poles … The click of his shutter has been heard on every Alp and in every desert. He has hunted down every landscape on the globe. Every bird and every beast has been captured by the camera … Every pimple on the earth's skin has been photographed, and wherever the human eye roves or roams it detects the self-conscious air of the reproduced. The aspect of novelty has been filched from the visible world. The earth is eye-worn.[81]

Irish people sent and brought back to Ireland picture postcards from their holidays abroad. Like tourists *to* Ireland, they were also likely to follow well-worn routes in search of attractions that had already been singled out, pictured and evaluated by others. Gaze's travel company, based in London but with branches in Dublin and Killarney, advertised bookings to 'all parts of the World' from their Killarney Office, specifically mentioning trips to the Paris 1900 Exhibition and the Passion Play at Oberammergau in Germany.[82] Postcards sent to Ireland from abroad included significant numbers of images of well-known and well-established sights such as Notre Dame Cathedral in Paris, the Colosseum in Rome and Lake Geneva in Switzerland. Irish tourists followed routes already well-trodden through places such as France, Italy and the Swiss Alps, the latter in particular a 'must-see' destination for travellers in Europe since the Grand Tours of the eighteenth century.

Christina Jessop's brother Jack visited the Swiss Alps in 1907 and documented his journey in detail on a series of postcards to his sister in Ireland. From his commentary it is clear that the sole purpose of his journey was tourism, and his aims as a tourist seem to have combined conscientious observation of the places he visited, a search for specific iconic sights and experiences associated with the area, and walking, climbing and pleasurable social interactions. His postcards describe, on the back of images of snow and mountains, the weather, travel conditions, geography, scenery and occasionally even wildlife that he saw and experienced. On one card he wrote excitedly 'A glacier at last!' The cards themselves were often designed to provide as much specific information as possible, frequently including on the images the names and heights of the mountains shown.

Jack was travelling with a group of friends, some of whom also sent cards to Christina suggesting he was also very much interested in having a good time on his trip. One of them told her that they had visited Geneva 'to see Mont Blanc but Jack brought me to so many cafes we saw several ranges of mountains instead. The heat is terrific and we are trying to counteract it by drinking iced beer'. Another joked that it was 'an absolute impossibility for me to keep Jack in order. He has broken at least 50 hearts all over the country'. Jack himself, like their other brother Charley in Alaska, tried to convey a sense of the vividness of his experiences to his sister. He wrote of having a 'Café complet' while waiting for his boat, of passing through Felsentor with its 'huge masses of stone', and of 'sitting down not very far from this scene' on the front of a card showing the Maderanertal valley, adding on the back: 'It is the ideal of Alpine scenery … This is Switzerland', thus conflating Switzerland with its tourist attractions in the same way that tourists to Ireland might mistake Killarney for the whole country.

Jack 's foreign travel also seems to have made him feel a stronger sense of his own Irish identity. According to Berghoff and Korte,

> tourism plays a prominent role in the formation of national identities and stereotypes. The encounter with the unfamiliar forces the traveler to reflect on his or her home country, to define his or her own place in the world and to erect borderlines between him or herself and the foreign.[83]

He made a point of signing off some of his postcards with Irish versions of his name, 'Seaghán' or 'Seán', drank a bottle of Guinness (underlining the word) when he arrived in Basel, and reported that at one stage all the people around them were 'gibbering' in French, German and English which allowed him and his friends 'to fall back on Irish'.

Most of Jack's postcards feature picturesque scenery, and some show middle-class tourists appreciating it (Figure 54), but as he returned through Belgium on his way home he also sent two cards showing the kind of 'picturesque types' that were so popular with consumers of picture postcards. These cards show local milkmaids, smiling young women pouring milk into churns and loading the churns onto a cart pulled by dogs (see Figure 55). Dog-drawn carts were a tradition that survived in Belgium and some other countries into the early twentieth century as a means of delivering milk and other goods, but would have seemed exotic to a tourist such as Jack. The cards he sent were produced by the Brussels-based Van Cortenbergh company, but such images were issued by a range of publishers, including Raphael Tuck who published a series in 1908–1909 titled *Dog Life in Belgium* which included several images of milk carts being pulled by dogs.

Figure 54. *Rigi-Kulm (1800 m) und die Berner-Hochalpen*, Edition Photoglob Co., Zurich. Christina Jessop's card collection.

Figure 55. Untitled, Phototypie Van Cortenbergh, Lille-Bruxelles. Christina Jessop's card collection.

Figure 56. *London Life, an Italian Organ Grinder*, Raphael Tuck. Christina Jessop's card collection.

Ireland therefore was not the only country frequently reduced to the picturesque and the exotic. A large proportion of images of 'abroad' in Irish Edwardian postcard collections show quaint-looking people wearing peasant or traditional costumes and engaged in pre-industrial occupations, as well as pretty old-fashioned cottages, romantic little streets in old towns, evocative ruins, castles, cathedrals and the stately homes of the aristocracy, and beautiful scenery, lush or bleak, showing few signs of modern human activities. Modern urban life is shown, of course, but the picturesque is often superimposed on that too. A Tuck oilette card sent to Christina Jessop in 1905 and titled *London Life* is subtitled *An Italian Organ Grinder* and shows a painting of an old man with a long white beard carrying his organ and hat along a London street (see Figure 56). Tuck's *London Life* series also contained images of ice cream, flower and oyster stalls, a street potter and a Punch and Judy show, but also a policeman directing traffic, a sandwich man and a news vendor, a messenger boy, a pavement artist, a shoe polisher outside a tube station, and images of fashionable individuals and crowds strolling along the streets, emerging from a theatre, boating in Battersea Park or attending a ball at Covent Garden.

Tuck's images of other societies, like their representations of Ireland, tended to portray a more limited range of social classes and occupations. Some of their most popular series were issued under the title *Wide Wide World*, and examples frequently occur in the collections examined. *Wide Wide World* included many town and country scenes from all over the world, usually picturesque in their presentation, as well as images of historic buildings such as the Taj Mahal in Agra and the Arch of Titus in Rome, although more modern civic and commercial buildings were also featured. The cards that focused on people, not surprisingly, tended to highlight what might be seen as strange or exotic. The series *Aborigines of Australia*, for instance, which was reissued in Australia and Britain several times from 1908 on, shows traditionally dressed or semi-naked figures hunting, throwing a boomerang, fishing or performing a ritual dance.[84] Such cards were often presented as educational, and perhaps envisaged as sets that children might be encouraged to collect to broaden their knowledge of different countries. Some also included informative text. Thirteen-year-old Delia Green was sent a *Wide Wide World* card in 1908 which showed *A Havasupai Indian Girl*, from the series *Indian Women* (see Figure 57). The young woman in the image is shown against a background of river and mountains and wearing colourful clothing and a feather headdress. The back of the card bears the text 'the Havasupai Indians are intelligent and industrious, though small in number. They inhabit the Havasn or Cataract Canyon in Arizona – part of the famous Grand Canyon of the Colorado River'.

A HAVASUPAI INDIAN GIRL.

Figure 57. *A Havasupai Indian Girl*, Raphael Tuck. Green family collection.

Another unposted *Wide Wide World* card found in the same collection, and used as early as 1906 according to the Tuck DB website, is one of the *Jamaica* set. It shows an idyllic image of a house set in a lush garden and is titled *Great House, Vale Royal, Trelawney* (Figure 58). In front of the house is a large tree, and the card bears the text 'this tree is a noted specimen of the Poncinia Regia. The Great House is the home of the overseer of the sugar plantations'. It would be very difficult for an Irish postcard purchaser or recipient to see the Havasupai woman, like the Irish peasant, as anything but 'other', despite her coming from an 'intelligent and industrious' group. Her clothes are too exotic looking, and her pose against the wild, apparently uninhabited landscape and the evening sky suggests, as with Irish images already discussed, the decline of an older order. She is already from the past. The overseer of the Jamaican sugar plantation, on the other hand, is represented by his Georgian-style house and lush English-looking garden with its notable botanical specimen, and the suggestion is that he is a relatable and contemporary important person. This is despite the fact that the sugar industry in Jamaica was in catastrophic decline since the abolition in the 1830s of the slavery on which it had been built, and that therefore his type is at least as likely to be heading for extinction.

Figure 58. *Great House, Trelawney*, Raphael Tuck. Green family collection.

Figure 59. 'Please drop in ….', Hely's, Dublin. Ellen Duff's card collection.

As noted already in relation to images of Irish people, picturesque 'types' shade very easily into crude stereotypes, and some of the worst were the representations of African Americans which also found their way into Ireland and Irish postcard collections. The major mainstream postcard publishers such as Valentine's and Raphael Tuck issued numerous series of what they termed 'coon' cards, usually cartoon caricatures with exaggerated features involved in activities such as eating watermelons, stealing chickens and running away from crocodiles. As Brooke Baldwin has stated in 'On the Verso: Postcard Messages as a Key to Popular Prejudices' (1988), in the United States in the early twentieth century 'Black caricatures and racial stereotypes were considered appropriate illustrations for holiday greetings, exchanges of neighbourhood gossip, expressions of concern for bed-ridden loved ones, and declarations of both familial and romantic love'.[85] Although probably less common than in America, they were used in Ireland for similar purposes. Figure 59 shows an example illustrated by Frank Rigney for Hely's in Dublin for one of their 'write-away' cards. The words 'Please drop in' are placed beside a cartoon image of a boy hanging from a branch under which is an open-mouthed crocodile. The sender, Molly, has merely completed the sentence, making no reference to the accompanying image, suggesting that it was seen as just an unremarkable comic card, entertaining and useful for her purpose.

As stated at the start of this chapter, Irish people in the early twentieth century were travelling much more than they had ever done previously, expanding and complicating their world view as a result. Picture postcards played an important role in maintaining communication between families and friends separated by emigration as well as those on shorter leisure journeys. Images sometimes helped people to express what they found difficult to write, or lightened the poignant message on the back, or made it easier to explain the wonder of the tourist sight or experience, while the small space for writing meant that none of this need take up too much time. Also, even for those who did not travel, the picture postcards sent by others, or even just imported into Ireland, became one of the richest and most accessible sources of information about the world, communicating not only facts but also attitudes and values and contributing significantly to their construction of both themselves and others, and the relationship between the two.

Picture postcards, it is clear, had the potential to strongly influence the formation of Irish concepts of 'us' and 'them', concepts which could have far-reaching consequences in terms of racism and attitudes towards non-Irish groups. Similarly, of course they helped construct ideas of Ireland, ideas that sometimes dismayed Irish people and that some tried to control, but that many also internalized and even mobilized in the service of tourism. To quote Urry and Larsen again, they were 'world making'.

Notes

1. L. Paul-Dubois, *Contemporary Ireland* (Dublin: Maunsel, 1908), 350.
2. Thomas E. Jordan, 'The Quality of Life in Victorian Ireland, 1831–1901', *New Hibernia Review / Iris Éireannach Nua*, 4/1 (2000), 103–121, 114.
3. Jordan, 'Quality of Life', 115.
4. Mulhall, *A New Day Dawning*, 49.
5. Paul-Dubois, *Contemporary Ireland*, 354.

6. David Fitzpatrick, 'Ireland Since 1870', in Roy Foster, ed., *The Oxford Illustrated History of Ireland* (Oxford: Oxford University Press, 2000), 213–274, 213.

7. Fitzpatrick, 'Ireland Since 1870', 215.

8. Fitzpatrick, 'Ireland Since 1870', 216.

9. National Archives: Census of Ireland 1901/1911 <http://www.census.nationalarchives.ie/reels/nai003791804/> accessed 11 August 2020.

10. Jordan, 'Quality of Life', 120.

11. Paul-Dubois, *Contemporary Ireland*, 358–359.

12. Plummer F. Jones, *Shamrock-Land: A Ramble through Ireland* (New York: Moffat, Yard & Company, 1908), 289.

13. Robert Lynd, *Home Life in Ireland* (Chicago: A. C. McClurg; London: Mills & Boon, 1910), 48.

14. Fitzpatrick, 'Ireland Since 1870', 216.

15. Jordan, 'Quality of Life', 120.

16. Paul-Dubois, *Contemporary Ireland*, 358–359.

17. Paul-Dubois, *Contemporary Ireland*, 358–359.

18. Fitzpatrick, 'Ireland Since 1870', 216.

19. Jones, *Shamrock-Land*, 287.

20. Gilderdale, *Hands Across the Sea*, 329.

21. McCabe, *Dear Miss B.*, 26, 28.

22. The Canadian census of 1911 cites his occupation as 'miner', and he is based in New Westminster, Vancouver.

23. Michael James Brand, *Transience in Dawson City, Yukon, during the Klondike Gold Rush*, (PhD thesis submitted to the Simon Fraser University, 2003), 7–8.

24. Brand, *Transience in Dawson City*, 50.

25. Brand, *Transience in Dawson City*, 5, 51.

26. Brand, *Transience in Dawson City*, 33.

27. Brand, *Transience in Dawson City*, 85.

28. Brand, *Transience in Dawson City*, 9.

29. Dan Breen and Tom Spalding, *The Cork International Exhibition 1902–1903: A Snapshot of Edwardian Cork* (Newbridge: Irish Academic Press, 2014), 234.

30. R. T. Lang, ed., *Black's Guide to Ireland* (London: Adam and Charles Black, 1906), xv.

31. Jones, *Shamrock-Land*, 24; John Cooke, ed., *Murray's Handbook for Ireland* (London: Edward Stanford, 1906), 12, 460.

32. Cooke, *Murray's Handbook*, 9.

33. Cooke, *Murray's Handbook*, 10–11.

34. Cooke, *Murray's Handbook*, 13.

35. Cooke, *Murray's Handbook*, 13.

36. Cooke, *Murray's Handbook*, 15.

37. Cooke, *Murray's Handbook*, 430.

38. William H. A. Williams, *Creating Irish Tourism: The First Century, 1750–1850* (London, New York, Melbourne, Delhi: Anthem Press, 2010), 35.

39. Williams, *Creating Irish Tourism*, 56.

40. Cooke, *Murray's Handbook*, 440; Cork, Bandon and South Coast Railway Company, *Glengarriff, "Prince of Wales Route" and Killarney* (Cork: Guy & Co., ND), Cork archive Box D 17.2 1999.102/4.7.

41. Williams, *Creating Irish Tourism*, 112–114.

42. See Mark Samuel and Kate Hamlyn, *Blarney Castle: Its History, Development and Purpose* (Cork: Cork University Press, 2007), 67–72.

43. Cooke, *Murray's Handbook*, 369.

44. Hartmut Berghoff and Barbara Korte, 'Britain and the Making of Modern Tourism an Interdisciplinary Approach', in Hartmut Berghoff, Barbara Korte, R. Schneider and C. Harvie, eds, *The Making of Modern Tourism: The Cultural History of the British Experience, 1600–2000* (Basingstoke and New York: Palgrave Macmillan, 2002), 10.

45. Dean MacCannell, *The Tourist. A New Theory of the Leisure Class* (New York: Schocken Books, 1989), 43.

46. MacCannell, *The Tourist*, 43–45.

47. MacCannell, *The Tourist*, 45.

48. MacCannell, *The Tourist*, 41.

49. Williams, *Creating Irish Tourism*, 89.

50. Williams, *Creating Irish Tourism*, 90; John Urry and Jonas Larsen, *The Tourist Gaze 3.0* (London, California, New Delhi and Singapore: Sage, 2011). Kindle book, loc 342. Urry also dates 'the birth of the tourist gaze in the west to around 1840. This is the moment when the "tourist gaze", that peculiar combining together of the means of collective travel, the desire for travel and the techniques of photographic reproduction becomes a core component of western modernity.' (Urry, loc. 401)

51. Cork Public Museum, D17.14 2002.387.

52. James Douglas, quoted in Staff, *The Picture and its Origins*, 79.

53. Carline, *Pictures in the Post*, 44.

54. Carline, *Pictures in the Post*, 59.

55. Cork Public Museum, 2015-08-11 10.52.10.

56. Cork Public Museum 17.12 2002.321.

57. Williams, *Creating Irish Tourism*, 122.

58. Williams, *Creating Irish Tourism*, ix–xi.

59. Williams, *Creating Irish Tourism*, xii.

60. Williams, *Creating Irish Tourism*, 83.

61. Julian Treuherz, *Victorian Painting* (London: Thames and Hudson, 1993), 66.

62. Williams, *Creating Irish Tourism*, 84.

63. Williams, *Creating Irish Tourism*, 183.

64. Quoted in Williams, *Creating Irish Tourism*, 190.

65. Cooke, *Murray's Handbook*, 4–9.

66. Angela Mehegan, 'The Cultural Analysis of Leisure: Tourism and Travels in Co. Donegal', *Circa*, 107 (Spring 2004), 58–62, 59–60.

67. Williams, *Creating Irish Tourism*, 83.

68. Cork Public Museum D17.7 2001.136.

69. TuckDB Postcards website, <https://tuckdbpostcards.org/items/87068> accessed 7/2/20.

70. Brian P. Kennedy, 'The Traditional Irish Thatched House: Image and Reality, 1793–1993', in Adele M. Dalsimer, ed., *Visualising Ireland. National Identity and the Pictorial Tradition* (London: Faber and Faber, 1993), 165–179, 165.

71. TuckDB Postcards website, <https://tuckdbpostcards.org/items/71222> accessed 16 August 2020.

72. TuckDB Postcards website, <https://tuckdbpostcards.org/search?utf8=%E2%9C %93&q=british+character&commit=> accessed 16 August 2020.

73. Cork Public Museum 17.7 2001.187.

74. Lynd, *Home Life in Ireland*, 215.

75. Lynd, *Home Life in Ireland*, 216.

76. Justin Carville, 'Photography, Tourism and Natural History: Cultural Identity and the Visualisation of the Natural World', in Michael Cronin and Barbara O'Connor, eds, *Irish Tourism: Image, Culture and Identity* (Clevedon: Channel View Publications, 2003), 215–240, 233.

77. Carville, 'Photography, Tourism and Natural History', 234.

78. Carville, 'Photography, Tourism and Natural History', 235.

79. Cork Public Museum, D18.12 2003.47.7; D19.15 2005.22.12ne.

80. Urry and Larsen, *The Tourist Gaze*, 167.

81. James Douglas, quoted in Staff, *The Picture Postcard and its Origins*, 79.

82. Cork, Bandon and South Coast Railway, *Prince of Wales Route*.

83. Berghoff and Korte, 'Britain and the Making of Modern Tourism', 8.

84. TuckDB Postcards website, <https://tuckdbpostcards.org/items/86473> accessed 16 August 2020.

85. Brooke Baldwin, 'On the Verso: Postcard Messages as a Key to Popular Prejudices', *Journal of Popular Culture*, 22/3 (1988), 15–28, 17.

A suitable hobby for young ladies: Postcards and women's lives in Edwardian Ireland

Picture postcard collections, especially informal ones, can offer valuable insights into the day-to-day lives, social circles, entertainment, work, interests and values of women during the Edwardian period. They are particularly helpful in what they can tell us about women in the middle and 'respectable' working classes, those who were not from the small social elite whose actions and life-events merited public recording and celebration, nor from the group at the other end of the social spectrum whose lives were so poor and desperate that their names appear in workhouse and court records. Even at the time, those who wrote about Ireland tended to dismiss its middle classes, both men and women, as either non-existent or uninteresting. In 1904 for instance Filson Young, in the middle of a stream of other generalizations, declared that 'the Irish are all serfs or aristocrats; they have no middle class at all'.[1] And Plummer Jones wrote in his chapter 'The Irish Woman – Aristocrat and Peasant' in *Shamrock-Land* (1908),

> broadly speaking, there are but two classes in Ireland – the aristocracy and the peasantry. The inconsequential middle class is modern and artificial, and is found chiefly in north, or 'alien' Ireland, and in the growing commercial cities like Belfast, Londonderry and Dublin ... The women of this commercial or farming middle class in Ireland are in no marked manner different from the women of similar classes elsewhere; it is the Irish woman aristocrat who is the most interesting study in the world, if, indeed, it is not the Irish peasant woman.[2]

For the historian, postcard collections offer one of the relatively few windows into the lives of the broad group between the aristocratic and peasant classes. They suggest the sort of popular culture they were exposed to and the media messages that contributed to their world view, as well as how they interacted with these and with each other.

As mentioned already, the images on the cards in all the personal collections examined for this book feature numerous examples of 'views' and 'picturesque' people, both Irish and foreign, attractive women, cute children and animals, flowers, artwork reproductions and comedic cartoons, all indicating particular personal and group tastes. Christina's collection contains only a few comic cards, for instance, while Ellen collected many of them, and both of them (or their correspondents) seem to have been very fond of actress cards, as indeed were all of the collectors studied here with the exceptions of Brigid Byrne and John O'Reilly. Both Christina and the Green family collected a small number of religiously themed images, such as photographs of the Pope or other prominent Catholic churchmen, but such cards do not appear at all in Ellen's collection. Christina's collection is the only one containing messages and addresses written in the Irish language, but all the collections feature cards with Ireland-themed images and motifs such as shamrocks, particularly that of Brigid Byrne, possibly because she seems to have spent a great deal of time away from Ireland and therefore was often sent greetings from there. There is no reference to women's suffrage on any of the cards examined, despite the fact that it was one of the talked-about issues of the day and such cards were in circulation.[3] There are cards and added text which refer to other topical political issues, such as the Home Rule movement, but these feature only in Christina's and John O'Reilly's collections, and are absent from the rest. John O'Reilly's collection makes an interesting comparison to the other, women's, collections, in that it contains a higher proportion of comic and 'write-away' cards, often based on the themes of flirting or excessive alcohol consumption, and the images and jokes are frequently referred to in the added text, suggesting that they were deliberately chosen in order to communicate a particular message. One example, for instance, shows a drunken man lying on the ground, and the sender has written on the back of the card 'Hope this doesn't happen to you soon?' The text added to the cards also tends more towards the use of slang expressions than that in the other collections (people are frequently referred to as 'A1', for instance) and includes more numerous observations on national, local and union politics. Similarities and differences between individual collections are usually of limited value however, unless there are a large number of collections examined, and it is more fruitful to examine the cards generally in relation to a range of broader themes relevant to the lives of women in early twentieth-century Ireland. This chapter will therefore look at the postcard collections under the following headings: Family and Social life, Work and Education and The Consumption of Popular and Celebrity Culture. The final section will discuss the ways in which women were constructed in popular postcard imagery.

Family and social life

As has been discussed already in Chapter 2, one of the most popular functions of picture postcards was the maintenance of relationships, and this was often via the heavy use of phatic dialogue, a form of communication whose primary purpose was engagement with others rather than the delivery of information. As a result, many of the messages on postcards were understandable only to their intended recipients at the time, and are even more opaque to the modern reader. They nevertheless help to construct a sense of the richness of interpersonal communication at the time. The postcard collections examined are full of family news: examples in Christina's collection, for instance, include messages such as 'Jim got a scholarship in Fermoy' or 'Denis is quite well again (I suppose you heard he drank some iodine and nearly did away with himself)'. In Christina's case these messages are more easily interpreted than many others, as her cards can be contextualized using other sources such as family history. Jim was her fiancé's younger brother and Denis was the small son of his sister, Agnes. These and many other cards, sent to her from various members of the Wilson family in Queenstown, can be seen as keeping her up-to-date with their family news in the run-up to her later move to Queenstown and her marriage into the family, functioning to consolidate bonds between the young Dublin women and her future in-laws. The Carmody sisters in Ennis similarly used picture postcards to maintain their family closeness while geographically separated, sending long newsy messages, some more like letters than typical postcard texts, containing gossip, references to fabrics and clothes patterns and queries and reports on health and educational achievements. Real photo postcards of family members could also be sent as a means of communicating a particular experience or, again, updating others on family news. Thus Jack, Christina's fiancé, sent her from Belfast a picture of himself and three other young men enjoying what looks like a trip to the countryside, writing on the back 'Isn't this a lot of beauties?' Another correspondent, Imelda Dillon, sent her a photo postcard from Birmingham, Alabama, of a small child, beside which she wrote: 'This is my little brother Wentworth. Taken just after we came back.' Real photo cards were a way of making experiences and people more real and vivid to the recipients, and thus helping to bridge physical distances between them.

Despite the medium's lack of privacy, people did not just write platitudes on postcards: heartfelt emotions were sometimes expressed. Julia, for example, wrote to Brigid Byrne in 1903: 'I hope you are real well and still on the lands of the living. If so please write soon as I am longing to hear from you. I never forget u.' After her sister got married and left their shared apartment, Christina's friend Margery wrote to her in 1907: 'You must feel very lonely. I wish I were near you', and another of Christina's correspondents, Mary, frequently reported feeling very lonely and on one occasion told her that she had had the 'blues' for a week.

In *Ireland at the Crossroads*, Filson Young also wrote about what he saw as the Catholic Church's too-strict suppression of social and sexual relationships in Ireland, and he was not the only commentator who thought this was a problem at the time.[4] This, however, is not so evident from the postcard collections, which feature lots of jokey, cheeky variations on the subject of flirtation and forbidden or naughty lovers' meetings, especially in Ellen's and John's collections. A typical example from Ellen's collection, sent to her in 1906, is titled *Over the Garden Wall* and shows a very cross-looking woman waving an umbrella at a man scrambling over a wall (hat abandoned on the ground) while a girl sits guiltily looking at the ground. Senders also sometimes mischievously interacted with the published imagery and text. Mention has already been made of the card in Ellen's album showing a seductively reclining woman with the words 'From Herbert' scrawled across the torso and thigh of her dress (see Figure 10). Another card, postmarked from Wicklow in 1905, is titled *Fol-The-Rol-Lol*, and features a photograph of a man and woman dancing closely together with the verse underneath:

> MacDuff met a girl at Nuneaton
> Her figure had plenty of meat on!
> She said: 'marry me, Mac,
> And you'll find that my back
> Is a nice place to warm your cold feet on!

The sender has cheekily written 'Warm just now' on the back, signed only with his or her initials. A generic tourist card sent to John in Ballinrobe, County Mayo features an image of numerous couples embracing by moonlight, titled *Everyone is doing it at Tourmakeady* (see Figure 60). His correspondent wrote on the back 'Anything such as the opposite to be had in B'robe'?[5]

Figure 60. *Everybody is doing it at Tourmakeady*, Joseph Asher, London. John O'Reilly/ Bessie Caulfield collection.

Even those whose cards and messages were more restrained provide a great deal of evidence of active and varied social lives involving a range of people, both men and women. In Christina's collection there are many mentions of Gaelic League activities, and indeed commentators have noted at the time and since that the Gaelic League helped to rejuvenate the social life of young Irish people, particularly in rural areas. Christina's friends in Queenstown report enjoying Gaelic classes and *feiseanna*, while in Dublin a great deal of her time seems to have been absorbed by Keating Branch meetings and attendance at Irish-language dramas put on by League members. The Gaelic League, for the time, was unusually open to the participation of women on equal terms to men, and to women in leadership roles, so that, as Biletz has argued, it 'contributed significantly to enlarging the public role of women'.[6]

Many other social activities are also mentioned throughout all the collections, such as going to weddings, balls, including fancy dress balls, dancing generally, skating, boating and visits to the theatre and to various exhibitions and fairs. People also seem to have casually socialized regularly in each other's homes: for instance, one of her Dublin friends wrote to Christina in 1906 asking her to come over to her house the following evening with her sister and 'bring some fancy work with you'. Travel had become common for work and tourist purposes as discussed in Chapter 5, but also to visit friends and family who lived some distance away. Christina's card collection suggests that she travelled frequently between Dublin and Queenstown, and that her friends and relatives were similarly mobile, travelling a great deal also between Ireland and Britain.

Religion also contributed to the social lives of Christina's friends, although there are few specific references on the cards to regular communal rituals such as Sunday Mass, which by the early twentieth century was a central aspect of life for Irish Catholics. However, excursions to Mount Melleray, a Trappist monastery near Cappoquin in County Kilkenny which included accommodation and tours for guests, are mentioned often. Religious matters tend to be referred to casually in ways that suggest that it was a taken-for-granted aspect of life at the time in Ireland. Thus Mary in Queenstown complained to Christina in April 1905, 'Hope you are getting over Lent alright. I am nearly a corpse from it.' and three weeks later told her, probably somewhat mischievously, 'We are having a Retreat here on Sunday week so we will be very good.' The secular fun of religious holidays was also enjoyed. In 1905, for instance, Liz wrote from Youghal: 'I hope you have a jolly Easter … I hope you won't eat too many eggs.'

During the period examined, the Carmody sisters at different stages either lived at home with their mother and brother or away at school, while the Greens seem to have remained a family group that included both parents, and it is difficult to ascertain the social constraints on Brigid Byrne. However, Christina's, Ellen's and John's collections were put together by young, unmarried people all earning their own money and no longer living with their parents, and perhaps their social lives reflect a relatively unusual freedom for the time.

Work and education

By 1900 women in Ireland had the right to own property and some could vote in local government elections, but they had no parliamentary franchise and a woman's role was generally seen as in the private rather than the public sphere. Thus women working for wages outside the home (and suffragettes demanding the right to vote) often attracted negative commentary, especially if they were married with children. Despite the establishment of the Irish Women's Suffrage and Local Government Association in 1876 and the Irish Women's Suffrage League in 1908, Tony Farmar has argued that 'for most people (male and female) the position of women was clearly in the home. Most men took the view that woman's suffrage was probably against the natural law'. He quotes the 'plain man's view' from the *Freeman's Journal* in June 1907:

> The 'smart' woman and sometimes the advanced woman sneer at the old-fashioned notion that a woman's life should be lived for her husband and her children. The man who is worth his salt realizes that his first duty is by the toil of his brains or his hands to make and keep a home for his wife and family. The woman can have no higher duty than to make that home happy.[7]

The Catholic Church also emphasized the importance of women remaining in the home, and encouraged them to adopt the Virgin Mary as their role model. An article in *The Irish Rosary* in 1898 criticized those women

> who always seem to be ill at ease in their homes, and who gladly catch at every passing pretext for spending their time outside their safe protection! Hence the widespread frivolity of the young, the decadence of family affection, the multiplied dangers to youth, and the too frequent evidences of domestic unhappiness.[8]

Lambert McKenna, a prominent Irish Jesuit writer on social issues, also claimed in 1913 that the modern world was heading for ruin 'in pressing women into the rough and tumble fight for existence, in putting before her, as her ideal, the modern virago instead of the gentle maid of Nazareth, in setting her up, not as a help but as a rival of man'.[9]

Many women, by choice or otherwise, did not marry nor have children, and many wives and mothers were forced to seek paid work out of economic necessity, but nevertheless, Eileen Breathnach argues, 'For the middle and upper middle class urban woman, convention dictated that work and career were no part of her life even for those who failed to marry or enter a convent, in which case the family was expected to provide support.'[10] Rosemary Cullen Owens similarly states that

> into the early decades of the twentieth century 'paid' work was accepted as necessary only for certain categories of women, mainly those from poor laboring and small farming backgrounds. The work available was generally domestic service, low-paid factory work or seasonal agricultural labour.[11]

However she adds that 'following the expansion of female education, a small but significant number of middle-class women began to enter the workforce from the 1890s, concentrated in newly emerging white-collar clerical jobs, teaching and nursing'.[12] And indeed, another article from *The Irish Rosary* in 1900 titled 'A Residence for Business Girls' begins with a statement that conjures up a spectacle of crowds of young women caught up in a daily rush-hour commute to work:

> The day has gone by when the sons only left the country home to seek a career and find their fortunes in the capital [London]. Nowadays parents must part also with

their daughters, and are obliged too often to see them … add another to the ever-increasing numbers who fill the trams and swell the throng every morning in the week on their road to business in the city.[13]

The fact of women working outside the home was therefore increasingly recognized, if not necessarily welcomed, and according to Cullen Owens by the early twentieth century even 'a permanent pensionable career was becoming an acceptable role for a Catholic woman'.[14]

All the women whose collections were looked at here, other than those in the Green family, were either in employment outside their home or, as in the case of Rennie Carmody, in full-time education to be a teacher. Christina Jessop's cards, as mentioned already, can be contextualized far more than the other collections, so a more detailed reconstruction of her working life is possible. During most of the period of her postcard collection Christina worked as an apothecary to the South Dublin Union (or workhouse) in James's Street, a fifteen- to twenty minute-walk from where she lived at 33, South Earl Street.[15] Although the postcards were sent to her home address, many of them include the letters LPSI or MPSI after her name, the senders choosing to highlight the fact that she was a licentiate or, later, a full member of the Pharmaceutical Society of Ireland. The line between work and leisure was further blurred as the cards were occasionally used to communicate for work purposes. In 1905, for instance, Christina's brother Jack, also an apothecary and based in the village of Skerries at the time, sent her the message 'Please post me on a dozen bandages', written on the back of a picture of Dublin Zoo.[16] On other cards the problem of juggling work and free time is suggested: in July 1905 a friend in Queenstown urges her to 'do her best' to get Sunday off as she tells her they have been boating during the lovely weather.[17]

Female apothecaries were relatively unusual at the time. According to Margaret Ó'hÓgartaigh, while women successfully applied for membership of the British Pharmaceutical Society from as early as 1879, by 1908 they still constituted only 1 per cent of its membership, and about 60 per cent of those worked in hospitals and institutions, as Christina did, possibly because of difficulties private pharmacies perceived in getting the public to accept a front-of-house female apothecary.[18] Ó'hÓgartaigh also argues that problems for would-be female apothecaries lay 'as in medicine … not in qualifying, but in establishing oneself'.[19] In 1896, when she was seventeen, Christina began attending evening classes at the City of Dublin Technical Schools and Science and Art Schools in Lower Kevin Street. She also simultaneously worked a four-year apprenticeship with the apothecary Thomas A. Furlong at a dispensary at 17 Upper Merrion Street. In 1900 she received a certificate from the Pharmaceutical Society of Ireland, certifying that she had been examined in Botany, Materia Medica, Chemistry and Pharmacy, and was qualified to act as a Pharmaceutical Chemist. She was only the second female in Ireland to do so, and the rarity of her qualification for a female is highlighted by the fact that an 's' had to be manually inserted before the word 'he' on the printed certificate (see Figure 61).

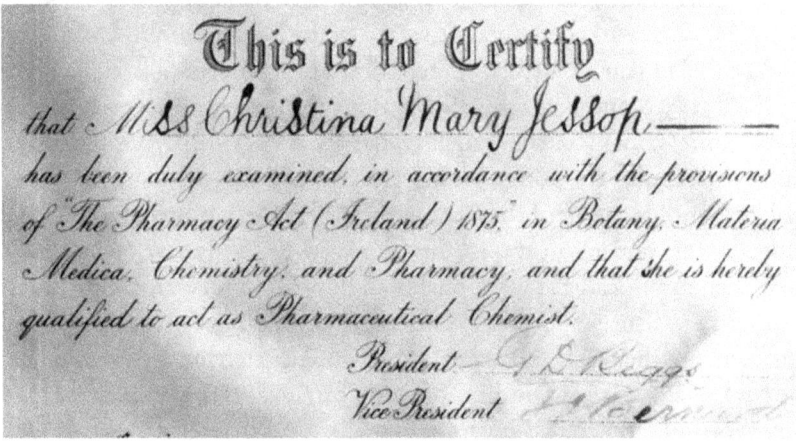

Figure 61. Christina Jessop's certificate stating her qualification as a pharmacist. Private collection.

Christina was both motivated and unusually privileged to acquire her pharmacist's qualification and job. Her father was 61 when he died in 1900, the year she qualified, and her mother died in 1903 at the age of 60, leaving Christina and her siblings to support themselves financially. Her father had been Assistant Master of the South Dublin Union from 1872 until his death, so that the family were sufficiently well off to pay for the education of their children. Christina also had the advantage that her father probably knew people who could help his daughter in her chosen career, so that she was able to serve her apprenticeship and afterwards find work. Her brother Jack had also already qualified as a pharmacist and worked as apothecary to the District Dispensary on South Earl Street, the building which also housed the family's living accommodation.

Writing of female pharmacists in Ireland who qualified in the 1920s, a generation after Christina, Ó'hÓgartaigh suggests that 'Irish female pharmacists may have been attracted to a profession where their presence, while not encouraged, was, at least, acceptable.'[20] Those who supported increasing the proportion of women working in pharmacy highlighted what they saw as the compatibility between what was required to do a good job as an apothecary and women's 'natural' characteristics. A paper written in 1905 by Sister Mary Ignatius for *The American Journal of Nursing* forcefully put this case. She argued that women were more inclined than men to pay attention to detail, and that the tradition of female pharmacy extended back to 'Mother Eve, who knew the names of the herbs from the first, knew also their especial properties and how to apply them to the needs of her family, and ... handed on her knowledge to her children's children'.[21] She also claimed that women were neater than men and less 'wasteful or destructive in handling materials and utensils', and that therefore it made more economic sense to employ them. Having thus mobilized motherhood, tradition and a peculiarly feminine care for detail, she finished her argument with a claim which was sure to appease even the most stalwart Edwardian traditionalist: 'Moreover, it is generally conceded that where an educated, cultured woman presides peace and good order are generally to be found.'[22]

The references obtained by Christina for her job applications suggest similar attitudes. The apothecary to whom she had been apprenticed, Thomas Furlong, said that she was 'a most reliable, neat and efficient compounder, at all times punctual and attentive to her duties'. Her Chemistry lecturer, Peter Bertram Foy, claimed she was 'a most gifted and careful student' as well as a 'conscientious and skilful worker', and J. P. Quinn, a medical officer from the Grand Canal-Street Dispensary where she worked in 1900 and 1901, praised her 'thorough efficiency and extreme kindliness of manner, as well as … promptitude and punctuality'.[23] Pharmacy there-fore, like teaching and nursing, could be seen as a profession particularly suited to femininity as it was then constructed. However, it also provided Christina with a greater level of freedom and independence than that en-joyed by most young unmarried middle-class women. On the 1901 census, for instance, when she was 22 years old, she was recorded as 'head of house-hold', staying alone in a four-roomed residence in the Dispensary at 8, Grand Canal Street, her then workplace. At some stage before 1903, pos-sibly through their shared studies or work, she met Jack Wilson, a young man from Queenstown who also became a pharmacist, and they married in June 1908. Some of the postcards Jack sent to Christina in 1907 commu-nicate information to her about a premises they could rent in Queenstown to establish their own pharmacy, which they subsequently did. Christina and Jack had their first child in 1909 and their second in 1911, but she is still recorded on the 1911 Census of Ireland as a Pharmaceutical Chemist, as is her husband.[24] Her qualifications and experience were essential for her economic survival after 1922, when Jack died and she was left alone to bring up their six young children.

Christina was more privileged both socially and financially than the other working postcard collectors looked at here. Ellen Duff, for instance, was a waitress, recorded as aged 27 on the 1911 census and working and living at Fleming's Restaurant, 1, South Great Georges Street in Dublin, the address to which most of her postcards were sent. The restaurant manager and Ellen's boss was 31-year-old Elizabeth Middleton.[25] Number 1, South Great Georges Street no longer exists, and it has not been possible to find out anything about Fleming's restaurant, but according to Máirtín Mac Con Iomhaire the fact that it was managed by a woman suggests that it may have been a restaurant at the lower end of the market.[26] Like Christina's job in the Grand Canal Dispensary, Ellen's included accommodation on the premises, although she had none of Christina's privacy or space as she shared with six other women, one of them her boss, in a restaurant building which in total consisted of five rooms. Her waitressing job was very likely to have been low-paid and have long hours, but her postcard collection suggests a young woman with a lively social life and an interest in many things, particularly theatre and theatre celebrities. There is no reference on any of Ellen's postcards to her work, other than a friend hoping they can both get time off for holidays at the same time.

Christina's sister Rose was recorded on the 1901 census as a dressmaker. Kathleen Clarke, who later became a founder member of Cumann na mBan and then a politician, was also a dressmaker and a contemporary of the Jessop sisters, and she referred to dressmaking in her autobiography as one of the few fields in which girls could make a living at the time.[27] Dressmaking could be very profitable, and indeed Clarke built up her own very successful business in Limerick, but dressmakers could also be poorly paid outworkers for clothing factories, finishing and embellishing garments from home, or, Mary Daly suggests in her book *Dublin, The Deposed Capital, a Social and Economic History, 1860–1914* (1984) 'self-employed workers doing repairs and making garments for a small number of personal customers. Their earnings were presumably low and highly uncertain while unemployment must have been a common phenomenon'.[28] Rose's situation is not known, but by the time the 1911 census was taken she had given up her job and was married with small children, and no occupation is recorded for her.

According to Daly, employment opportunities for women in dress-making declined from around 1871 due to the increased mass production of cheap ready-made clothes, made possible by the invention of the sewing machine and the emergence of department stores.[29] However, there were still many women employed as dressmakers, and many more women began to work in drapers' shops, where textiles for making clothes were sold, but also, increasingly, ready-to-wear garments: according to Caitriona Clear 'the number of women drapers rose by 40 per cent between 1891 and 1911'.[30] Margaret Wilson, Christina's 53-year-old future mother-in-law, and her 20-year-old daughter are both recorded on the 1901 census as drapers by occupation. Margaret, whose maiden name was Higgins, ran Higgins' drapery shop in Harbour Row in Queenstown from a building which she possibly inherited and which was also the Wilson family home. Her husband James Wilson worked as secretary of the Gas Company.[31] Interestingly, the only male whose postcards were examined here, John O'Reilly, seems to have been a draper's assistant who worked and lived in a series of shops in small towns throughout Galway and Mayo during the years of his postcard collection. Clear states that shop assistants 'often "lived in", [lived on the business premises] particularly in provincial towns where accommodation was hard to find', and until unions 'put a stop to it in the early twentieth century, shops kept assistants on their feet until 10 or 11 pm'.[32] Based on comments on his postcards, John and/or his friends seem to have been active in the Drapers' Assistants' Association (DAA), a trade union founded in 1901 with the aims of achieving for its members 'a minimum wage, fixed hours and payment for overtime, sick benefits, a weekly half-holiday' and the abolition of the living-in system, which placed workers under 'constant supervision and subjected to the discipline of the employer for practically twenty-four hours a day ... often housed in over-crowded unhealthy dormitories, sometimes being locked in at night'.[33] John received a card from a friend in New York, dated possibly 1911 (the number is unclear), saying 'Hope the D.A.A. is still going on good and that ye have no black legs in town now'.[34]

Christina's postcard collection also offers some insight into another profession significantly populated by women, teaching. Fifty per cent of National School teachers in 1900 were women, paid only eighty per cent of the salaries of male teachers, but the job was respected, secure and pensionable.[35] Rennie Carmody was training in Southampton to be a teacher during the period examined, and there are also cards in the Cahir album sent to and from Bessie Caulfield, a National School teacher living in Inver in Bangor Erris in County Mayo, but none of these offers particular insight into their teaching experience. Christina, however, received several postcards from Margery Leonard, a teacher whose messages suggest a difficult working life and lack of the security of a government job. In 1905 Margery lived in lodgings in Edgeworthstown in County Longford and in 1906, at the age of 30, she moved with her widowed mother to Finea, a small village on the border of Counties Westmeath and Cavan.[36] She wrote to Christina in 1905 saying that she now had 'four different classes & one is about 6 miles off, in the Co. Westmeath'. She went to Athlone to do a course in Kindergarten in August 1907, but on the 1911 census she and her mother are recorded as sharing a two-roomed dwelling in Finea, and no occupation is recorded for either of them.[37] Margery nevertheless seems to have been enthusiastic about her teaching: in March 1906 she told Christina about a concert in which she was involved, telling her it was 'a wonderful success. Everyone was delighted especially the pupils'. According to Clear, 'private teaching was the default occupation of genteel women, just as domestic service was for laboring class women'.[38] Whether this was Margery's situation or not is unclear, but her postcards combined with the Census information highlight some of the difficulties that many middle-class women may have faced in earning a living.

Ideas about the social roles of men and women also influenced how girls were educated. Many, especially in the middle classes, prioritized the education of boys over girls, since the prevailing view was that girls would marry or at least remain in the domestic sphere, requiring therefore only basic levels of literacy and numeracy, whereas boys would have to provide financially for themselves and their families. Nevertheless, a small but increasing number of middle-class parents began to see secondary education for girls as desirable for various reasons, although frequently, as Breathnach argues, its 'object was to equip girls with accomplishments considered suitable for young ladies'.[39] The passing of the Intermediate Education Act in 1878 provided a structure for both boys' and girls' secondary schooling and a system for funding schools based on the awarding of prizes based on examination results. According to Cullen Owens, this system 'gave a new generation of young women access to the world of competitive examinations, with recognition and reward for academic endeavour'.[40]

As discussed already, Christina attended courses in science in the Kevin Street Technical School for her pharmacy qualification, but her previous convent secondary school education, even though it was in the relatively progressive Dominican College in Eccles Street, seems to have been typical of that provided for girls as opposed to boys. Boys could do subjects such as Latin and Greek, and Science and Mathematics to a high level, whereas girls' schools often did not have the resources to offer these subjects.[41] Christina's Junior Grade Intermediate certificate from 1894 records her passing English, French, Arithmetic, and Domestic Economy, with Honours in Drawing and Music.[42] According to Deirdre Raftery, Judith Harford and Susan M. Parkes, by 1885 there were eighty-nine girls' schools receiving results fees from the Intermediate Board, including the Eccles Street Dominican College, but while girls could do any of the subjects on offer, a number of subjects became 'girls' subjects' only; these were botany, theory of music, and domestic economy and hygiene. One of the dilemmas for girls' schools was whether to offer a curriculum for girls which would be the same as that for boys or whether the distinct needs of girls should be recognised.[43]

Some members of the Catholic hierarchy in Ireland were determined to prevent the broader education of girls for other than the domestic sphere. According to Breathnach, in 1895 the Bishop of Limerick in his prize day speech in Laurel Hill Convent asserted, 'We have no girl graduates here, nor even Intermediate students but we are working away on old Catholic rules and principles and I am not aware that we lose anything thereby.'[44] Despite the Catholic beliefs and values evident from her postcard collection, however, Christina as an adult seems to have had little problem with abandoning such 'old Catholic rules and principles' in order to do what she felt she wanted or needed to do.

The Catholic Church continued to have a significant influence on the education of both boys and girls into the twentieth century. Secondary schools were denominational and privately run, and Catholic girls' schools were run by religious orders such as the Dominicans, the Ursulines and the Loreto Order. Christina's teenage friend May Crimmins sent her many postcards from her boarding school, Loreto Abbey in Rathfarnham. One card is a real photo card of her hockey team ('here I am' she wrote on the back) and on many of them she asks when Christina will visit her at the school. According to Mary Hatfield, Loreto advertised 'their students' successful transformations into genteel ladies at student exhibitions and prize ceremonies. Their curricular offerings privileged foreign language tuition, dance, music and other feminine accomplishments'.[45] The girls were also closely supervised:

> One of the regulations introduced, which continued in Loreto schools during the twentieth century, was the constant presence of an adult with the pupils. A nun slept in the student dormitories, accompanied girls on their way to class and chapel and presided over meals. Anxieties about moral corruption, bad language and disobedience prompted this highly regulated environment.[46]

School life was permeated with Catholicism. May wrote more than once of having 'just come out of retreat' and almost always signed her cards 'May E. de M.', 'E. de M.', an abbreviation of 'Enfant de Marie', identifying

herself as a member of the Children of Mary, a Catholic devotional society. May was still able to make space in her life for popular culture, however, and one of the cards on which she announced her emergence from
retreat (and signed as 'May E. de M.') features a painting of a woman by
the Italian painter Angelo Asti from a series published by Raphael Tuck.
The subject's seductive appearance and about-to-fall-off robe suggest that
May have managed to escape the nuns' supervision, if only briefly (see
Figure 62).

Figure 62. Angelo Asti, *Rosalind*, Raphael Tuck. Christina Jessop's card collection.

Entertainment and celebrity culture

Stephanie Rains has written of the leisure culture that became increasingly prominent in Ireland and elsewhere towards the end of the nineteenth century, evidenced by 'the rise of music halls, department stores, day-trip tourism and of course the media itself', of which picture postcards constituted a significant aspect by the early twentieth century.[47] Kevin Rockett also mentions the increased circulation of the modern press, which 'brought into Ireland ideas and images which had been produced in the first instance for Britain's industrial working class'.[48] Irish people were therefore more exposed than ever before to international trends in popular culture, and the imagery and added messages of the postcard collections examined here reference popular tourist resorts, fashions, dances and theatrical productions, as well as the celebrities associated with them. Dublin and other Irish cities presented commercial public entertainment in theatres and music halls, the latter distinguished from the former in permitting drinking and eating in the auditorium and including 'circuses, boxing matches, and topical sketches' in their programmes.

> Irish halls employed local performers, but were also part of a circuit followed by famous British acts such as Marie Lloyd and Harry Lauder ... All classes attended shows at the halls, though they were condemned by churchmen and temperance campaigners. By 1910 music halls were the premier entertainment venue for Ireland's growing urban population, though most Irish halls were now owned by British conglomerates.[49]

The British musical comedies that toured in Irish theatres and music halls tended to be funny, sentimental, unchallenging and largely indistinguishable from each other, featuring formulaic stories, often with a rags-to-riches theme, and catchy tunes.[50] The enthusiasm they could generate, however, is indicated by a card sent to Micko Carmody in Ennis from Dublin in 1906, from someone who attended the musical comedy *The Catch of the Season* (see Figure 63). The front of the card features a photograph of the stars of the show, Ellaline Terriss and Seymour Hicks, and on the back the following text was written:

1597 D MISS ELLALINE TERRISS AND MR. SEYMOUR HICKS. ROTARY PHOTO.

Figure 63. *Miss Ellanine Terriss and Mr Seymour Hicks*, Rotary. Carmody family collection.

You can imagine you are at the 'Catch of the Season' when you see this. It's from the last scene, they are going to be married. Imagine the front rows of the upper circle 1/ – part is booked at 1/6, no access to Parterre unless by ticket. The house is crowded.

Gossip about stars and reviews of the shows were printed in Irish newspapers, although, as with George Cecil's 'Musical Matters' (1909) in
the *Cork Examiner*, many of these articles were clearly syndicated from
English sources. The tone of Cecil's writing was similar to that of many
others on the subject, sarcastic and amused:

> London's musical comedies, which, as a rule, are devoid of music and comedy, are,
> as the modern vernacular has it, going strong. 'Our Miss Gibbs', 'The Acadians' and
> 'Dear Little Denmark', still attract the *jeunesse doree*, and the heroines of each piece
> smirk from countless picture postcards.[51]

Despite his fastidiousness, Cecil recognized the immense popularity of
these shows, and the large market for images of their actress stars in particular. As Viv Gardner has argued, 'the photographic postcard industry
became enormously important in the commodification and mass circulation of performers' images'.[52] Postcards functioned efficiently on one level
to promote shows and performers, available for sale not only from all the
usual postcard outlets but also in theatres.[53] However, they also played an
essential role in the creation and perpetuation of a huge celebrity culture
in the era before cinemas and mass-produced, widely distributed films.
Stage performances could only reach a relatively limited urban audience,
but photographic picture postcards of their stars made it easy for people
living in even remote areas who had never seen a stage performance to collect and engage with their images. Newspapers and other periodicals fed
into this culture by regularly reporting on the doings of these stars, especially their romantic lives. A typical example is an article in the *Freemans
Journal* in September 1908 reporting on rumours that the English actress
Marie Studholme was planning to marry for a second time. The writer
called Studholme the 'inventor of the "toothsome smile"' and went on to
claim that she had 'taken the record as a picture postcard favourite'. He or
she also favourably assessed the actress as having 'more animation, more
good humour, than her rivals – at least in her photographs – in addition
to being the very pink of prettiness'.[54] Reports such as this both assumed
and further cultivated public interest in the lives and appearance of theatre stars, driving up the production and sales of their postcard images,

which in turn, of course, fostered an even more widespread hunger for information about them. The Cork Museum postcard collection contains a photographic postcard of Marie Studholme, signed by the star herself and dated 1909 (see Figure 64). Possibly she signed it when Frank Curzon's London production of the musical *My Mimosa Maid, A Riviera Musical Incident in Two Acts* opened for six nights in the Cork Opera House in February 1909. Studholme played Paulette, the Head Girl on the Mimosa Plantation on which it was set, and on advertisements for it her name appeared above and in much larger type than that of any of the other performers, and even of Curzon himself (see Figure 65).

From the card collections looked at for this book, it seems that young Irish women were avid collectors of such actress images. As Veronica Kelly has noted in her article 'Beauty and the Market: Actress Postcards and their Senders in Early Twentieth-Century Australia' (2004), actress postcard imagery was aimed primarily at female fans, 'catering less for the male gaze than to a demographic of youthful female desire for idealized self-fashioning'.[55] Christina's collection features actresses and singers, most of them English, who were popular throughout the British Empire, such as Marie Studholme, Gabrielle Ray, Nina Sevening, the Dare sisters, Phyllis and Zena, Gertie Millar, Isabel Jay, Doris Stocker and many others. Although one card shows the American star Maude Fealy posed dramatically and staring intently at the camera as if playing a specific role, many actress postcard images from the period are not linked specifically to stage performances, but are carefully constructed portraits of smiling or slightly wistful pretty young women, usually gowned elaborately in pale-coloured frills, ribbons and lace, as in the image of Doris Stocker sent to Christina on 10 August 1905 (Figure 66). Sometimes they are posed sitting in a basket or on a swing or involved in some playful activity. Kelly quotes the theatre critic and journalist Herbert Farjeon on the various presentations of Edwardian actresses on postcards:

> [Farjeon] recalled seeing rows and rows of glossy musical comedy beauties in the alluring windows of the stationers. Some of them were smiling to display their dazzling white teeth, some peering coyly over parasols, some swinging on swings, some perching on crescent moons, some reveling in snow, some with their doggies, some punting, some canoeing, some in pyjamas, some in furs.[56]

Figure 64. *Marie Studholme*, Rotary. Cork Public Museum archive, postcard collection
19.2.2003.72.22.

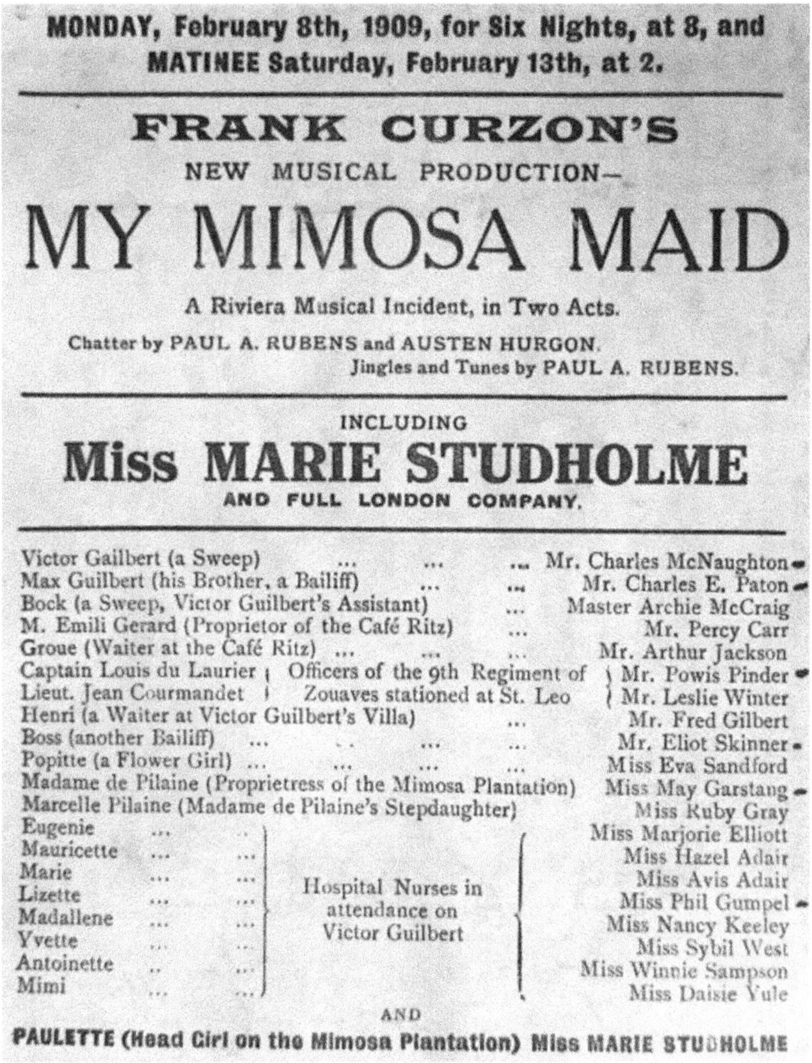

MONDAY, February 8th, 1909, for Six Nights, at 8, and MATINEE Saturday, February 13th, at 2.

FRANK CURZON'S

NEW MUSICAL PRODUCTION—

MY MIMOSA MAID

A Riviera Musical Incident, in Two Acts.

Chatter by PAUL A. RUBENS and AUSTEN HURGON.
Jingles and Tunes by PAUL A. RUBENS.

INCLUDING

Miss MARIE STUDHOLME

AND FULL LONDON COMPANY.

Victor Gailbert (a Sweep)	Mr. Charles McNaughton
Max Guilbert (his Brother, a Bailiff) ...	Mr. Charles E. Paton
Bock (a Sweep, Victor Guilbert's Assistant) ...	Master Archie McCraig
M. Emili Gerard (Proprietor of the Café Ritz) ...	Mr. Percy Carr
Groue (Waiter at the Café Ritz)	Mr. Arthur Jackson
Captain Louis du Laurier ⎱ Officers of the 9th Regiment of ⎰	Mr. Powis Pinder
Lieut. Jean Courmandet ⎰ Zouaves stationed at St. Leo ⎱	Mr. Leslie Winter
Henri (a Waiter at Victor Guilbert's Villa) ...	Mr. Fred Gilbert
Boss (another Bailiff)	Mr. Eliot Skinner
Popitte (a Flower Girl)	Miss Eva Sandford
Madame de Pilaine (Proprietress of the Mimosa Plantation)	Miss May Garstang
Marcelle Pilaine (Madame de Pilaine's Stepdaughter)	Miss Ruby Gray
Eugenie ... ... ⎫	Miss Marjorie Elliott
Mauricette ... ... ⎪	Miss Hazel Adair
Marie ... ... ⎪ Hospital Nurses in	Miss Avis Adair
Lizette ... ... ⎬ attendance on	Miss Phil Gumpel
Madallene ... ... ⎪ Victor Guilbert	Miss Nancy Keeley
Yvette ... ... ⎪	Miss Sybil West
Antoinette ... ... ⎪	Miss Winnie Sampson
Mimi ... ... ⎭	Miss Daisie Yule

AND

PAULETTE (Head Girl on the Mimosa Plantation) Miss MARIE STUDHOLME

Figure 65. Advertisement, unknown origin. Cork Public Museum archive, postcard collection 19.2.1.

Figure 66. *Miss Doris Stocker*, Raphael Tuck. Christina Jessop's card collection.

And, as Kelly herself states, actress postcards also 'show the photograph manipulated, situated, and adorned in many ways, both to endow "artistic" quality and to manufacture useful variations of the original image to suit differing tastes and budgets'.[57] Thus, to broaden and enhance their appeal, photographs could be combined with others or with illustrated motifs and decoration and text, and glitter and colour were often added to the surface by hand.

The actress cards collected by the Carmodys in Ennis overlap considerably with Christina's, featuring also such popular staples as the Dare sisters, Gabrielle Ray, Gertie Millar and Maude Fealy. Somebody in the Green household in Belfast seems to have had a particular fondness for the English actress and dancer Mabel Love, as the first few pages of their album is devoted to postally unused cards showing her in different poses with a range of props and costumes, for instance standing with a straw basket in front of a rustic fence, leaning over a stone balustrade, lying on a fur rug, sitting beside a spinning wheel, and brandishing a giant feather fan. In all these she looks very young and sweet, with her hair loose, full and curly, and her expression alternating between slightly wistful and smiling. The Green's album and also Ellen's album both feature many of the same stars as Christina's and the Carmodys', such as Marie Studholme, Maude Fealy, Gertie Millar and the Dare sisters. Ellen, however, seems to have been a particularly dedicated actress card collector, with an extensive and eclectic mixture of names from musical comedy but also more 'serious' theatre circles appearing in her album: Olive May, Sybil Carlisle, Lillah McCarthy, Dorothea Baird, Edna May, Bettie Bellknap, Gaynor Rowlands, Gertrude Elliott, Ghita Corri, Grace Lane, Hilda Hanbury, Miss Robinson, Madge Vincent, Evie Greene, Marie Tempest, Madge Crichton and Madge Kendal. The occasional image of a male actor or theatre producer appears in all these collections, but they are rare compared to the number of cards featuring female performers. Ellen, for instance, preserved two images of elderly male actor/managers, Charles Wyndham and W. H. Kendal, but none showing younger male actors. The Carmody collection has one image of Dudley Stuart as Raffles in the play *Raffles, The Amateur Cracksman*, which, according to text on the back of the card was performed by a London company in the Town Hall in Ennis on Monday 6, 1911. The Green's album features three male performers, Seymour Hicks, Martin Harvey and Henry Irving (born 1838), and Christina also owned a card showing Forbes Robinson, another relatively elderly English actor and theatre manager. For whatever reason, these young female collectors, and many others like them, seem to have been primarily fascinated by images of youthful female rather than male stars, and as Kelly states, 'The early twentieth century is predominantly characterized by the mass production of cards of the female performer – the actress.'[58] Christina also has one other postcard of a male performer, Cahal

O'Byrne, a popular singer and storyteller who was also a member of the
Gaelic League in Belfast (see Figure 67). O'Byrne was photographed for
the card in Revivalist Gaelic costume and he signed it on the front in the
Irish language. It is a testimony to the pervasiveness and appeal of international celebrity culture, and to the challenges faced by nationalist groups
such as the Gaelic League, that this is the only card from the period in any
of the collections showing an Irish performer.

Figure 67. *Cahal O'Byrne*, publisher/printer unclear. Christina Jessop's card collection.

Ellen was also interested in another form of celebrity, that of the aristocracy. She had in her collection several photographic postcards, probably a set, published by Hely's of Dublin, showing the elaborate and expensive society wedding in 1905 of John Crichton-Stuart, the Marquis of Bute and his Irish bride Augusta Bellingham, of Castle Bellingham in County Louth. The wedding took place in Kilsaran Parish Church and one of Ellen's postcards shows the bride and groom leaving the church and greeting a large group of fashionably dressed well-wishers. The photographic composition also includes the dynamic figure of another photographer leaning in to capture the image (see Figure 68). Although the Irish aristocracy traditionally did not welcome public interaction, the newly married couple must have been comfortable with cultivating a celebrity identity to have allowed Hely's to publish photographic postcards of their wedding, which also included a photograph of their immediate family posed at the entrance to Castle Bellingham. They also commissioned one of the first known films of a wedding, although this seems to have been primarily for private family viewing rather than public consumption.[59]

Figure 68. *Bride and Bridegroom Leaving Church. The Bute-Bellingham Wedding,* Hely's Dublin. Ellen Duff's card collection.

The construction of women in popular postcard imagery

Edwardian actress postcards, as Kelly has argued, presented in general a very narrow version of an 'idealized and glorified' femininity based on 'youth, luxury, simplicity, and costumed grace'.[60] Actresses in postcard imagery were lit so that they looked smooth-skinned and glowing, and their clothes and accessories were chosen to show off not just their forms but the kinds of fabrics and detailed decorative work that signalled both femininity and material luxury. Gold, glitter, tinting and thick blobs of white paint were also often used to highlight details and enhance the sense of the rich surfaces of their clothing and jewellery (Figure 2; Figure 10). In her book, *A Magazine of Her Own? Domesticity and Desire in the Woman's Magazine, 1800–1914* (1996) Margaret Beetham has argued that in the women's magazines that developed during the nineteenth century femininity was constructed around the importance of personal appearance, and women were encouraged to achieve the appropriate standard of appearance through consumption: 'Women were not born but made and made themselves.'[61] Fashion, hair and beauty products, clothes, corsets, jewellery and accessories were all sold to women on the basis that they had the ability, but also the responsibility, to create an acceptably feminine image if they constantly worked at it and bought the appropriate products. Femininity therefore became also associated with consumption – women were characterized as shoppers, spending the money earned by men.

Actress images, with their elaborate and carefully put-together costumes, epitomized this concept of a femininity based on the work of consumption, while at the same time their subjects seemed to be permanently at leisure, relaxing, languishing or at play. Kelly has pointed out the contradiction here, as of course these actresses by definition were working women, and posing for photographs, even if those photographs appeared to show them resting or playing, was part of their work.[62] The work of other women in the production of these cards, such as the sweat-work that produced their jewelled and tinted effects, was also hidden. Leisure had come to be seen as a characteristic of ideal middle- and upper-class femininity, associated with the idea that a woman's place was in the domestic, private sphere as opposed to the male-dominated public world of work.

Despite their beauty and luxurious dress, the actresses in postcard images generally seemed accessible and relatable, their subjects mostly appearing young, friendly and wholesome. They were also the kinds of images that were unproblematic to send openly through the post and to gift to young female relatives. They provided what seemed like a safe, conventional version of femininity to which fans could aspire, even if the stars' lifestyles were far removed from those of most women, such as Christina and Ellen, who nevertheless seem to have been fascinated by them. It is not difficult to imagine, for instance, that Ellen felt flattered when her friend suggested, on the back of an image of the beautifully coiffed and accessorized actress Olive May, that she looked like her: 'I thought this picture bore some resemblance to you … what do you think?' (see Figure 12). According to Jane Beckett and Deborah Cherry, these images

> were powerful influences on the formation of Edwardian femininity. Women were encouraged to model themselves on the 'stars' of the theatre and music-hall, to emulate a particular 'look'. Camille Clifford's distinctive shape and face, circulated on postcards and posters, sold corsets and magazines. The images of Marie Lloyd and other famous artists sold toothpaste and hair products.[63]

Actress postcards fed into a nascent celebrity culture that throughout the twentieth and early twenty-first centuries has increasingly been perceived as enormously socially powerful, and is now the focus of a vast (and growing) literature on beauty ideals, gender norms and what Olivier Driessens considers the 'celebritization' of society and culture.[64]

Picture postcards also featured plenty of decorative anonymous or even imaginary women. Photographs of pretty, fashionably dressed women were entwined around or filled up the letters of the initials or names of places and people, as on the card sent to Christina in August 1906 (see Figure 69). Many other women were shown dressed in classically inspired robes with flowers in their hair, looking dreamily at the viewer. In 1905 Delia Green was sent *A Moonstruck Maiden*, a card by CW Faulkner, showing an illustrated image of a woman and an owl sitting on the curve of a smiling crescent moon hanging over a snowy landscape (see Figure 70). Even in this fantasy image sent to a young girl, the same sort of appearance conventions are observed as in the actress postcards, with the amiable-looking maiden tightly corseted and carefully costumed, although in this case showing more of her legs than would usually be considered acceptable for a woman. In the first decade of the twentieth century, Raphael Tuck produced numerous sets of postcards of women, photographic and illustrated, variously titled *Beautiful Women, Fair Women, Lovely Women, Fair Maidenhood, Beauty's Power, A Classic Beauty, American Beauties, In Beauty's Realm, Jolies Femmes, Birthday Glamour, Glamorous Easter* and *Glamour Studies*, among others. Such titles left consumers in no doubt as to the centrality of personal appearance in the evaluation of women. Many of these images were sentimental, featuring dreamy-looking subjects accompanied by flowers and sometimes children, occasionally set within fantasy or even religious compositions. Other cards showed glamorous women who were laced and fashionably dressed, while others again were portrayed looking languidly seductive or even cheekily provocative.

Figure 69. *Greetings from Queenstown*, Hartmann/Eason's Dublin. Christina Jessop's card collection.

Figure 70. *A Moonstruck Maiden*, CW Faulkner, London. Green family collection.

Young Irish Catholic women who collected such cards, and there seem to have been many of them, would have found their presentation of ideal femininity somewhat at odds with the views generally promoted by their Church. Canon Patrick Sheehan (1852–1913), for instance, whose novels became very popular throughout Ireland and internationally after 1900 when his bestseller *My New Curate* was serialized, regularly and severely punished personal vanity in his young female characters.[65] The Reverend Bernard O'Reilly throughout his bestselling handbook, *The Mirror of True Womanhood; A Book of Instruction for Women in the World*, first published in 1877 and reissued many times, presented numerous warnings against the moral pitfalls of female vanity and the love of display.[66] And Mary Colum in her autobiography *Life and the Dream, Memories of a Literary Life in Europe and America* recalled that the convent school she attended in Monaghan in the late nineteenth and early twentieth centuries 'set itself to eradicate whatever girlish vanity about their appearance their pupils might naturally have, with the result that [by age eighteen] I had very little concern with my looks and only an intermittent interest in clothes'.[67] However, in 1899 *The Irish Rosary* published an article warning Catholic women against being 'dowdy', asserting that 'the Catholic woman who goes into society perfectly dressed … has it in her power to wield a greater influence for good than that possessed by her so-called "pious" sister who sits in a corner in a gown dating from the year before last'.[68] This added an interesting moral purpose to the kind of fashion consumption promoted in popular media, and suggests that women then, as now, were seen as valid targets of criticism in relation to their appearance, regardless of how they chose to present themselves.

As well as the array of beautiful women shown on picture postcards, mocking representations of conventionally unattractive women were also popular. A Tuck card from 1905, from the series *Books and Their Readers*, features an illustration of a large, dishevelled-looking woman in a torn apron with a black eye and a sticking plaster on her cheek reading the book *A Pair of Blue Eyes* by Thomas Hardy (see Figure 71). The card was posted from Mullingar in 1906 to a Miss Diamond in Newtowncashel in County Longford. The intended humour here lies in the contrast between the unappealing appearance of the woman and the romantic title of the novel, and indeed the sender has written under the image ' "She" looks romantic', as if the woman's lack of conventional feminine attractiveness disqualified her from being female. Such an image, and indeed the added text, is rather shocking to modern eyes, as the representation invites questions about domestic violence, and it seems strange now that it was published as a joke in a mainstream medium at the time. Designers and publishers of Edwardian picture postcards were however merciless in constructing jokes around women who did not fit the stereotype of young, shapely and charming, and the popularity of such jokes and evidence such as the sender's interaction with *A Pair of Blue Eyes* suggest the power and pervasiveness of the discourse of the importance of physical beauty in a woman. Unattractive women were also often pitted against pretty ones in postcard images, so there are many images of plain-looking wives frowning at husbands who are looking at younger attractive women, or stern-looking aunts or governesses preventing romantic meetings between their charges and their lovers.

Figure 71. *A Pair of Blue Eyes*, Raphael Tuck. From <https://tuckdbpostcards.org/items/68070>

Another female type that was frequently mocked on Edwardian post-cards was the 'pushy' woman, who was often represented as very large, towering over a much smaller, timid-looking man. Such representations played on what many people saw as the ridiculous and unnatural paradox of a dominant woman and a passive, obedient man. Their popularity can be seen as a manifestation of male anxiety in an era when women were increasingly seeking access to traditionally 'male' rights, such as the right to earn their own living. As Beetham has argued,

> the absolute correlation of gender and sexuality meant that the powerful binary oppositions which linked masculinity with activity/production and femininity with passivity/consumption worked across the categories of the economic and the sexual. Women's claim to the 'masculine' roles of breadwinner and independent self therefore threatened not only men's economic power but their sexuality. This anxiety was evident … in cartoons and jokes about mannish women.[69]

Anti-suffrage cards relied heavily and very specifically on the caricature of the bossy unattractive woman, but a threatening 'mannishness' in a woman was also often the target of mockery in other cards, and could be shown in a variety of ways.[70] Leap-year-themed cards, for instance, offered a great opportunity for this, since traditionally on 29 February women were allowed to take an initiative usually only permitted to men and ask a man to marry them. *Unshrinkable* (Figure 72) is an example first produced by Raphael Tuck in 1904, showing an image of a large lady with a small dog, accompanied by the text 'My Valentine. Leap Year Goods. "Unshrinkable".' 'Leap Year Goods' suggests the idea that the woman was left 'on the shelf' because no man wanted to ask her to marry him. This woman, with her square, masculine features and 'unshrinkable' tent-like figure, contrasts sharply with the beautiful, tightly corseted and passive-looking women of stage and fantasy, despite her carefully put-together outfit. She is represented, jokingly, as threatening to men, because of both her size and her temporary right to actively pursue a man for marriage.

Figure 72. *My Valentine. Leap Year Goods. 'Unshrinkable'.* Raphael Tuck. From
<https://tuckdbpostcards.org/items/80827/pictures/298130>

Anxiety was also evident in debates around the concept of the New
Woman, a term that could describe anything from female suffrage activists
and those who flouted gender and marriage conventions to those who displayed mildly unladylike behaviours such as smoking cigarettes or cycling.
Monica Cure, in *Picturing the Postcard. A New Media Crisis at the Turn of*

the Century (2018), cites the work of Ellen Jordan in explaining that the term 'New Woman' emerged 'at the end of the nineteenth century out of a complicated discourse of competing femininities sparked by a generation of English feminists who had profited from increased educational and vocational opportunities'.[71] According to Beetham, some people went so far as to declare that the New Woman did not actually exist, but was merely a product of novelists' imaginations.[72] The New Woman was unfavourably opposed to the 'true' or 'womanly' woman, but she could also be repackaged as the 'new woman of advertising culture, identified with the pleasures of consumption', and in this manifestation she posed a challenge to the 'New Woman who had demanded access to paid employment and productive labour'.[73] Cure discusses how the New Woman became associated with the very popular drawings of beautiful, superior-looking women produced by Charles Dana Gibson, images which 'conveyed a sense of personal independence but were a far cry from satirical depictions of masculinized suffragettes'.[74] Gibson Girls were conventionally beautiful, but they were represented as haughty and capable of manipulating men so that they could make advantageous marriages, 'thus obtaining a form of economic freedom'.[75] Gibson's images became much-sought-after commodities, and according to Cure inspired an entire postcard genre of beautiful but inaccessible women.[76] The Green postcard album contains a series of such cards illustrated by the Canadian-born artist Philip Boileau, and published by Reinthal and Newman of New York and Charles H Hauff of London. They show a range of sophisticated, fashionable and rather superior-looking women, with titles such as *A Thoroughbred, To-Day?* and *Those Bewitching Eyes*. *Over the Teacup* shows a woman in a large flamboyant hat holding a teacup and saucer in her elegant hands and staring knowingly and seductively at the viewer (see Figure 73). This type of manifestation of the New Woman appears several times in the postcard collections examined, whereas there are no images of more genuinely transgressive women such as suffragettes. It is not difficult to understand the appeal of such depictions of glamour, sophistication and even power to the girls and young women who collected postcards, and their avoidance of images of women who were widely lampooned as ugly, unfeminine and ridiculous. Gibson and Boileau 'girls', and many others like them, permeated popular culture throughout the world, providing a very influential model of femininity for countless women.

Figure 73. *Over the Teacup*, Wildt & Kray, London. Green Family collection.

While middle-class women were encouraged to confine themselves to domestic duties only, and popular imagery represented the ideal femininity as leisured, other groups of women were shown frequently on picture postcards and in other media as if working was their natural way of life, and they and their work were often idealized and romanticized, as in many of the images discussed earlier (Figures 27 and 48). Irish working women, such as milkmaids, spinners or turf carriers, were mostly shown as charming, happy and smiling, looking as picturesque and natural as their surroundings, even though they might be carrying large loads and walking barefoot through wet bogs. Women seen as 'exotic' foreigners were also often shown in terms of their occupation, such as the indigenous Alaskan fisherwoman in Figure 38 and the Belgian milkmaids in Figure 55. Other working women, such as domestic servants, factory workers, waitresses, governesses, nurses or teachers, rarely appeared on postcards in the pre–First World War era, and when they did it was often as part of a joke.

Picture postcards offer insights into the lives of ordinary Irish women in the early part of the twentieth century, including their social lives, which seem to have been livelier than is often suggested in other historic accounts. They provide greater understanding of the kinds of working lives which have not tended to be visible in the historical record, such as those of Christina and Ellen. They also suggest the kinds of popular culture consumed by women, which included the collection of vast numbers of actress postcards featuring the glamorous stars of (mainly) English musical comedy. Picture postcard imagery tended to present either impossibly idealized or joke versions of femininity, but this did not stop women from aspiring towards the former, like the imitation Gibson girls in Dublin mentioned on page 12, and laughing along at the latter, like the sender of *A Pair of Blue Eyes*. Like other media, picture postcards presented women with a variety of competing femininities, but the really popular cards seem to have fallen predominantly into these two categories. Huge numbers of female postcard collectors therefore seem to have been seduced by fantasies of glamour and leisure that they could only dream about in relation to their own lives, making it very difficult for those who wanted to challenge the rigidity of existing gender conventions, and indeed for proponents of alternative nationalist or religious models of cultural value.

Notes

1. Young, *Ireland at the Crossroads*, 5.
2. Jones, *Shamrock-Land*, 218.

3. Lisa Tickner, 'Suffrage Campaigns. The Political Imagery of the British Women's Suffrage Movement', in Jane Beckett and Deborah Cherry, eds, *The Edwardian Era* (London: Barbicon Gallery and Oxford: Phaidon, 1987), 109–113; National Print Museum, *Print, Protest, and the Polls: The Irish Women's Suffrage Campaign and the Power of Print Media, 1908–1918*, exhibition <https://www.nationalprintmuseum. ie/print-protest-and-the-polls-the-irish-suffrage-campaign-and-the-power-of-print-media/> accessed 16 August 2020.

4. Young, *Ireland at the Crossroads*, 117–122.

5. Tourmakeady, a small Mayo town, was the location from 1905 on of an Irish college whose summer schools were very popular with those associated with the Gaelic League and visitors generally interested in the revival of the Irish language and culture.

6. Biletz, 'Women and Irish-Ireland', 60.

7. Tony Farmar, *Privileged Lives. A Social History of Middle-Class Ireland 1882–1989* (Dublin: A. & A. Farmar, 2010), 61.

8. T.E. (1898) 'The Feast of the Annunciation', *The Irish Rosary*, II/3 (1898), 107–110, 110.

9. Lambert McKenna, *The Church and Labour* (New York: P.J. Kenedy, 1914), 45–46.

10. Eileen Breathnach, 'Women and Higher Education in Ireland (1879–1914)', *The Crane Bag*, 4/1, *Images of the Irish Woman* (1980), 47–54, 47.

11. Cullen Owens, Rosemary, A Social *History of Women in Ireland 1870–1970* (Dublin: Gill and Macmillan, 2005, 2014), loc 4840, Kindle Book.

12. Cullen Owens, *A Social History of Women in Ireland*, loc 4840.

13. C. R. Fortescue, 'A Residence for Business Girls', *The Irish Rosary* (1900), 614–615, 614.

14. Cullen Owens, *A Social History of Women in Ireland*, loc 5195.

15. *Thom's Business Directory of Dublin and Suburbs, for the year 1906*, p. 86.

16. Christina Jessop's Collection 050810_6482.

17. Christina Jessop's Collection 050726_6579.

18. Ó'hÓgartaigh, *Women in Pharmacy*, 162.

19. Ó'hÓgartaigh, *Women in Pharmacy*, 162.

20. Ó'hÓgartaigh, *Women in Pharmacy*, 161.

21. Sister Mary Ignatius, 'Women as Pharmacists in Public Institutions', *The American Journal of Nursing*, 6/2 (1905), 92–95, 93.

22. Sister Mary Ignatius, 'Women as Pharmacists', 95.

23. References for Christina Jessop, family collection.

24. Census of Ireland 1911, <http://www.census.nationalarchives.ie/reels/nai001910137/> accessed 16 August 2020.

25. Census of Ireland 1911, <http://www.census.nationalarchives.ie/reels/nai000177784/> accessed 16 August 2020.

26. Máirtín Mac Con Iomaire, 'Haute Cuisine Restaurants in Nineteenth and Twentieth Century Ireland', *Proceedings of the Royal Irish Academy: Archaeology, Culture, History, Literature*, 115C (2015), 371–403, 377.

27. Kathleen Clarke, *Revolutionary Woman* (Dublin: O'Brien Press, 1991, 2008), 24.

28. Daly, *Dublin*, 42–44.

29. Daly, *Dublin*, 42.
30. Caitriona Clear, *Social Change and Everyday Life in Ireland, 1850–1922* (Manchester: Manchester University Press, 2007), 31.
31. Census of Ireland 1901, <http://www.census.nationalarchives.ie/reels/naio03985863/>; <http://www.census.nationalarchives.ie/reels/naio03985855/> accessed 16 August 2020.
32. Clear, *Social Change*, 30–31.
33. Cullen Owens, *A Social History of Women in Ireland*, loc 4434.
34. Card sent to John O'Reilly from Joe Jennings, 9 August possibly 1911.
35. Clear, *Social Change*, 31.
36. Information based on cards and also 1911 Census of Ireland.
37. Census of Ireland 1911 <http://www.census.nationalarchives.ie/reels/naio03535452/>.
38. Clear, *Social Change*, 32.
39. Breathnach, *Women and Higher Education in Ireland*, 47.
40. Cullen Owens, *A Social History of Women in Ireland*, 922.
41. Deirdre Raftery, Judith Harford and Susan M. Parkes, 'Mapping the Terrain of Female Education in Ireland, 1830–1910', *Gender and Education*, 22/5 (2010), 565–578, 570.
42. Christina Jessop's Intermediate Certificate, 1894, family collection.
43. Raftery, Harford and Parkes, 'Mapping the Terrain of Female Education', 570.
44. Breathnach, *Women and Higher Education in Ireland*, 48.
45. Mary Hatfield, 'The School and the Home: Constructing Childhood and Space in Dublin Boarding Schools', in Georgina Laragy, Olwen Purdue and Jonathan Jeffrey Wright, eds, *Urban Spaces in Nineteenth-Century Ireland* (Liverpool: Liverpool University Press, 2018), 84–105, 94.
46. Hatfield, 'The School and the Home', 93.
47. Stephanie Rains, 'Mass Media, High Society and the Invention of Celebrity', *Irish Media History* (2017) <https://irishmediahistory.com/tag/lady-of-the-house/> accessed 19 July 2020, paragraph 3.
48. Rockett, 'Disguising Dependence', 22.
49. Neal Garham, 'Music Halls', in Connolly, *The Oxford Companion*, 394.
50. Viv Gardner, 'Gertie Millar and the "Rules for Actresses and Vicars' Wives"', in Martin Banham and Jane Milling, eds, *Extraordinary Actors* (Exeter: Exeter University Press, 2004), 97–119, 105.
51. George Cecil, 'Musical Matters', *The Cork Examiner* (28 October 1909).
52. Viv Gardner, 'Defending the Body, Defending the Self: Women Performers and the Law in the "Long" Edwardian Period', in Maggie B. Gale and Kate Dorney, eds, *Stage Women, 1900–50* (Manchester: Manchester University Press, 2019), 138–160, 143; Gardner, 'Gertie Millar', *passim*.
53. *Evening Herald* (8 September 1906).
54. *Freemans Journal* (12 September 1908).
55. Kelly, 'Beauty and the Market', 99–116, 111.

56. Kelly, 'Beauty and the Market', 103.

57. Kelly, 'Beauty and the Market', 104.

58. Kelly, 'Beauty and the Market', 99.

59. Scotland on Screen, website, <https://scotlandonscreen.org.uk/browse-films/007-000-002-519-c> accessed 25 July 2020.

60. Kelly, 'Beauty and the Market', 100, 110.

61. Margaret Beetham, *A Magazine of Her Own? Domesticity and Desire in the Woman's Magazine, 1800–1914* (London and New York: Routledge, 1996), loc 4445, Kindle book.

62. Kelly, 'Beauty and the Market', 106.

63. Jane Beckett and Deborah Cherry, 'Working Women. Overdressed/Underpaid: Women Workers and the Production of Femininity', in Jane Beckett and Deborah Cherry, eds, *The Edwardian Era* (London: Barbicon Gallery and Oxford: Phaidon, 1987), 82.

64. Olivier Driessens, 'The Celebritization of Society and Culture: Understanding the Structural Dynamics of Celebrity Culture', *International Journal of Cultural Studies*, 16/6 (2013), 641–657.

65. For example, Canon Sheehan, *My New Curate. A Story Gathered from the Stray Leaves of an Old Diary* (Dublin and Cork: The Talbot Press, 1899), 204–209.

66. Bernard O'Reilly, *The Mirror of True Womanhood; A Book of Instruction for Women in the World* (New York: P.J. Kenedy, Excelsior Catholic Publishing House, 1886), 123.

67. Colum, *Life and the Dream*, 86.

68. G.V.C., 'Piety and Dowdyism', *The Irish Rosary*, 514–517 (1899), 515.

69. Beetham, *A Magazine of Her Own?* loc 3043.

70. Donna Gilligan, 'Anti-Suffragette Postcards, c.1913', *Artefacts*, 3/26 (2018), <https://www.historyireland.com/volume-26/anti-suffragette-postcards-c-1913/> accessed 14 August 2020.

71. Monica Cure, *Picturing the Postcard. A New Media Crisis at the Turn of the Century* (Minneapolis: University of Minnesota Press, 2018), loc 1331, Kindle book.

72. Beetham, *A Magazine of Her Own?* loc 2095.

73. Beetham, *A Magazine of Her Own?* loc 2245; loc 3018.

74. Cure, *Picturing the Postcard*, loc 1390.

75. Cure, *Picturing the Postcard*, loc 1390.

76. Cure, *Picturing the Postcard*, loc 1401.

Conclusion

During the Edwardian period, picture postcards were enormously popular and pervasive in Ireland as they were elsewhere, and as a visual medium they constituted a significant if sometimes overlooked influence on people. The reasons for their success are many: their cheapness, their portability, their visual appeal and variety, their potential for manipulation so that messages could be customized for individual or mass communication, their mass production in a standardized format and of course the fast and efficient national and international postal systems to which they were perfectly adapted, and via which they facilitated and sped up millions of transactions between people in their private and working lives. All these factors worked just as well in the Irish context as they did elsewhere, and in Ireland the format was either adapted to specifically Irish needs, or probably more commonly, imported cards were cheerfully and unproblematically consumed and enjoyed in exactly the same ways as they were all over the world, just as imported media products are in Ireland today.

Picture postcards changed how people interacted with each other in their personal, business and political lives, and they were also the route by which vast amounts of popular imagery from all over the world entered and circulated around Ireland. They were so cheap and accessible that they were practically unavoidable, and for every voice raised in criticism of them many more people used and consumed them with great enthusiasm. They were much more a part of daily life than is remembered today, when even their use for holiday communications is disappearing, so that comparisons with modern electronic mass communication media such as texting, email and social media are at least as relevant to them as discussions about souvenirs and personal mementos, although these of course are also important in understanding the phenomenon that they became in the early twentieth century.

Irish companies did their best to exploit the profit-making potential of the picture postcard boom, and many of them, such as Lawrence, Hely's and Fergus O'Connor, seem to have done well and achieved a high consumer visibility, but they still had to coexist with giants such as Raphael Tuck and Valentines who continued to dominate the market and directly competed with them even in the production of Irish-themed cards. Irish people bought and were gifted and sent cards that were published in Ireland, but probably not as many as they got from non-Irish publishers, and even those published in Ireland were often modifications of imported cards, and indeed foreign-published cards often obtained their imagery from Irish companies. A single postcard could be based on a photograph taken in one country, modified and captioned in at least one other, printed in another and published in yet another. The picture postcard therefore was a thoroughly international phenomenon.

Postcard producers borrowed images and formats from traditions such as painting, but the much wider range of people involved in the production of postcards, the greater number of purposes to which they could be put and their broader consumer demographic meant that the conventions were stretched and altered and often abandoned altogether in the interest of other agendas. Images were plagiarized and manipulated as required, and there were endless reiterations of a relatively narrow range of national, gender and class stereotypes. Card production was largely dictated by the market, so popular cards were repeatedly reissued while at the same time a great deal of effort and money was also invested in the ongoing production of novelty variations in order to keep people interested and buying.

People collected picture postcards for a range of reasons and with varying degrees of seriousness. Many original Edwardian collections have been broken up by later collectors, and the casual personal or family postcard album, put together by unimportant unknown people, is unfortunately probably both the most likely to have been broken up and the most valuable to the historian in its original intact form. A complete collection from the period allows the establishment of a context in which to understand the added text as well as the cards' imagery, and thus gain insight into the lives of people usually invisible to history. Later collections of Edwardian cards, whether put together for personal or public reasons, are less useful in many ways, as each card functions as an individual isolated 'statement', although they can be useful in the sense of providing access to a range of informal utterances from the period, and in gaining an overall idea of how a particular geographical area, for instance, was constructed in a wide range of related imagery. All the collections examined here show a great variety of subject matter, mostly nothing to do with Ireland. A significant proportion of the cards were posted abroad, although many of those with images of far-flung places were not. The overall mix of imagery is of the type seen nowadays on social media sites such as Instagram or Facebook: personal, funny, sentimental, beautiful, romantic etc., varying in proportion depending on the collection. The picture postcard was also ideal for the publication of popular stories and news items such as disasters, spectacular events and celebrity visits or marriages, delivering the message mainly in visual form with any added text kept simple and succinct. It was also an effective way of communicating political propaganda to a wide audience, although publishers could never completely control how consumers might manipulate or use the cards once they bought them, possibly transforming a message into something very different as a result.

Irish people embraced the communicative potential of imported picture postcards with enthusiasm, customizing the cards they sent by adding individual messages that either interacted with or ignored the pre-printed text and images, just as people did elsewhere. They realized that imagery combined with text could enhance the communication of the reality of an experience, of being in a particular place, whether that experience was everyday and mundane, or exotic. They also learned to exploit the postcard's particular suitability for making social and other arrangements and for general relationship maintenance, as well as for libel, mockery, propaganda and political protests, such as those against the Boer War or as part of the Mail-in-Irish campaign. Because picture postcards were used for so many different purposes, and came to play such a central role in so many aspects of people's day-to-day lives, they are especially useful for their insights into these lives, insights which might have been difficult to obtain via more formal historical sources. The collections looked at here suggest a vibrant, busy Irish population constantly engaged in social activities and the consumption of imported popular culture, and a country that was rapidly modernizing, and that part of this modernizing was its othering of the remnants of its traditions for touristic and nationalistic purposes. Christina Jessop's collection shows the importance of the Gaelic League and the Irish language revival in the lives of some people, although it is not even referenced in any of the other collections. The collections overall highlight the contradictions of real life, in which people seem to express contradictory views and reality seldom conforms to even widely recognized social ideals, such as that of the woman who stayed at home and confined herself to domestic duties. During the Edwardian period, as now, people attempted to shape their own lives as best they could to suit their circumstances, despite the rhetoric of various commentators.

Picture postcards also constructed Ireland in contradictory ways that to a certain extent reflected much of the complexity of the real-life country, although in other ways caricatured it. Their imagery and text both celebrated and criticized the British empire and its role in Ireland, rejoicing in royal visits and imperial monuments, but also featuring nationalist monuments, evictions and calls to Irish nationalism. They promoted *and* ridiculed the concept of Home Rule, and publicized Irish revivalism and British musical comedy actresses. They constructed a melancholy 'old Ireland' from ruined castles, sunsets and wizened peasants, but they also featured images of modern urban centres bustling with advertisement-decked trams and crowds of fashionably dressed shoppers and commuters. They repeated popular stereotypes so often that they probably gave them a gloss of truth: Irish rural poverty was regularly idealized, exoticized and personified by pretty cheerful colleens, for instance, and Irishmen were disproportionately drunken and stupid, and far too frequently accompanied by a pig. Picture postcards did not generally reflect the lives of those who collected them, who presumably did not expect them to. Their construction of Irish society, and of other societies, was reductive and distorted but nevertheless must have been enchanting to many people. Because of their accessibility and appeal it may also have been convincing.

The picture postcard construction of women was also simplified and stereotyped. Most of the women represented on popular postcards, whether 'real' actresses or anonymous or imaginary 'beauties', were young and attractive, passively or playfully posed for the enjoyable consumption of the viewer, who very often seems herself to have been a young woman. These were contrasted with conventionally unattractive women, who were most frequently presented as the butt of jokes and/or as threatening to men, the latter a motif that would be increasingly used in anti-suffragette imagery, no examples of which were found in any of the collections examined. Edwardian picture postcards relentlessly reinforced the importance of conventional feminine beauty and presented innumerable aspirational figures on which young women could model themselves. Actress images in particular tended to feature their subjects as permanently at leisure and luxuriously dressed and accessorized, an association of femininity with a level of conspicuous consumption that must have seemed very different to the lives of many Irish women, and to the values imbued in them by their church and schools.

Based on the quantity in circulation, their wide accessibility and their potential for influencing opinions and values, picture postcards must be seen as an important cultural phenomenon in early twentieth-century Ireland. However, as historical sources they need to be examined as the multifaceted objects they are and in context, and not as images of a past reality. Pictures of all sorts have always presented a visual argument rather than a faithful reflection of the world, and the picture postcard brought this to a whole new level. Mass production and international distribution meant that publishers could manipulate and combine images and their titles at will in order to satisfy the demands of the market while keeping costs down. Postcard imagery, illustrated and photographic, often therefore took on a life of its own, becoming separated from its original purpose and significance in order to serve other functions and create new meanings. In this way it constructed a sort of parallel postcard world, a fantasy version of reality designed primarily for maximum appeal to the market. As has been shown, however, early twentieth-century Irish postcard consumers did not just passively consume what was presented to them, but by their additions and manipulations actively created new meanings in ways that can be compared to the use of interactive digital media in the early twenty-first century.

Bibliography

Postcard collections

Christina Jessop's album, Margaret O'Leary, private collection.

Cobh Museum archive, postcards and ephemera collection, High Road, Cobh.

Cork Public Museum archive, postcard collection, Cork Public Museum, Fitzgerald's Park, Cork.

Ellen Duff's album, Portlaoise County Library, Portlaoise, County Laois, Ireland.

John O'Reilly/Bessie Caulfield collection, Mary and Arthur O'Donnell, private collection.

The Carmody family collection, Hilda Haugh, private collection.

The Green family album, Ann Wilson private collection.

Websites

Irish Newspaper Archives, available at <https://www.irishnewsarchive.com/>.

Linen Hall Library Collection, available at <http://www.postcardsireland.com/about>.

National Library of Ireland: Lawrence Collection online catalogue, available at <http://catalogue.nli.ie>.

TuckDB Postcards, available at <https://tuckdbpostcards.org/>.

Books and articles

Andrews, C. S., *Dublin Made Me*, Kindle edition (Dublin: Lilliput Press, 2001).

Atkins, Guy, 'The Edwardian Social Network', *History Today*, 63/6 (2013), <http://www.historytoday.com/guy-atkins/edwardian-social-network> accessed 14 August 2020.

Atkins, Guy, *Come Home at Once* (London: Transworld Publishers, 2014).

Baldwin, Brooke, 'On the Verso: Postcard Messages as a Key to Popular Prejudices', *Journal of Popular Culture*, 22/3 (1988), 15–28.

Becker, Barbara, and Karen Malcolm, 'Suspended Conversations that Intersect in the Edwardian Postcard', in Nina Norgaard, ed., *Systemic Functional Linguistics in Use* (Odense: Odense Working Papers in Language and Communication, 29, 2008), 175–198.

Beckett, Jane, and Deborah Cherry, 'Working Women', in Jane Beckett and Deborah Cherry, eds, *The Edwardian Era* (London: Barbicon Gallery and Oxford: Phaidon, 1987), 70–87.

Beetham, Margaret, *A Magazine of Her Own? Domesticity and Desire in the Woman's Magazine, 1800–1914* (London and New York: Routledge, 1996).

Behan, A. P., 'History from Picture Postcards', *Dublin Historical Record*, 46/2 (1993), 129–140.

Belk, Russell W., and Melanie Wallendorf, 'Of Mice and Men: Gender Identity in Collecting', in Susan M. Pearce, ed., *Interpreting Objects and Collections* (London and New York: Routledge, 1994), 240–251.

Berghoff, Hartmut, and Barbara Korte, 'Britain and the Making of Modern Tourism: an Interdisciplinary Approach', in Hartmut Berghoff, Barbara Korte, R. Schneider and C. Harvie, eds, *The Making of Modern Tourism: The Cultural History of the British Experience, 1600–2000* (Basingstoke and New York: Palgrave Macmillan, 2002).

Biletz, Frank A., 'Women and Irish-Ireland: The Domestic Nationalism of Mary Butler', *New Hibernia Review*, 6 (Spring 2002), 59–72.

Bradley, Ian, *Celtic Christianity: Making Myths and Chasing Dreams* (Edinburgh: Edinburgh University Press, 1999).

Brand, Michael James, *Transience in Dawson City, Yukon, during the Klondike Gold Rush*, (PhD thesis submitted to the Simon Fraser University, 2003).

Breathnach, Eileen, 'Women and Higher Education in Ireland (1879–1914)', *The Crane Bag*, 4/1, *Images of the Irish Woman* (1980), 47–54.

Breen, Dan, and Tom Spalding, *The Cork International Exhibition 1902–1903: A Snapshot of Edwardian Cork* (Newbridge: Irish Academic Press, 2014).

Browne, Christopher, *Getting the Message. The Story of the British Post Office* (Stroud, Gloucestershire: Alan Sutton, 1993).

Byatt, Anthony, *Picture Postcards and Their Publishers* (Malvern, Worcs: Golden Age Postcard Books, 1978).

Carline, Richard, *Pictures in the Post. The Story of the Picture Postcard and Its Place in the History of Popular Art* (London: Gordon Frazer, 1971).

Carville Justin, 'Photography, Tourism and Natural History: Cultural Identity and the Visualisation of the Natural World', in Michael Cronin and Barbara O'Connor, eds, *Irish Tourism: Image, Culture and Identity* (Clevedon: Channel View Publications, 2003), 215–240.

Carville Justin, *Photography and Ireland* (London: Reaktion Books, 2011).

Clarke Kathleen, *Revolutionary Woman* (Dublin: O'Brien Press, 1991, 2008).

Clear, Caitriona, *Social Change and Everyday Life in Ireland, 1850–1922* (Manchester: Manchester University Press, 2007).

Clery, Arthur, 'The Gaelic League', *Studies: An Irish Quarterly Review*, 8/31 (1919a), 398–408.

Clery, Arthur, *Dublin Essays* (Dublin and London: Maunsel, 1919b).

Colum, Mary, *Life and the Dream, Memories of a Literary Life in Europe and America* (Garden City, New York: Doubleday & Company, 1947).

Colum, Padraig, *My Irish Year* (New York: James Pott & Co., 1912).

Connolly, S. J. ed., *The Oxford Companion to Irish History* (Oxford, New York: Oxford University Press, 2004).

Cooke, John, ed., *Murray's Handbook for Ireland* (London: Edward Stanford, 1906).

Coombes, Annie E., 'The Franco-British Exhibition', in Jane Beckett and Deborah Cherry, eds, *The Edwardian Era* (London: Barbicon Gallery and Oxford: Phaidon, 1987), 152–166.

Cork, Bandon, and South Coast Railway Company, *Glengarriff, "Prince of Wales Route" and Killarney* (Cork: Guy & Co., ND).

Cox, David J., and Kim Stevenson, Candida Harris and Judith Rowbotham, *Public Indecency in England 1857–1960 'A Serious and Growing Evil'* (London and New York: Routledge, 2015).

Crozier-de Rosa, Sharon, *Shame and the Anti-Feminist Backlash: Britain, Ireland and Australia, 1890–1920* (New York: Routledge, 2018).

Cullen Fintan, *Ireland on Show. Art, Union and Nationhood* (Surrey: Ashgate, 2012).

Cullen Owens, Rosemary, *A Social History of Women in Ireland 1870–1970* (Dublin: Gill and Macmillan, 2005, 2014).

Cure, Monica, *Picturing the Postcard. A New Media Crisis at the Turn of the Century* (Minneapolis: University of Minnesota Press, 2018), Kindle book.

Curtis, L. Perry Jr. *Apes and Angels: The Irishman in Victorian Caricature* (Washington, D.C and London: Smithsonian Institution, 1997).

Daly, Mary, *Dublin, The Deposed Capital, a Social and Economic History, 1860–1914* (Cork: Cork University Press, 1984).

Dawson, William, 'My Dublin Year', *Studies: An Irish Quarterly Review*, 1/4 (1912), 694–708.

Day Good, Katie, 'From Scrapbook to Facebook: A History of Personal Media Assemblage and Archives', *New Media & Society*, 15 (2013), 557–573.

Debord, Guy, translated by Donald Nicholson-Smith, *The Society of the Spectacle* (New York: Zone Books, 1967, 1994) <http://www.antiworld.se/project/references/texts/The_Society%20_Of%20_The%20_Spectacle.pdf>, accessed 10 October 2014.

De Nie, Michael, *The Eternal Paddy: Irish Identity and the British Press, 1798–1882* (Madison: University of Wisconsin Press, 2004).

Dixon, F. E., 'Pioneer Publishers of Dublin Picture Postcards', *Dublin Historical Record*, 32 (1979), 146–147.

Driessens, Olivier, 'The Celebritization of Society and Culture: Understanding the Structural Dynamics of Celebrity Culture', *International Journal of Cultural Studies*, 16/6 (2013), 641–657.

Dunleavy, Gareth W., 'Hyde's Crusade for the Language and the Case of the Embarrassing Packets', *Studies: An Irish Quarterly Review*, 73 (Spring, 1984), 12–25.

Farmar Tony, *Privileged Lives. A Social History of Middle-Class Ireland 1882–1989* (Dublin: A. & A. Farmar, 2010).

Ferguson, Sandra, ' "A Murmur of Small Voices": On the Picture Postcard in Academic Research', *Archivaria*, 60 (September 2006), 167–184. <http://journals.sfu.ca/archivar/index.php/archivaria/article/view/12520/13654> accessed 19 September 2014.

Ferguson, Stephen, *The Post Office in Ireland, an Illustrated History* (Dublin: Irish Academic Press, 2016).

Ferriter, Diarmaid, *The Transformation of Ireland 1900–2000* (London: Profile Books, 2005).

Finnan, Joseph P., 'Punch's Portrayal of Redmond, Carson and the Irish Question, 1910–18', *Irish Historical Studies*, 33/132 (2003), 424–451.

Fitzpatrick, David, 'Ireland Since 1870', in Roy Foster, ed., *The Oxford Illustrated History of Ireland* (Oxford: Oxford University Press, 2000), 213–274.

Fortescue, C. R., 'A Residence for Business Girls', *The Irish Rosary*, IV/12 (1900), 614–615.

Fraser, John, 'Propaganda on the Picture Postcard', *Oxford Art Journal*, 3/2 (1980), 39–47.

G.V.C., 'Piety and Dowdyism', *The Irish Rosary*, III/10 (1899), 514–517.

Gardner, Viv, 'Gertie Millar and the "Rules for Actresses and Vicars Wives"', in Martin Banham and Jane Milling, eds, *Extraordinary Actors* (Exeter: Exeter University Press, 2004), 97–119.

Gardner, Viv, 'Defending the Body, Defending the Self: Women Performers and the Law in the "Long" Edwardian Period', in Maggie B. Gale and Kate Dorney, eds, *Stage Women, 1900–50* (Manchester: Manchester University Press, 2019), 138–160.

Geary, Christaud M., and Virginia Lee Webb, eds, *Delivering Views: Distant Cultures in Early Postcards* (Washington and London: Smithsonian Institution Press, 1998).

Gibbons, Luke, 'John Hinde and the New Nostalgia', in *Transformations in Irish Culture* (Cork: Cork University Press/Field Day, 1996), 37–43.

Gifford Daniel, *American Holiday Postcards, 1905–1915, Imagery and Context* (Jefferson, North Carolina and London: McFarland & Company, 2013).

Gilderdale, Peter, *Hands Across the Sea: Situating an Edwardian Greetings Postcard Practice* (PhD thesis submitted to the Auckland University of Technology, 2013).

Gilderdale, Peter, 'Stoic *and* Sentimental: The Emotional Work of the Edwardian Greetings Postcard', *Journal of New Zealand Studies*, NS22 (2016), 2–18.

Gillen, Julia, 'Writing Edwardian Postcards', *Journal of Sociolinguistics*, 17/4, 488–521 <https://eprints.lancs.ac.uk/id/eprint/65539/1/Writing_Edwardian_Postcards_post_print.pdf> accessed 14 August 2020.

Gillen, Julia, and Nigel Hall, 'The Edwardian Postcard: A Revolutionary Moment in Rapid Multimodal Communications', paper presented at the British Educational Research Association Annual Conference Manchester, 2–5 September 2009 <http://www.leeds.ac.uk/educol/documents/189190.pdf> accessed 14 August 2020.

Gilligan, Donna, 'Anti-Suffragette Postcards, c.1913', *Artefacts*, 3/26 (2018), <https://www.historyireland.com/volume-26/anti-suffragette-postcards-c-1913/> accessed 14 August 2020.

Hatfield, Mary, 'The School and the Home: Constructing Childhood and Space in Dublin Boarding Schools', in Georgina Laragy, Olwen Purdue and Jonathan Jeffrey Wright, eds, *Urban Spaces in Nineteenth-Century Ireland* (Liverpool: Liverpool University Press, 2018), 84–105.

Henchy, Deirdre, 'Dublin 80 Years Ago', *Dublin Historical Record*, 26/1 (1972), 18–36.

Holt, Tonie, and Valmai, *Picture Postcards of the Golden Age, a Collector's Guide* (London: MacGibbin & Kee, 1971).

Horgan, Donal, *The Victorian Visitor in Ireland, Irish Tourism 1840–1910* (Cork: Imagimedia, 2002).

Humphries, Steve, *Victorian Britain Through the Magic Lantern* (London: Sidgwick & Jackson, 1989).

Hyde, Douglas. 'The Necessity for De-Anglicising Ireland', 1892, <https://www.thefuture.ie/wp-content/uploads/1892/11/1892-11-25-The-Necessity-for-De-Anglicising-Ireland.pdf> accessed 19 April 2014.

Inglis, Tom, *Moral Monopoly: Rise and Fall of the Catholic Church in Modern Ireland* (Dublin: University College Dublin, 1998).

Jones, Plummer F., *Shamrock-Land: A Ramble through Ireland* (New York: Moffat, Yard & Company, 1908).

Jordan, Thomas E., 'The Quality of Life in Victorian Ireland, 1831–1901', *New Hibernia Review / Iris Éireannach Nua*, 4/1 (2000), 103–121.

Joyce, James, *Dubliners* (New York: B.W. Huebsch, 1917).

Kelly Veronica, 'Beauty and the Market: Actress Postcards and Their Senders in Early Twentieth-Century Australia', *New Theatre Quarterly*, 20/2 (2004), 99–116.

Kennedy, Brian P., 'The Traditional Irish Thatched House: Image and Reality, 1793–1993', in Adele M. Dalsimer, ed., *Visualising Ireland. National Identity and the Pictorial Tradition* (London: Faber and Faber, 1993), 165–179.

Kennedy, Kieran A., Thomas Giblin and Deirdre McHugh, *The Economic Development of Ireland in the Twentieth Century* (London and New York: Routledge, 1988).

Kiberd, Declan, and P. J. Mathews, eds, *Handbook of the Irish Revival. An Anthology of Irish Cultural and Political Writings 1891–1922* (Dublin: Abbey Theatre Press, 2015).

Killen, John, *John' Bull's Famous Circus. Ulster History through the Postcard 1905–1985* (Dublin: The O'Brien Press, 1985).

King, J., *King's Bibliography of Irish Pictorial Post Cards* (London: J. King, 1903).

Klich, Linda, and Benjamin Weiss, *The Postcard Age, Selections from the Leonard A. Lauder Collection* (London: Thames and Hudson, 2012).

Kress, Gunther, and Theo van Leeuwen, *Reading Images: The Grammar of Visual Design* (London: Routledge, 1996).

Lang, R. T., ed., *Black's Guide to Ireland* (London: Adam and Charles Black, 1906).

Lee, Joseph, *The Modernisation of Irish Society 1848–1918: From the Great Famine to Independent Ireland* (Dublin: Gill and Macmillan, 1973 and 1989).

Leerssen, Joep, *Remembrance and Imagination: Patterns in the Historical and Literary Representation of Ireland in the Nineteenth Century* (Cork: Cork University Press, 1996).

Logan, J. D., *The Making of the New Ireland, an Essay in Social Psychology* (Toronto: Gaelic League, 1909).

Lynd, Robert, *Home Life in Ireland* (Chicago: A. C. McClurg; London: Mills & Boon, 1910).

Mamiya, Christin J., 'Greetings from Paradise: The Representation of Hawaiian Culture in Postcards', *Journal of Communication Inquiry*, 16/86 (1992), 86–101.

Mathews, P. J., *Revival. The Abbey Theatre, Sinn Féin, the Gaelic League and the Co-operative Movement*, Field Day Monographs (Cork: Cork University Press, 2003).

Mathews, P. J. ' "Doing Something Irish": From Thomas Moore to Riverdance', UCD scholarcast, Series 1 (Spring 2008), 2–11 <http://www.ucd.ie/scholarcast/transcripts/Doing_Something_Irish.pdf> accessed 15 October 2014.

Mac Con Iomaire, Máirtín, 'Haute Cuisine Restaurants in Nineteenth and Twentieth Century Ireland', *Proceedings of the Royal Irish Academy: Archaeology, Culture, History, Literature*, 115C (2015), 371–403.

MacCannell, Dean, *The Tourist. A New Theory of the Leisure Class* (New York: Schocken Books, 1989).

McCabe, Brian, *"Dear Miss B" – A Collection of Edwardian Postcards* (Naas: Kildare County Council; Brian McCabe, 2014).

McCole, Niamh, 'The Magic Lantern in Provincial Ireland, 1896–1906', *Early Popular Visual Culture*, 5 (November 2007), 247–262.

McKenna, Lambert, *The Church and Labour* (New York: P. J. Kenedy, 1914), 45–46.

McMahon, Timothy, *Grand Opportunity. The Gaelic Revival and Irish Society, 1893–1910* (Syracuse: Syracuse University Press, 2008).

Meaney, Gerardine, Bernadette Whelan and Mary O'Dowd, *Reading the Irish Woman: Studies in Cultural Encounters and Exchange, 1714–1960* (Liverpool: Liverpool University Press, 2013).

Mecklenburg-Fainger, Amy, *Scissors, Paste and Social Change: The Rhetoric of Scrapbooks of Women's Organisations, 1875–1930* (PhD thesis submitted to Ohio State University, 2007).

Mecklenburg-Fainger, Amy, *Trifles, Abominations, and Literary Gossip: Gendered Rhetoric and Nineteenth-Century Scrapbooks*, Genders 1998–2013, University of Colorado, Boulder, 2012, available at <https://www.colorado.edu/gendersarchive1998-2013/2012/02/01/trifles-abominations-and-literary-gossip-gendered-rhetoric-and-nineteenth-century>.

Mehegan, Angela, 'The Cultural Analysis of Leisure: Tourism and Travels in Co. Donegal', *Circa*, 107 (Spring, 2004), 58–62, 59–60.

Mifflin, Jeffrey, 'Historical Photograph Albums, Archives, and the Shape of Experience and Memory', *The American Archivist*, 75 (Spring/Summer 2012), 225–240.

Milne, Esther, *Letters, Postcards, Email. Technologies of Presence* (New York, London: Routledge, 2010), Kindle Book.

Mulhall, Daniel, *A New Day Dawning: A Portrait of Ireland in 1900* (Cork: The Collins Press, 1999).

Murphy, James H., *Abject Loyalty: Nationalism and Monarchy in Ireland during the Reign of Queen Victoria* (Washington, DC: Catholic University of America Press, 2001).

Murphy, Niall, *A Bloomsday Postcard* (Dublin: The Lilliput Press, 2004).

O'Brien, Kate, *Presentation Parlour* (Dublin: Poolbeg, 1963; 1994).

O'Brien, Mark, *The Fourth Estate: Journalism in Twentieth-Century Ireland* (Manchester: Manchester University Press, 2017).

Ó Donnabháin, Barra, 'An Appalling Vista: The Celts and the Archaeology of Later Prehistoric Ireland', in Angela Desmond, Gina Johnson and Margaret McCarthy, eds, *New Agendas in Irish Prehistory: Papers in Commemoration of Liz Anderson* (Dublin: Wordwell, 2000), 189–196.

O'Donovan Perry, *Love from Cork, Postcards of the City and County* (Cork: Collins Press, 2013).

O'Hagan, Lauren Alex, '"Home Rule Is Rome Rule": Exploring anti-Home Rule Postcards in Edwardian Ireland', *Visual Studies*, 2020, <https://doi.org/ 10.1080/1472586X.2020.1779612>.

Ó'hÓgartaigh, Dr Margaret, *Quiet Revolutionaries, Irish Women in Education, Medicine and Sport, 1861–1964* (Dublin: The History Press Ireland, 2011).

O'Leary, Niamh, 'Not Just Four Generations in the Profession – But the First Woman Pharmacist Too!', *IPU Review* (February 1993), 38–39.

O'Reilly, Bernard, *The Mirror of True Womanhood; A Book of Instruction for Women in the World* (New York: P.J Kenedy, Excelsior Catholic Publishing House, 1886).

O'Toole, Laurence, *Pornocopia: Porn, Sex, Technology and Desire* (London: Serpent's Tail, 1999).

Ott, Katherine, and Susan Tucker, *The Scrapbook in American Life* (Philadelphia: Temple University Press, 2006).

Paseta, Senia, *Before the Revolution: Nationalism, Social Change and Ireland's Catholic Elite, 1879–1922* (Cork: Cork University Press, 1999).

Paul, Rev., 'The Catholic Vigilance Association, its Aims and Results', in *The Torch, Catholic Truth Annual and Conference Record* (Dublin: Catholic Truth Society, 1919), 54–63.

Paul-Dubois, L., *Contemporary Ireland* (Dublin: Maunsel, 1908).

Pearce, Susan M., *Museums, Objects and Collections* (Washington, DC: Smithsonian Institutions Press, 1992).

Pilkington, Lionel, *Theatre and Ireland* (Basingstoke: Palgrave Macmillan, 2010), 14–15.

Pollen, Annebella, 'Sweet Nothings: Suggestive Brighton Postcard Inscriptions', 2009 <https://cris.brighton.ac.uk/ws/portalfiles/portal/260032/Pollen+-+Photography+and+Culture+article+-+for+repository.pdf> accessed 14 August 2020.

Prochaska, David, and Jordana Mendelson, eds, *Postcards: Ephemeral Histories of Modernity* (Pennsylvania: Pennsylvania State University Press, 2010).

Raftery, Deirdre, Judith Harford and Susan M. Parkes, 'Mapping the Terrain of Female Education in Ireland, 1830–1910', *Gender and Education*, 22/5 (2010), 565–578.

Rains, Stephanie, *Commodity Culture and Social Class in Dublin 1850–1916* (Dublin: Irish Academic Press, 2010).

Rains, Stephanie, 'Mass Media, High Society and the Invention of Celebrity', *Irish Media History* (2017) <https://irishmediahistory.com/tag/lady-of-the-house/> accessed 19 July 2020.

Rickards, Maurice, *The Encyclopedia of Ephemera, A Guide to the Fragmentary Documents of Everyday Life for the Collector, Curator, and Historian* (New York: Routledge, 2000).

Rockett, Kevin, 'Disguising Dependence: Separatism and Foreign Mass Culture', *Circa*, 49 (January–February 1990), 20–25.

Rockett, Kevin, 'Cinema', in S. J. Connolly, ed., *The Oxford Companion to Irish History* (Oxford, New York: Oxford University Press, 2004), 98–99.

Rockett, Kevin, and Emer Rockett, *Magic Lantern Panorama and Moving Picture Shows in Ireland, 1786–1909* (Dublin: Four Courts Press, 2011).

Rogan, Bjarne, 'An Entangled Object: The Picture Postcard as Souvenir and Collectible, Exchange and Ritual Communication', *Cultural Analysis*, 4/1 (2005), 31–57.

Samuel, Mark, and Kate Hamlyn, *Blarney Castle: Its History, Development and Purpose* (Cork: Cork University Press, 2007).

Saothrái, Séamas O., 'Wish You Were Here?', *Books Ireland*, 17 (October 1977), 201.

Sheehan, Canon, *My New Curate. A Story Gathered from the Stray Leaves of an Old Diary* (Dublin and Cork: The Talbot Press, 1899).

Sigel, Lisa Z., *Governing Pleasures: Pornography and Social Change in England, 1815–1914* (New Brunswick, New Jersey and London: Rutgers University Press, 2002).

Siggins, Brian, *The Great White Fair, the Herbert Park Exhibition of 1907* (Dublin: The History Press Ireland, 2007).

Sister Mary Ignatius, 'Women as Pharmacists in Public Institutions', *The American Journal of Nursing*, 6/2 (1905), 92–95.

Smithson, Annie M. P., 'Christmas in Donegal', *The Irish Monthly*, 54/642 (1926), 633–641.

Staff, Frank, *The Picture Postcard and Its Origins* (London: Lutterworth Press, 1966).

T.E. 'The Feast of the Annunciation', *The Irish Rosary*, II/3 (1898), 107–110, 110.

Thaw, E. V., 'The Art of Collecting', *The New Criterion*, 36/6 (2012) <https://www.newcriterion.com/issues/2002/12/the-art-of-collecting> accessed 14 August 2020.

The Citizen, 'Picture Post-Cards', *Art and Progress*, 1/1 (1909), 11–12.

Tickner, Lisa, 'Suffrage Campaigns. The Political Imagery of the British Women's Suffrage Movement', in Jane Beckett and Deborah Cherry, eds, *The Edwardian Era* (London: Barbicon Gallery and Oxford: Phaidon, 1987), 100–116.

Treuherz, Julian, *Victorian Painting* (London: Thames and Hudson, 1993).

Turpin, John, '1798, 1898 & the Political Implications of Sheppard's Monuments', *History Ireland*, 6/2 (1998), 44–48.

Urry, John, and Jonas Larsen, *The Tourist Gaze 3.0* (London, California, New Delhi and Singapore: Sage, 2011). Kindle book.

Wang, Victoria, John V. Tucker and Kevin Haines, 'Phatic Technologies in Modern Society', *Technology in Society*, 34 (2012), 84–93.

Williams, William H. A., *Creating Irish Tourism: The First Century, 1750–1850* (London, New York, Melbourne, Delhi: Anthem Press, 2010).

Wilson, Ann, 'Constructions of Irishness in a Collection of Early Twentieth-Century Picture Postcards', *The Canadian Journal of Irish Studies*, 39/1 (2015), 92–117.

Wilson, Ann, 'Image Wars: The Edwardian Picture Postcard and the Construction of Irish Identity in the Early 1900s', *Media History*, 24/3–4 (2018), 320–334.

Wilson, Ann, 'Picture Postcard Politics: The Expression of Dissent via Picture Postcards in Edwardian Ireland', in L. O'Hagan, ed., *Rebellious Writing: Contesting Marginalisation in Edwardian Britain* (Bern: Peter Lang, 2020), 297–319.

Yeats, W. B., *Autobiographies* (London: Macmillan, 1966).

Young, Filson, *Ireland at the Crossroads. An Essay in Explanation* (London: Grant Richards, 1904).

Index

Reimagining Ireland

Series Editor: Dr Eamon Maher, Technological University Dublin

The concepts of Ireland and 'Irishness' are in constant flux in the wake of an ever-increasing reappraisal of the notion of cultural and national specificity in a world assailed from all angles by the forces of globalisation and uniformity. Reimagining Ireland interrogates Ireland's past and present and suggests possibilities for the future by looking at Ireland's literature, culture and history and subjecting them to the most up-to-date critical appraisals associated with sociology, literary theory, historiography, political science and theology.

Some of the pertinent issues include, but are not confined to, Irish writing in English and Irish, Nationalism, Unionism, the Northern 'Troubles', the Peace Process, economic development in Ireland, the impact and decline of the Celtic Tiger, Irish spirituality, the rise and fall of organised religion, the visual arts, popular cultures, sport, Irish music and dance, emigration and the Irish diaspora, immigration and multiculturalism, marginalisation, globalisation, modernity/postmodernity and postcolonialism. The series publishes monographs, comparative studies, interdisciplinary projects, conference proceedings and edited books. Proposals should be sent either to Dr Eamon Maher at eamon.maher@ittdublin.ie or to ireland@peterlang.com.

Vol. 69   Michel Brunet, Fabienne Gaspari and Mary Pierse (eds): George
               Moore's Paris and His Ongoing French Connections
               ISBN 978-3-0343-1973-7. 279 pages. 2015.

Vol. 70   Carine Berbéri and Martine Pelletier (eds): Ireland: Authority
               and Crisis
               ISBN 978-3-0343-1939-3. 296 pages. 2015.

Vol. 71   David Doolin: Transnational Revolutionaries: The Fenian Invasion of
               Canada, 1866
               ISBN 978-3-0343-1922-5. 348 pages. 2016.

Vol. 72   Terry Phillips: Irish Literature and the First World War: Culture,
               Identity and Memory
               ISBN 978-3-0343-1969-0. 297 pages. 2015.

Vol. 73   Carmen Zamorano Llena and Billy Gray (eds): Authority and
               Wisdom in the New Ireland: Studies in Literature and Culture
               ISBN 978-3-0343-1833-4. 263 pages. 2016.

Vol. 74   Flore Coulouma (ed.): New Perspectives on Irish TV Series: Identity
               and Nostalgia on the Small Screen
               ISBN 978-3-0343-1977-5. 222 pages. 2016.

Vol. 75   Fergal Lenehan: Stereotypes, Ideology and Foreign
               Correspondents: German Media Representations of Ireland,
               1946–2010
               ISBN 978-3-0343-2222-5. 306 pages. 2016.

Vol. 76   Jarlath Killeen and Valeria Cavalli (eds): 'Inspiring a Mysterious
               Terror': 200 Years of Joseph Sheridan Le Fanu
               ISBN 978-3-0343-2223-2. 260 pages. 2016.

Vol. 77   Anne Karhio: 'Slight Return': Paul Muldoon's Poetics of Place
               ISBN 978-3-0343-1986-7. 272 pages. 2017.

Vol. 78   Margaret Eaton: Frank Confessions: Performance in the Life-Writings
               of Frank McCourt
               ISBN 978-1-906165-61-1. 294 pages. 2017.

www.ingramcontent.com/pod-product-compliance
Lightning Source LLC
Chambersburg PA
CBHW071459110726
47908CB00003B/671